Let Us C++

Second Edition

By

Yashavant Kanetkar

BPB PUBLICATIONS
B-14, CONNAUGHT PLACE, NEW DELHI-1

SECOND REVISED EDITION 2010 REPRINTED 2012

ISBN : 10 : 81-7656-106-1 / 13 : 978-81-7656-106-8

Distributors:

COMPUTER BOOK CENTRE
12, Shrungar Shopping Centre, M.G. Road,
BANGALORE-560001 Ph: 25587923, 25584641

MICRO BOOKS
Shanti Niketan Building, 8, Camac Street
KOLKATTA-700017 Ph: 22826518/9

BUSINESS PROMOTION BUREAU
8/1, Ritchie Street, Mount Road,
CHENNAI-600002 Ph: 28410796, 28550491

BPB PUBLICATIONS
B-14, Connaught Place, NEW DELHI-110001
Ph : 23325760, 23723393, 23737742

BPB BOOK CENTRE
376, Old Lajpat Rai Market, DELHI-110006
Ph: 23861747

MICRO MEDIA
Shop No.5, Mahendra Chambers, 150 D.N. Rd,
Next to Capital Cinema V.T. (C.S.T.) Station,
MUMBAI-400001 Ph: 22078296, 22078297

DECCAN AGENCIES
4-3-329, Bank Street,
HYDERABAD-500195 Ph: 24756400, 24756976

INFO TECH
G-2, Sidhartha Building , 96, Nehru Place,
NEW DELHI-110019
Ph: 26438245, 26415092, 26234208

INFO TECH
Shop No. 2, F-38, South Extention Part-I
NEW DELHI-110049
Ph: 24691288

Published by Manish Jain for BPB Publications, B-14, Connaught Place, New Delhi-110001 and printed by him at Balaji Printing Press, New Delhi

Dedicated to

Nalinee & Prabhakar Kanetkar

About The Author

Through his original works in the form of books and Quest Video courseware DVDs on C, C++, Data Structures, VC++, .NET, Embedded Systems, etc. Yashavant Kanetkar has created, moulded and groomed lacs of IT careers in the last decade and half. In recognition of his immense contribution to IT education in India, he has been awarded the "Best .NET Technical Contributor" and "Most Valuable Professional" awards by Microsoft. His current passion includes Device Driver and Embedded System Programming. Yashavant holds a BE from VJTI Mumbai and M.Tech. from IIT Kanpur. Yashavant's current affiliations include being a Director of KICIT and KSET. He can be reached at kanetkar@ksetindia.com or through http://quest.ksetindia.com/

Acknowledgments

The joy of creativity! Probably, that's why I am drawn to writing. I believe that at some stage of book writing the book starts taking a life of its own. Once it does that the author just has to kneel down, claw at the earth, overturn the soil and pray for the rain. The book is capable of unfolding itself. There is no need for the author to take credit for it.

This has been one long book project and naturally many people got associated with it. Any bouquets for the merit in this book should go to their door. Any brickbats, I am ready to catch myself.

Shakeel Ali helped in two ways: We together straightened out poorly written or confusing text. He alone pulled, pushed and shoved the code in this book till he got it perfectly right.

Nandita Hingwe solved all the exercises in the book and made sure that the questions make sense to the reader. Figures in this book too are all hers.

I am grateful to all the students who attended my C++ lectures and seminars and helped me to improve my understanding of numerous C++ concepts. More than anything else I learnt from them that if you are open to new ideas your circle of friends can go much beyond where your car can drive.

It's befitting that somebody who has helped me so much in so many ways while I was toiling away at this book gets to create the first impression of this book. Credit for the cover idea goes to my wife, Seema.

Contents

Preface To Second Edition

Things have changed a lot since I wrote the first edition of this book, about a decade ago. That time C++ was the new kid on the block. Today it is a mature, powerful and a popular choice for programmer's community. I wanted to reflect this change in this new edition. So I took each program in the book, checked whether it works with popular compilers of today like Visual Studio and gcc, modified them when they didn't and finally I am presenting them to you. The text too has been modified to accommodate the changes made in the programs.

One of the biggest hurdles faced by programmers learning C++ is that they are most of the time doing C programming with a C++ compiler. This is one aspect that I wanted to change, because if this is not done you would never be able to exploit the real power that C++ lays at your door-steps. Hence, in the very first chapter itself I have discussed how one should *think* about any problem in C++ way. I am hopeful you would appreciate this approach and benefit from it.

For a novice it is difficult to decide which development environment to choose, how to obtain it, install it and start using it. Towards this end, I have dedicated one full chapter (Chapter 2). I am sure if you go through this chapter you would be up and running quickly rather than spending hours on end figuring out the installation and compilation procedure yourselves.

All in all, I would say that this is a C++ book written to help you learn this wonderful language with latest development tools in the right perspective. All the best and I hope you would enjoy reading it.

Yashavant Kanetkar

Preface To First Edition

Completing this book is one of the hardest things that I have ever done. It took me almost two years to get it into the form you are reading. Every time I read the earlier draft I had to almost always rewrite the whole thing. Two reasons for this: one C++ is abstract, second it is complex. Most C++ programmers are former C programmers. I too migrated to C++ from C. Hence, unless I could contrast any new C++ feature with how it was being done in C and tell readers how it could be done better in C++ I felt I would be failing in my duty.

C++ is decorated (?) with a lot of bombastic jargon. One of my aims here was to keep this jargon at bay and concentrate on the underlying concepts instead. At most places I have tried to show how things work and more importantly why do they work that way.

If you ask me to name the most important characteristic of this book I would say *simplicity*. Be it the code or the text, I have tried to make it as simple as I could. As far as the code is concerned I wanted to present simple examples that can be easily edited, compiled and run. My goal was not to demonstrate how good a programmer I am by adding gloss to these programs, but to illustrate specific programming concepts.

You will also notice that very few programming examples in this book are code fragments. I have found that a program that can actually compile and run, no matter how simple it is, helps improve one's understanding of a subject a great deal more than just code fragments.

I have found that simple exercises are exceptionally useful to complete the reader's understanding of a topic. So you will find one at the end of each chapter.

More than anything else I have tried to design the book for a programmer struggling with a new and complex programming language. I have poured my best efforts into these pages. I trust you would find the book useful.

CHAPTER

ONE

Introduction To OOP

What is object-oriented programming (OOP)? This question is little difficult to answer because the software industry has a fascination for terminologies and catch words. Not long ago, words like "artificial intelligence", "WAP" and "Java" were used as if they were to offer a path to heaven. The same overuse seems to be happening to the phrase "object-oriented". Since it has been proven that object-oriented techniques offer a way to write better programs, everybody seems to be slapping the label "object-oriented" on their software products.

Hence it is important for us to understand what is OOP, why do we need it, what does it do that traditional languages like C, Pascal and Basic don't and what are the principles behind OOP. This chapter addresses these issues and provides an overview of the features to be discussed in the rest of the book. What we say here will necessarily be general and brief. Don't worry if you don't catch everything in this chapter on the first pass; OOP is a bit complex and understanding it takes time. We will be going over these features again in subsequent chapters. There's lot of ground to cover here, so let's get started.

The purpose of a programming language is to express the solution to a problem with the help of an algorithm (step by step procedure). The success of the solution depends on how the solution models (represents) the problem. Different approaches have evolved over the years to model solutions to problems. The primary amongst them are Structured programming model (also called Procedural programming model) and Object-oriented programming model. Of late, the structured programming model is being replaced by object-oriented programming model. To understand these models we need to begin by taking a peek at the history of programming models.

The Beginning...

The earliest computers were programmed in binary. Mechanical switches were used to load programs. With the advent of mass storage devices and larger and cheaper computer memories, the first high-level computer programming languages came into existence. With their arrival, instead of thinking in terms of bits and bytes, programmers could write a series of English-like instructions that a compiler could translate into the binary language of computers.

These languages were simple in design and easy to use because programs at that time were primarily concerned with relatively simple tasks like calculations. As a result, programs were pretty short, limited to about a few hundred lines of instructions.

As the computers' capacity and capability increased, so also did the ability to develop more complex computer programs. However, the earlier programming languages were found wanting in performing the complex programming tasks. These languages suffered from the following limitations:

(a) There were no facilities to reuse existing program code. Wherever the same piece code was required, it was simply duplicated.

(b) The control of execution within a program was transferred via the dangerous *goto* statement. As a result, there was too much jumping around in the program, often without any clear indication of how, where and why the control is flowing.

(c) All variables in the program were global. Tracking down spurious changes in global data in long convoluted programs was a very tedious job.

(d) Writing, understanding and maintaining long programs became a programmer's nightmare.

(e) In short, we can call this methodology of developing programs as *Unstructured* programming.

Structured Programming

To overcome the limitations mentioned above, a quest began to develop new languages with new features that would help to create more sophisticated applications. The breakthrough occurred in late 1960's and early 1970's with the introduction of structured programming. The long programs that the programmer found difficult to comprehend could now be broken down into smaller units of few hundred statements. Functions/subroutines/procedures were introduced in these languages to make the programs more comprehensible to their human creators. A program was now divided into functions, with each function having a clearly defined purpose. How structured programming overcame the limitations experienced in unstructured programming is given below.

(a) Reuse of existing program code – Wherever the same piece code is required at multiple places in a program, the function containing that code is used. As a result, there is no need to repeat the same code at multiple places.

(b) Excessive use of *goto* statement – The excessive use could be minimized with the introduction of powerful control instructions that could transfer the control within the program in an easy-to-understand manner.

(c) Unexpected changes in global variables – With introduction of functions, need for global variables got minimized.

(d) Complexity of programs – Complexity became more manageable as structured programming permitted better organization of the program.

A structured program is built by breaking down a solution into smaller pieces (also called as divide and conquer technique) that then become functions within that program. Each function can have its local variables and logic. The execution begins with one function and then all other functions are called directly or indirectly from this function. This is shown in Figure 1.1.

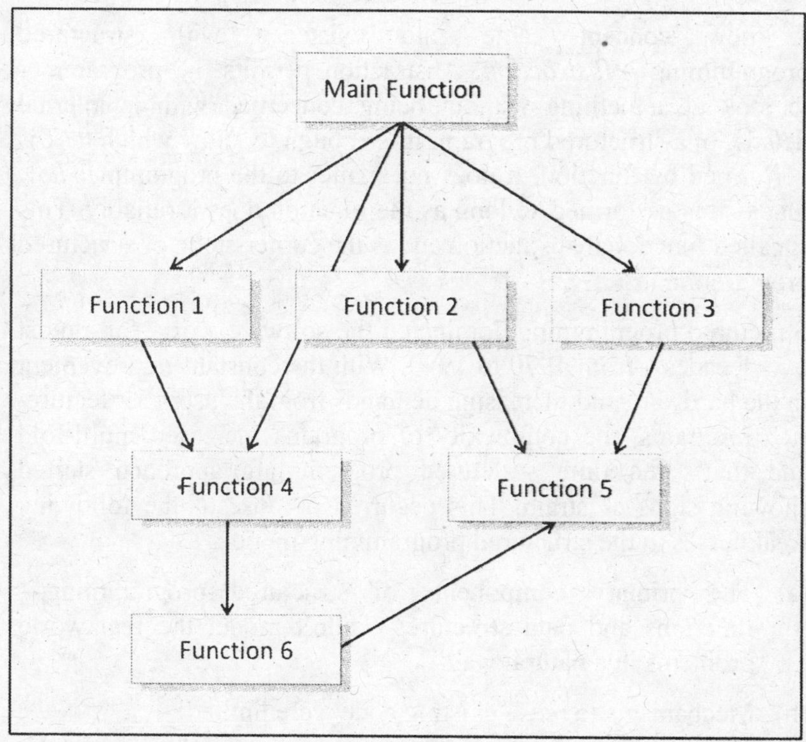

Figure 1.1

In structured programming, there is less need of global variables, which are now replaced by local variables that have a smaller and more controllable scope. Information is passed between functions using parameters and functions can have local variables that cannot be accessed outside the function's scope.

By isolating processes within functions, a structured program minimizes the chance that one function will affect another. This also makes it easier to locate problems, if any. Structured programming helps you to write cleaner code and maintain control over each function. All this makes the development and maintenance of code easier as well as efficient.

A new concept came into existence with structured programming—*Abstraction*. Abstraction permits the programmer to look at something without being concerned with is internal details. In a structured program, it is enough to know which task is performed by function. It does not matter to the programmer *how* that task is performed so long as the function does it reliably. This is called functional abstraction and is the corner-stone of structured programming.

Structured programming dominated the software world for almost two decades—from 1970 to 1990. With the constant improvement in the hardware and increasing demands from the users for feature-rich programs, the complexity of programs increased multi-fold and that's the time structured programming approach started showing signs of strain. This occurred because of the following weaknesses in the structured programming model:

(a) The primary components of structured programming—functions and data structures—didn't model the real world problems in a natural way.

(b) Mechanisms to reuse existing code were limited.

(c) Maintaining, debugging and upgrading large programs were a difficult task.

The solution to these limitations is discussed in the next section.

Object Oriented Programming

The real-world problems and their solutions are not organized into values and procedures separate from one another. Problem solvers do not perceive the world that way. They deal with their problem domains by concentrating on the objects and letting the characteristics of those objects determine the procedures to apply to them. To build a house, grow a tomato, or repair an engine, first you think about the object and its purpose and behavior. Then you select your tools and procedures. The solution fits the problem.

Thus the world is object-oriented, and the object-oriented programming methodology expresses computer programs in ways that model how people perceive the world. Because programmers are people, it is only natural that their approach to the work of the world reflects their view of the world itself.

The object-oriented methodology is built on the foundation laid by the structured programming concepts and data abstraction. Data abstraction does for data what functional abstraction does for operations. With data abstraction, data structures can be used without having to be concerned about the exact details of implementation. For example, floating-point numbers are abstracted in programming languages. You are not required to know how a floating-point number is represented in binary while assigning a value to it. Likewise, you are not bothered how binary multiplication takes place while multiplying floating-point numbers. Abstraction for floating-point numbers has existed in programming languages since long. However, it is only recently that languages have been developed that let you define your own abstract data types.

The fundamental change in OOP is that a program is designed around the data being operated upon, rather than around the operations themselves. This is to be expected once we appreciate that the very purpose of the program is to access or manipulate data. The basic idea behind object-oriented language is to combine into a single unit, both, the data and the functions that operate on the data. Such a unit is called an object.

An object's functions, called member functions or methods in C++, typically provide the only way to access its data. If you want to access a data item in an object, you call a member function in the object. It will read the item and return the value to you. You can't access the data directly.

If you want to modify the data in an object, you know exactly what functions interact with it—the member functions in the object. No other functions can access the data. This simplifies writing, debugging, and maintaining the program.

A C++ program typically consists of a number of objects which communicate with each other by calling one another's member functions. The organization of a C++ program is shown in Figure 1.2.

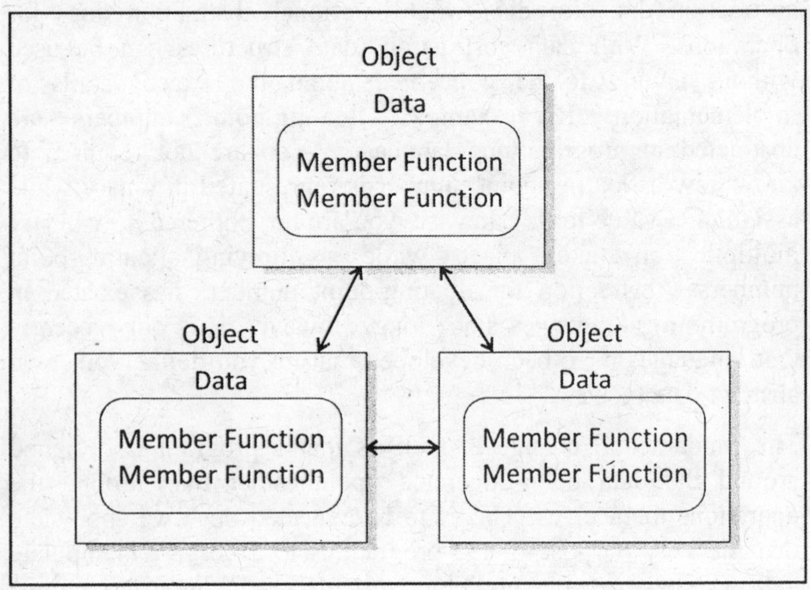

Figure 1.2

When you approach a programming problem in an object-oriented manner, you no longer ask how the problem will be divided into functions, but rather how it will be divided into objects. Thinking in terms of objects, rather than functions, has a surprisingly helpful effect on how easily programs can be designed. This results from the close match between objects in the programming world and objects in the real world.

The match between programming objects and real world objects is the happy result of combining data and functions. The resulting objects offer a revolution in program design. No such close match between programming constructs and the concepts being modeled exists in a procedural language.

There is more to OOP than just binding the data and functions together. Given below are some of the new concepts introduced in OOP:

(a) Data hiding

(b) Encapsulation

(c) Inheritance

(d) Containership

(e) Polymorphism

(f) Templates

(g) Exception handling

(h) Reflection

Don't get daunted by this list of new features. Some of these are explained in brief in the next section. A detailed explanation of each of these concepts is given in chapters to follow.

Characteristics Of Object-Oriented Languages

Object-oriented programming uses a vocabulary that is unfamiliar to the procedural programmer. Let us now briefly examine this vocabulary with regards to the major elements of object-oriented languages.

Objects

In structured programming a problem is approached by dividing it into functions. Unlike this, in object-oriented programming the problem is divided into objects. Thinking in terms of objects rather than functions makes the designing of program easier. Following are few candidates that can be treated as objects in respective situations:

- Employees in a Payroll processing system
- Data structures like linked lists, stacks, queues etc.
- GUI elements like windows, menus, icons etc.
- Hardware devices like disk drive, keyboard, printer, etc.
- Various elements in computer games like cannons, guns, animals, etc.
- Customers, sales persons in a sales tracking system
- Computers in a network model

Classes

Most languages offer primitive data types like *int*, *long* and *float*. Their data representation and response to arithmetic, assignment and relational operators are defined as part of the language. However, not all the information about real world objects can be represented using these limited built-in data types. The programmer often needs to create his own data types by defining a *class* for it.

For example, there can be a user-defined data type to represent dates. The compiler and the computer do not know about dates. Programmers have to define the behaviour of dates by designing a Date *class*. This class expresses the format of a date and the operations that can be performed on it. The way, we can declare many variables of the primitive type *int*, we can define many objects of the *Date* class. A class serves as a blueprint or a plan or a template. It specifies what data and what functions will be included in objects of that type. Defining a class doesn't create any objects, just as the mere existence of a type *int* doesn't create any variables.

Inheritance

OOP permits you to create your own data types (classes) just like the types built into the language. However, unlike the built-in data types, the user-defined classes can use other classes as building blocks. Using a concept called *inheritance*; new classes can be built on top of the old ones. The new class referred to as a *derived* class, can inherit the data and functions of the original, or the *base* class. The new class can add its own data elements and functions in addition to those it inherits from its base class.

For example, we can build a set of classes that describe a library of publications. There are two primary types of publications—periodicals and books. We can create a general *Publication* class by defining data items for the publisher name, the number of pages and the accession number. Publications can be retrieved, stored and read. These would be the functions of *Publication* class.

Next we can define two classes named *Periodical* and *Book*. Both these classes can be derived from the base class *Publication*. This is natural because a periodical as well as a book would have properties like publisher name, number of pages and the accession number.

In addition to this, a periodical also has a volume and issue number and contains articles written by different authors. Data items for these should be included in the definition of the *periodical* class. The *Periodical* class will also need a function, subscribe.

Data items for the *Book* class will include the names of its author a cover type (hard or soft) and its ISBN number. This class would also have a function called *subscribe*. As you can see, the *Book* class and the *Periodical* class share the characteristics of *Publication* class while having their own unique attributes. This entire scenario is depicted in Figure 1.3.

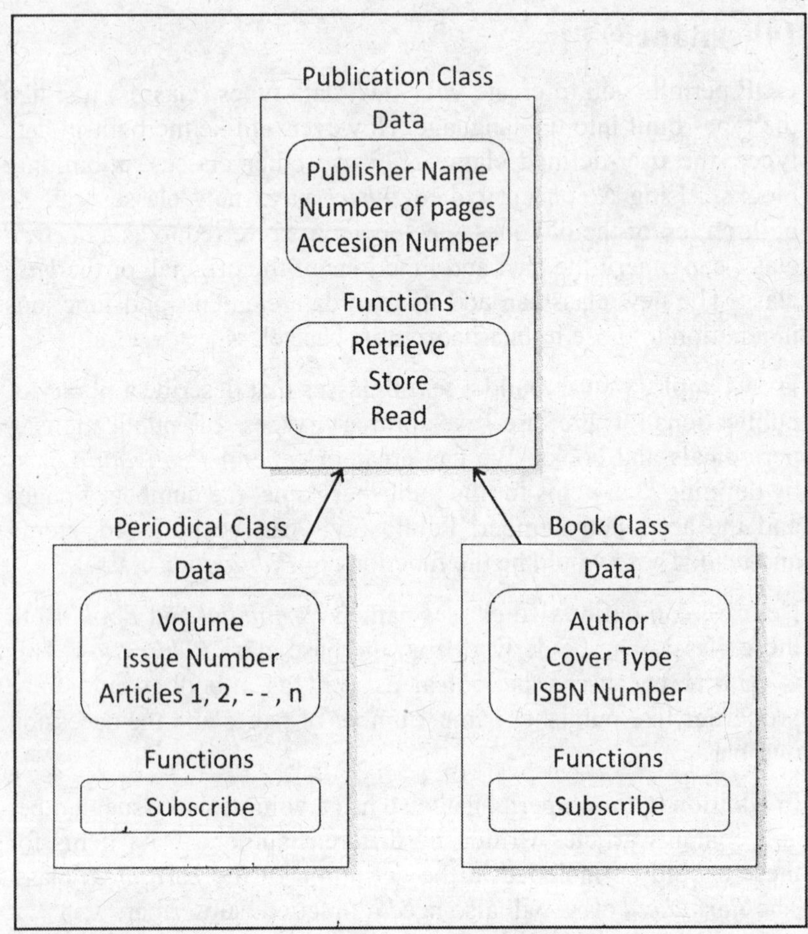

Figure 1.3

Polymorphism

Extending the same example of the Publication, Periodical and Book, let us now understand another important concept. Our base class, Publication, defines methods for storing and retrieving data. A periodical may be stored in a binder, while a book is usually placed on a shelf. Furthermore, the way to find a specific periodical is different from finding a book. Periodicals are located through a guide to periodical literature, while books are found using a card catalogue system. Based on this we can design a 'find through periodical literature' function for a periodical and a 'find through card catalogue' function for a book. OOP provides an elegant facility called *polymorphism* to handle such situations. In our example, the retrieval method for a periodical is different from the retrieval method for a book, even though the end result is same. Polymorphism permits you to define a function for retrieving a publication that can work for both periodicals and books. When a periodical is retrieved, the retrieve function that is specific to a periodical is used, but when a book is retrieved, the retrieve function associated with a book is used. The end result is that a single function name can be used for the same operation performed on related derived classes even if the implementation of that function varies from class to class. This concept of polymorphism (one thing with several distinct forms) can be extended even to operators, as we would see in later chapters.

Containership

In a typical super-market each item on sale can be represented using a class. These items in turn belong to different categories like cosmetics, food, cold-drink, clothes, books, electronics, etc. Such relationships can be represented using containership. For example objects like cold-cream, face-wash, shampoo are contained inside a category object called cosmetics. You will be able to observe this containership relationship in many real-world problems.

Reusability

Object-oriented programs are built from reusable software components. Once a class is completed and tested, it can be distributed to other programmers for use in their own programs. This is called reusability. If those programmers want to add new features or change the existing ones, new classes can be derived from existing ones. The tried and tested capabilities of base classes do not need to be redeveloped. Programmers can devote time to writing new code instead of wasting time in rewriting existing code. This way software becomes easier to test, since programming errors can be isolated within the new code of derived classes.

For example, you might have written (or purchased from someone else) a class that creates a menu system. You are happy with the working of this class and you don't want to change it, but you want to add the capability of displaying *help* for each menu item. To do this, you simply create a new class that inherits all the capabilities of the existing one but adds *help* feature. This ease with which existing software can be reused is a major benefit of OOP.

Object Oriented Design

The concepts that we learnt above are fine, but where should we begin learning them? Certainly not by diving straight-away into the grammar and other nitty-gritty's of the language. That way you would never be able to grasp the essence of OOP and C++. As a result, you might end up doing C++ programming mechanically and would miss out on the real substance of this fabulous language and all that it offers to us. In our opinion, the best place to begin is to understand the very basis of all modern programming languages—i.e. Object-Oriented Design (OOD). There are three major steps involved in any OOD. These are as follows:

(a) Identify the actors / players / entities that are involved in the problem that you are trying to solve.

(b) Identify the relationships that exist between these actors.

(c) Identify the actions that are carried out by each actor.

Best way to understand these steps would be to try them out on some example problems. Let us begin with the first one.

Example 1 – Building An IDE

All the programs in this book are going to be built using Microsoft Visual C++ Express Edition IDE (Integrated Development Environment). When you launch this development tool, the window shown in Figure 1.4 would appear.

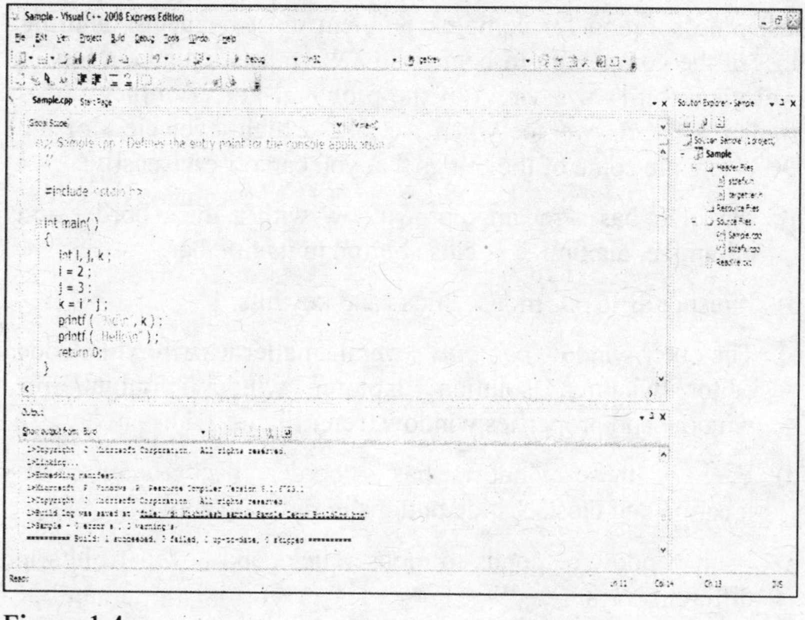

Figure 1.4

This powerful tool is called an Integrated Development Environment (IDE) because it lets us carry out various steps in application development like editing, compiling, linking, testing, debugging using the *same* tool. Imagine that one day, you are asked to create a tool like this! Where would you begin?

You are likely get overwhelmed with the complexity that has to be managed in this—create rectangular windows, manage their colors, write text in them using different fonts, let user interact with them using mouse and keyboard, etc. In addition to this the C++ keywords in the windows have to be shown in different colors (this feature is commonly called as syntax highlighting). And on top of all this, tools like Editor, Compiler, Linker, Debugger, etc. have to be integrated with these windows. One thing that is clear from this is—the solution to this problem is *complex*. So how do we proceed to design a solution for this problem?

Designing solution for complex problem must begin by ignoring most of the complexity to begin with. We must first take a higher level view (bird's eye view) of the problem. For example, in this problem what do we see when we take a high-level view of the IDE? Here are some of the things that you can observe easily:

(a) The IDE has a rectangular window with a thick border and minimize, maximize & close button in its title bar.

(b) It responds to our mouse clicks and key hits.

(c) The outer window *contains* several smaller *windows* like code editor window, solution explorer window, output/error window and properties window (refer Figure 1.1).

(d) Each of these windows has a border, background color, location and close & hide buttons in right top corner.

(e) Each window responds to mouse clicks and keyboard hits in different ways.

(f) Each window can be attached to any of the edges of the main window.

What we can gather from this is that there is lot of commonality amongst these windows. Capturing the commonality at early stage of design is what makes it possible to arrive at the solution efficiently. On the contrary, if we focus on the differences early in the design process, it would lead to unnecessary repetition of ideas during implementation. Result would be a sub-optimal design.

From the above discussion we can now identify actors, relationships between actors and the actions performed by the actors. These are mentioned below:

Actors

Window is the basic actor in this problem. Other actors are Solution Explorer window, Code Editor Window, Output/Error Window, Frame Window, which are all specialized windows. Each actor can be represented using a class.

Relationship Between Actors

(a) Solution Explorer Window, Code Editor Window, Output/Error window and Frame window can be inherited from a Window. Thus Window class would be the base class, whereas, Solution Explorer Window class, Output/error Window class, Frame Window class would become derived classes.

(b) All these specialized windows are contained in the master (outermost) window. The Frame window class would contain objects of other specialized window classes.

Actions Performed By Actors

Each window (actor) responds to mouse and keyboard interaction differently. The actions performed by each actor would become functions (*OnKeyHit* and *OnMouseClick*) in respective classes.

The actors involved in this problem, the relationship between them and the actions performed by the actors in this problem are shown in Figure 1.5.

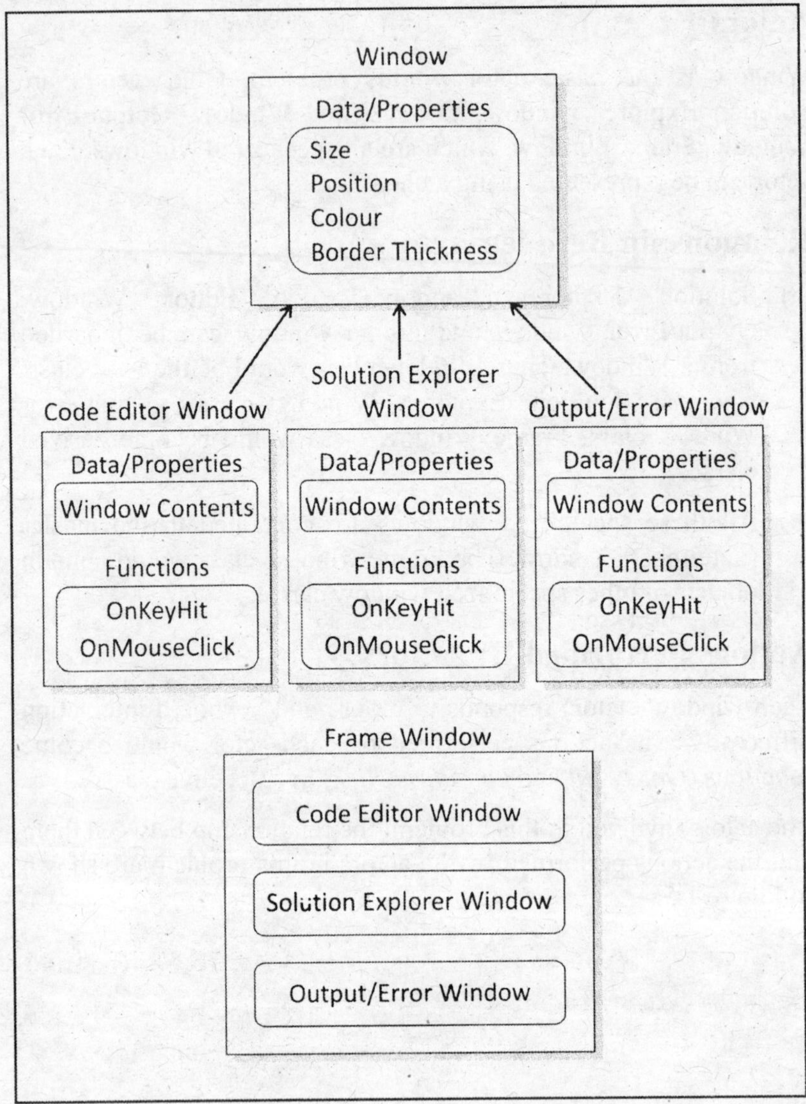

Figure 1.5

Once we are able to identify the basic types in a problem and understand relationships between them, we are well on our way to creating a good design for the problem at hand.

Example 2 – College Administration

Let us consider one more example. We all are familiar with the concept of college and its functioning. Let us try and identify the actors / players / entities that constitute a college. We would begin by stating some facts that are observed and experienced easily:

(a) A college has one or more departments.

(b) Each department runs one or more programs (for example, a program can be a degree of a diploma).

(c) Each program consists of one or more courses.

(d) Students take admission in the college for a particular program.

(e) A program has multiple students in it.

(f) A course in a program is taught by a professor.

(g) Each professor can teach multiple courses.

Now that we know the actors involved in functioning of a college and their inter-relationship, let us now see what activities these actors are engaged in:

(a) Students *purchase* a form for taking admission in programs offered by college.

(b) Students *submit* complete application forms along with the fees.

(c) College *scrutinizes* the application forms received and *approves* or *rejects* an application.

(d) Once college *approves* the admission, department *admits* a student.

(e) Department *prepares* time-table for each program offered by it.

(f) Professors *conduct* classes for different courses included a program for which the students have been admitted as per the time-table.

(g) Department *prepares* an examination schedule at the end of the course.

(h) Department *conducts* an examination as per the schedule.

(i) Professors *evaluate* the answer-papers and allot grades to each student in a program.

(j) Department *collects* grades in all subjects for each student and *declares* the result

The essence of this discussion has been captured in Figure 1.6. Each circle in the figure represents a concrete entity in the problem discussed here. Each line connecting these entities indicates that these entities are related in some way. Now let us capture the exact nature of relationship that exists between different entities and the actions that make these relationships possible.

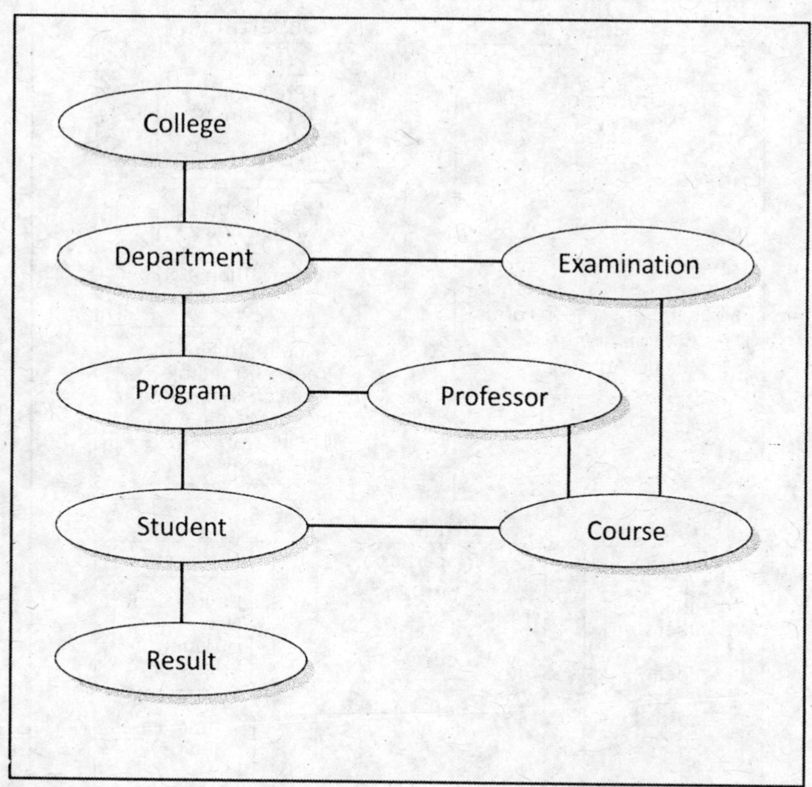

Figure 1.6

Figure 1.7 shows the properties and actions for different actors involved in this problem.

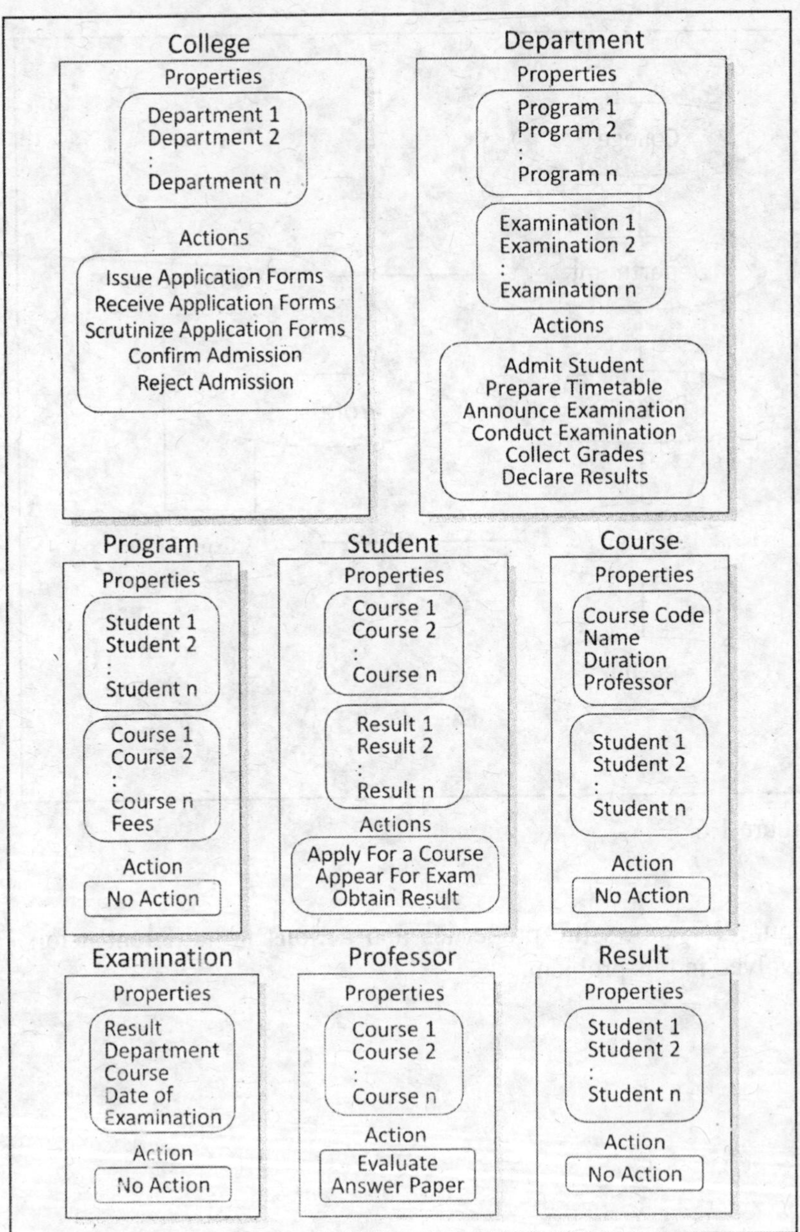
College
Properties
Department 1
Department 2
:
Department n
Actions
Issue Application Forms
Receive Application Forms
Scrutinize Application Forms
Confirm Admission
Reject Admission
Department
Properties
Program 1
Program 2
:
Program n
Examination 1
Examination 2
:
Examination n
Actions
Admit Student
Prepare Timetable
Announce Examination
Conduct Examination
Collect Grades
Declare Results
Program
Properties
Student 1
Student 2
:
Student n
Course 1
Course 2
:
Course n
Fees
Action
No Action
Student
Properties
Course 1
Course 2
:
Course n
Result 1
Result 2
:
Result n
Actions
Apply For a Course
Appear For Exam
Obtain Result
Course
Properties
Course Code
Name
Duration
Professor
Student 1
Student 2
:
Student n
Action
No Action
Examination
Properties
Result
Department
Course
Date of Examination
Action
No Action
Professor
Properties
Course 1
Course 2
:
Course n
Action
Evaluate Answer Paper
Result
Properties
Student 1
Student 2
:
Student n
Action
No Action

Figure 1.7

In object-oriented programming, the actors shown in Figure 1.7 are represented using user-defined data type called classes. To define a *class*, we must be able to clearly identify its properties and the actions performed by that class. This is precisely what we have done in Figure 1.7. These classes are a foundation of every OO language including C++, C#, Java and VB.NET. What we intend to do in the rest of this book is help you understand how to define these classes and establish relationships between them using the grammar rules (syntax) of C++ language. We would like to urge you to solve the exercise given at the end of this chapter before you go to the next chapter. That way you would be on a firm footing to grasp the material covered in chapters to follow.

Exercise

[A] State whether the following statements are True or False:

(a) Object oriented programming permits reusability of the existing code.

(b) Languages earlier than procedural programming languages made use of only global variables.

(c) In Object Oriented programming languages the only way to transfer control from one place in the program to another is by using the *goto* statement.

(d) It is easier to write, understand and maintain programs if they use Object Oriented Programming model as compared to Structured Programming model.

(e) As compared to procedures, data is not given enough importance in Procedural programming.

(f) Structured programming model does not represent the real world problem as well as the Object Oriented programming model.

(g) Object Oriented programming model permits functional abstraction as well as data abstraction.

(h) A class permits us to build user-defined data types.

(i) Objects are to classes as variables are to built-in data types.

(j) Deriving a new class from an existing class promotes reusability of code.

(k) Encapsulation facilitates a single function name to be used for the same operation performed on related derived classes.

(l) In polymorphism even though the function names are same, their implementation may vary from class to class.

(m) Multiple objects can be created from the same class.

[B] Fill in the blanks:

(a) The two major components of an object are _____ & ______.

(b) The ability of a function or operator to act in different ways on different data types is called _________.

(c) The process of building new classes from existing ones is called ________.

(d) If a class A inherits its properties from class B, then A and B are known as ______ class and _____ class, respectively.

(e) Pascal and C are _______ languages, whereas, C++ is _____ language.

[C] Answer the following:

(a) What is the basic difference between structured programming model and object oriented programming model?

(b) What is the difference between a class and an object?

(c) Give at least 5 examples of classes and objects.

(d) What do you mean by encapsulation?

(e) What do you mean by Inheritance?

(f) What do you mean by polymorphism?

[D] Answer the following:

(a) Consider an email client application. The purpose of this application is to put the world of online communication on your desktop. Using it you should be able to receive emails, compose new emails and send them to colleagues and friends. The application should also let you maintain an address book containing contact details of your friends and colleagues.

Identify the actors involved in this application, their relationship with one another and the actions performed by them.

(b) Suppose you are required to create an Enquiry tracker system for a car dealer. The purpose of this system is to help a car dealer to keep a track of enquiry about car purchase. When a customer makes a call to a dealer, the system should be able to store contact information of the customer, whether the customer has bought any car from the dealer in the past, mode of payment (cash/cheque/finance). The system should be able to generate a quotation for the model of a car that a particular customer is interested in. The quotation must contain detailed information about car model, its on-road price, insurance amount and prices of accessories. System should be able to furnish a day-wise report indicating the enquiries made and a quarterly report indicating the total number of cars sold.

Identify the actors involved in this system, their relationship with one another and the actions performed by them.

CHAPTER TWO

Before We Begin...

To understand C++ language and gain confidence in working with it you would be required to type programs in this book and then instruct the machine to execute them. To type any programs you need another program called Editor. Once the program has been typed it needs to be converted to machine language (0s and 1s) before the machine can execute it. To carry out this conversion we need another program called Compiler. Compiler vendors provide an Integrated Development Environment (IDE) which consists of an Editor as well as the Compiler.

There are several such IDEs available in the market targeted towards different operating systems. For example, Turbo C++ is a popular compiler that works under MS-DOS; Visual Studio 2008 and Visual Studio 2008 Express Edition are the compilers that work under Windows, whereas gcc compiler works under Linux. Note that Turbo C++ and gcc compilers can also be installed on machines running Windows OS.

Installation Of Compilers

Out of Turbo C++, Visual Studio 2008 Express Edition and gcc compilers, the last two are available free of cost. They can be downloaded from the following sites:

http://www.microsoft.com/exPress/download

http://www.cygwin.com

You are free to use any of the compilers mentioned above for compiling programs in this book. If you wish to know my personal choice, I would prefer Visual Studio Express Edition for two simple reasons—it is a modern compiler with easy to use GUI and it is available free of cost.

To help you go through the installation process of Visual Studio Express Edition smoothly I have also recorded a video. You can watch the same at the following link:

http://www.youtube.com/asangdani

The installation procedure of TC++ compiler is very simple. However, if you install TC++ compiler under Windows Vista, the window size becomes very small. So small is the screen size that you can hardly work with it. You can increase the size of TC++ window to occupy the entire screen. For this you will have to download an x86 emulator called DosBox from following link:

http://prdownloads.sourceforg.net/dosbox/dosbox0.72-win32-installer.exe?download

Once you have downloaded this emulator carry out the following steps:

(a) Install the DosBox software that you have downloaded.

(b) Create a folder called Turbo on your C: drive.

(c) Copy entire Turbo C++ software in this Turbo folder.

(d) Start DosBox by double clicking DosBox icon.

(e) You would be presented with two screens. You need to use the one which has a Z> prompt in it. Type the following command at Z> prompt.

```
mount  X C:\Turbo
mount  D C:\Turbo\TC
D:
cd Bin
TC
```

By typing the last command "TC" you are executing the Turbo C++ software. This would bring up the normal blue colored TC++ window. To increase the window size, just press Alt + Enter. Now the TC++ window will accommodate the entire screen.

(f) Go to the Options Menu (Alt O), select 'Directories' menu item and change the 'Include' and 'Library' directory such that they contain the following entries:

```
X:\TC\INCLUDE
X:\TC\LIB
```

(g) Once you have typed and saved program do not compile it using the usual Ctrl F9. Instead, compile it using the Compile Menu and execute it using Run Menu.

The following are the shortcut keys that can be used while working in Turbo C++ environment. If you use them it will improve your productivity.

- Press Alt + F, N to open a new file
- Press F2 to save the current file
- Press Ctrl + F9 to compile and run the program
- Press Alt + F5 to view the output of the program
- Press Alt + F3 to close the currently opened file
- Press Alt + X to exit Turbo C++

Compilation process used in TC++, Visual Studio and gcc is a bit different. So for your benefit I am giving below the detailed compilation and execution steps with each of these compilers.

Compilation Using TC++

Here are the steps that you need to follow to compile and execute programs using TC++...

(a) Start the compiler at **C>** prompt. The compiler (TC.EXE) is usually present in **C:\TC\BIN** directory.

(b) Select **New** from the **File** menu.

(c) Type the program.

(d) Save the program using **F2** under a proper name (say Program1.c).

(e) Use **Ctrl + F9** to compile and execute the program.

(f) Use **Alt + F5** to view the output.

Compilation Using Visual Studio 2008 / Visual Studio 2008 Express Edition

You need to carry out the following steps to compile and execute programs using any Visual Studio version:

(a) Start Visual Studio 2008 from Start | All Programs | Microsoft Visual Studio 2008 or start Visual Studio 2008 Express Edition from Start | All Programs | Microsoft Visual C++ 2008 Express Edition.

(b) Select File | New Project... from the File menu. Select Project Type as Visual C++ | Win32 Console Application from the dialog that pops up. Give a proper name of the project in Name TextBox (say Program1). Then click on OK and Finish.

(c) Type the program.

(d) Save the program using **Ctrl + S**.

(e) Use **Ctrl + F5** to compile and execute the program.

When you use Visual Studio to create a Win32 Console Application for any program the wizard would insert the following code by default:

```
#include "stdafx.h"
int _tmain ( int argc, _TCHAR* argv[ ] )
{
    return 0 ;
}
```

You can delete this code and type your program in its place. If you now compile the program using Ctrl F5 you would get the following error:

```
Fatal error C1010:
unexpected end of file while looking for precompiled header.
Did you forget to add '#include "stdafx.h"' to your source?
```

If you add #include “stdafx.h” at the top of your program then it would compile and run successfully. However, including this file makes the program Visual Studio-centric and would not get compiled with TC++ and gcc compilers. This is not good as the program no longer remains portable. To eliminate this error, you need to make a setting in Visual Studio. To make this setting carry out the following steps:

(a) Go to ‘Solution Explorer’.

(b) Right click on the project name and select 'Properties' from the menu that pops up. On doing so, a dialog shown in Figure 1.1 would appear.

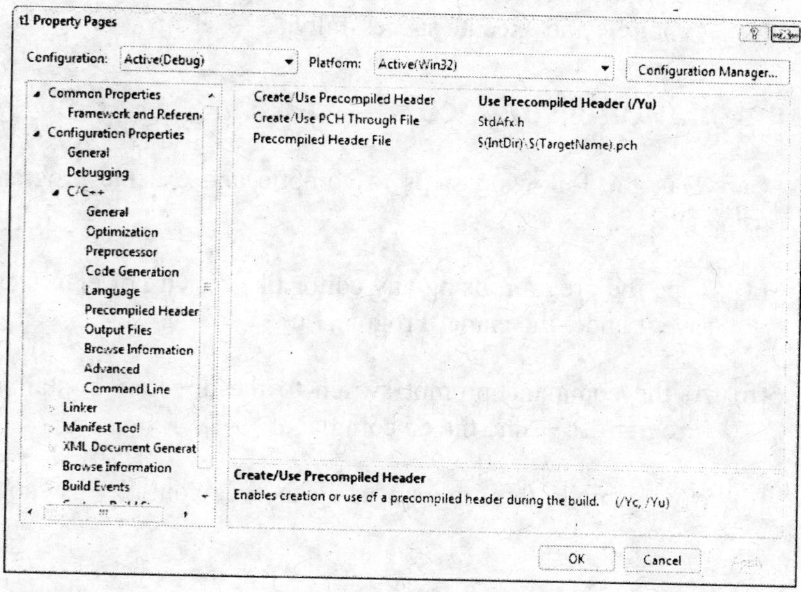

Figure 1.1

(c) From the left pane of this dialog first select 'Configuration Properties' followed by 'C/C++'.

(d) Select 'Precompiled Headers'

(e) From the right pane of the dialog click on 'Create/Use Precompiled Header'. On doing so in the value for this option a triangle would appear.

(f) Click on this triangle and a drop down list box would appear.

(g) From the list box select 'Not using Precompiled Header'.

(h) Click on OK button to make the setting effective.

Once this setting is made you can now compile the program using Ctrl F5. This time no error would be flagged and the program would compile and execute successfully.

Compilation Using gcc

Carry out the following steps to compile and execute programs using gcc:

(a) Type the program using any editor like vi, vim or emacs and save it under the name 'Program1.c'.

(b) At the command prompt switch to the directory containing 'Program1.c' using the **cd** command.

(c) Now compile the program using the **gcc** compiler as shown below:

```
# gcc Program1.c
```

(d) On successful compilation, **gcc** produces a file named 'a.out'. This file contains the machine code of the program which can now be executed.

(e) Execute the program using the following command.

```
# ./a.out
```

(f) Now you should be able to see the output of Program 1 on the screen.

A Word Of Caution

All programs given in the chapters to follow have been created assuming that you have installed Visual Studio on your machine. If you have installed TC++, then you would be required to make some minor changes pertaining to clearing of screen and positioning of cursor. Let me show this to you using a simple program that first clears the screen then positions the cursor at 10th row, 20th column and prints a message at this location. If we were to use TC++, the program would look like this…

```
#include <stdio.h>
#include <conio.h>
int main( )
{
    clrscr( ) ; /* clear existing contents on screen */
    gotoxy ( 20, 10 ) ; /* position cursor */
    printf ( "Hello" ) ;
}
```

A similar program in Visual Studio would take the following form:

```
#include <stdio.h>
#include <system.h>
void gotoxy ( short int col, short int row ) ;

int main( )
{
    system ( "cls" ) ; /* clear existing contents on screen */
    gotoxy ( 20, 10 ) ; /* position cursor */
    printf ( "Hello" ) ;
}
void gotoxy ( short int col, short int row )
```

```
{
    HANDLE hStdout = GetStdHandle ( STD_OUTPUT_HANDLE ) ;
    COORD position = { col, row } ;
    SetConsoleCursorPosition ( hStdout, position ) ;
}
```

With choice of the development tool, the installation procedure and the compilation process out of the way, I think we are ready to begin learning C++ formally. That is what the next chapter is all about.

CHAPTER THREE

Graduating To C++

I would assume that you have installed a C++ compiler to run the programs in this book. Most of the programs in this book have been developed and executed using the Visual Studio Express Edition compiler, but I trust that they would also work with other C++ compilers in the market. Visual Studio provides a good platform for learning C++. Its Integrated Development Environment (IDE) puts all the tools that you need for C++ program development into a single, convenient screen display. We won't be discussing here Visual Studio's programming environment, or explaining how loops, switches and functions work. It is assumed that you have at least a working knowledge of C. The aim here is to help a C programmer to become a proficient C++ programmer.

Like C, C++ began its life at Bell Labs, where Bjarne Stroustrup developed the language in the early 1980s. In his own words, "C++ was primarily designed so that programmers would not have to program in assembler, C, or various modern high-level languages. Its main purpose is to make writing good programs easier for the programmer." Stroustrup based C++ on C because of C's brevity, its suitability to system programming, and its widespread availability. C++'s OOP aspect was inspired by a computer simulation language called Simula67. Stroustrup added OOP features to C without significantly changing the C component. Thus C++ is a superset of C, meaning that any valid C Programming is a C++ program too. In order to add object-oriented features a number of new keywords were created for C++. These are:

asm	bool	catch	class
const_cast	delete	dynamic_cast	explicit
friend	inline	mutable	namespace
new	operator	private	protected
public	reinterpret_cast	static_cast	template
this	throw	try	typeid
using	virtual		

We would postpone the discussion of these keywords or the object-oriented features of C++ to subsequent chapters. In this chapter we would take a look at the non-object-oriented extensions provided in C++. We would take them up one by one. Before that we would arm ourselves with statements that can do simple input/output for us.

Consider the following statement:

```
cout << "God, Give me common sense!" ;
```

This statement causes the phrase in the quotation marks to be displayed on the screen. A complete description of this statement requires an understanding of objects, operator overloading, and other topics we won't discuss until later in the book, but here's a brief preview.

The identifier *cout* (pronounced "C out") is actually an object. It is predefined to correspond to the *standard output stream*. A *stream* is an abstraction that refers to a flow of data. The standard output stream normally flows to the screen display, although it can be redirected to other output devices. We will discuss streams in Chapter 11.

The operator << is called the *insertion* or *put to* operator. It directs the contents of the variable on its right to the object on its left. In our statement it directs the string constant "God, Give me common sense!" to *cout*, which sends it to display. (If you know C, you will recognise << as the left-shift bitwise operator and wonder how it can also be used to direct output. In C++ operators can be *overloaded*. That is, they can perform different activities, depending on the context. We'll learn about overloading in Chapter 4.)

Although the concepts behind the use of *cout* and << may be obscure at this point, using them is easy. They'll appear in almost every program in this book. Now that we know how output to the screen can be accomplished let us turn our attention to receiving input from the keyboard.

Contrary to *cout*, to receive input through the keyboard what is used is an identifier *cin*. The word *cin* (pronounced "C in") is an object, predefined in C++ to correspond to the *standard input stream*. This stream represents data coming from the keyboard (unless it has been redirected). The >> is the *extraction* or *get from* operator. It takes the value from the stream object on its left and places it in the variable on its right. Here's some sample code that shows *cin* at work.

```
#include <iostream>
using namespace std ;

int main( )
{
    char str[40] ;
    int m1, m2, m3, avg ;

    cout << "Enter your name: " ;
    cin >> str ;

    cout << "Enter marks in three subjects: " ;
    cin >> m1 >> m2 >> m3 ;
    avg = ( m1 + m2 + m3 ) / 3 ;

    cout << "Your name is " << str ;
    cout << endl << "And your average marks are " << avg << endl ;
    return 0 ;
}
```

Here is some sample interaction with the program.

```
Enter your name: Saurav Gupta
Enter marks in three subjects: 44 72 64
Your name is Saurav Gupta
And your average marks are 60
```

In the first line of this program we have included the file 'iostream.h'. In C++ the convention is to drop the .h while including the file.

The 'iostream.h' file contains declarations that are needed by *cout* & *cin* identifiers and << & >> operators. Without these declarations the compiler won't recognize *cout* & *cin* and will think that << & >> are being used incorrectly.

The next line, *using namespace std;*, will be present in nearly all the programs in this book. To understand the meaning of this statement we need to first understand what a namespace is. A namespace is nothing but a collection of identifiers (variable names and some other types of names that we haven't discussed yet) that all belong to a group or family. For example, all identifiers in the C++ standard library belong to a namespace called *std*.

There are two ways to refer to a specific identifier that belongs to a namespace. These are:

(a) Use the *using* statement at the beginning of the program as we have done in our program.

(b) Prefix the identifier with the name of the namespace followed by two colons. An example of this is shown below:

```
std::cout << "Enter your name: " ;
```

Naturally, the first way is a better way rather than preceding every *cout*, *cin* and *endl* with *std::*.

The first pair of *cout* and *cin* used in the program is straightforward. *cout* outputs a message asking for the name and *cin* receives that name in the string *str[ ]*.

Note the repeated use of the extraction operator >> in the second *cin* statement. This is perfectly legal. This is known as cascading of operators. It is a better idea than having three independent *cin*s. However, using this capability eliminates the opportunity to prompt the user between inputs. As you may have guessed cascading of insertion operators is also allowed.

Look at the last *cout* statement. You would find the use of an unfamiliar word in this statement, *endl*. This is known as a *manipulator*. It causes a linefeed to be inserted in the output stream. As a result, the phrase following it appears on a fresh line. The same effect could have been obtained by sending the newline character '\n' to the output stream through any of the following statements:

```
cout << "\n" << "And your average marks are " << avg ;
cout << '\n' << "And your average marks are " << avg ;
cout << "\nAnd your average marks are " << avg ;
```

These are workable statements. However, using *endl* to do the same job is perhaps a cleaner way of doing it.

And now a thousand-dollar question! Have we gained anything out of using *cin* and *cout* instead of *scanf( )* and *printf( )*? Certainly. In *scanf( )* and *printf( )* we have to always mention the format specifiers in the format string (*%d* for integer, *%s* for string etc.). This gets completely avoided while using *cin* and *cout*. Also, as you would see in Chapter 11, we can employ *cin* and *cout* to perform input/output for user-defined data types as well.

Function Prototypes

A function prototype is a declaration that defines the return type and the parameters of a function. Following are a few examples:

```
float square ( float ) ;
char * strconvert ( char *, int ) ;
double nthroot ( float, float ) ;
```

Each of this declaration clearly specifies the number, order and the type of arguments each function is going to receive during a call, and the type of the value that each function would return when the control comes back from it.

The compiler uses the prototype to ensure that the types of actual arguments that you pass in a function call are the same as the types of the formal arguments in the function definition. No C++ function can be called unless its prototype is available to the compiler to crosscheck the argument type and the return value. This is known as strong type checking.

In the following program if the file 'string.h' is not *#include*d, the prototype of the function *strupr( )* would not be available. Hence a call to this function would result in an error.

```
#include <string>
#include <iostream>
using namespace std ;
int main( )
{
    char str[ ] = "Hello" ;
```

```
    strupr ( str ) ;
    cout << str << endl ;
    return 0 ;
}
```

Comments

Unlike C, C++ supports two types of comments. C programmers are familiar with the /* */ style of commenting. Anything lying within the /*.. */ pair is ignored by the compiler. C++ additionally supports the // notation for commenting. For example,

```
c = 5.0 / 9 * ( f - 32 ) ; // conversion formula
```

Here, everything following // till the end of line is treated as comment. Usually /* */ style is used for commenting out a block of code, whereas, // is used for single line comments.

Flexible Declarations

C is quite rigid as far as declaration of variables is concerned. C requires that all variables be declared before the first executable statement. As against this, C++ allows definition of variables at the point where they are used. The following example illustrates this.

```
#include <iostream>
using namespace std ;

int main( )
{
    int f ;

    cin >> f ;
    int c = ( f - 32 ) * 5 / 9 ;
```

```
    cout << c ;

    for ( int j = 10 ; j <= 100 ; j++ )
        cout << endl << j << endl ;
    return 0 ;
}
```

Note that the variables *c* and *j* have not been declared at the beginning of the function *main( )* as would have been necessary in a C program. Instead, they have been declared where they are used to store a value. Declaring variables where they are used makes the program easier to understand, since you don't need to refer repeatedly to the beginning of the function to find the variable declarations. However, this practice should be used with discretion. Variables that are used in many places in a function are probably better defined at the start of the function.

structure, *union* And *enum* Syntax

Consider the following declarations:

```
struct employee
{
    char name[20] ;
    int age ;
} ;
union data
{
    char ch[2] ;
    int i ;
} ;
enum status { married, unmarried, divorced } ;
employee e ;
data d ;
status s ;
```

Note how the variables *e*, *d* and *s* have been defined. C++, unlike C, doesn't need the keywords *struct*, *union* and *enum* while defining the variables *e*, *d* and *s*. Thus the format for defining a structure variable is exactly same as the one used for a variable of a built-in data type such as *int*:

```
int i ;
employee e ;
```

This similarity is not accidental. One of the aims of C++ is to make the syntax and the operation of the user-defined data types similar to that of built-in data types.

There is another major difference between structures and unions of C++ as compared to those in C. Structures and unions of C++ can contain as their elements not only various data types but also functions. We would take up this aspect of structures and unions in Chapter 5 when we study something called *classes* in C++.

Anonymous *unions* And *enums*

A special type of *union* and *enum* has been added in C++. They are called *anonymous union* and *enum*. An anonymous union does not have a union name (tag), and its elements can be accessed directly without using a *union* variable. Following example illustrates this:

```
union
{
    int i ;
    char ch[2] ;
} ;
```

Both *i* and the array *ch[ ]* share the same memory locations and can be accessed directly simply by saying,

```
i = 10 ;
ch[0] = 'A' ;
```

Simply omitting the *union* name in the declaration does not make the *union* an anonymous *union*. For a *union* to qualify as an anonymous *union*, the declaration must not declare a variable of the *union* type.

On similar lines anonymous *enums* can be built as shown below:

```
enum { first, second, slleper, actwotier } ;
int t = second ;
```

The stream I/O classes presented in Chapter 11 define several anonymous enumerated types.

Typecasting

If we carry out an operation between an *int* and a *float* the *int* is promoted to a *float* before performing the operation. This conversion takes place automatically. A few more such automatic conversions are possible in C/C++. As against these automatic conversions, to carry out data conversions desired by the programmer typecasting is used. Two different types of typecasting syntaxes are supported in C++. These are given below:

```
int y = 1001, j = 365, n ;
n = ( y - 1 )  * j ;  /* results in wrong answer since integer
                         range is exceeded on multiplication */

n = ( y - 1 ) * ( long ) j ;  // C style typecasting, also supported by C++
```

```
n = ( y - 1 ) * long ( j ) ; // new C++ style typecasting
```

C supports only the first type of casting, whereas, C++ supports both. Instead of using typecasting we may as well have defined *j* as *long*. In this small fragment of code this would have worked. However, in a situation where we subsequently want to use *j* as an *int* there is no alternative to typecasting.

void Pointers

The keyword *void* can be used to define a pointer to a generic term. Unlike C, in C++ special care has to be taken to handle the assignment of *void* pointers to other pointer types. This is shown in the following code fragment.

```
void *p ;
char *s ;
p = s ;
s = p ;
```

Here, the second assignment would flag an error indicating a type mismatch. While you can assign a pointer of any type to a *void* pointer, the reverse is not true unless you specifically typecast it as shown below:

```
s = ( char * ) p ;
```

The :: Operator

:: is the scope resolution operator. Let us straightway put it to work in a program.

```
#include <iostream>
using namespace std ;
```

```
int a = 10 ;

int main( )
{
    int a = 15 ;
    cout << "\nLocal a = " << a << " Global a = " << ::a ;
    ::a = 20 ;
    cout << "\nLocal a = " << a << " Global a = " << ::a << endl ;
    return 0 ;
}
```

Here is the output of the program...

```
Local a = 15 Global a = 10
Local a = 15 Global a = 20
```

Suppose in a C program there are two variables with the same name *a*. Assume that one has been declared outside all functions (global) and another is declared locally inside a function. Now if we attempt to access the variable *a* in the function we always access the local variable. This is because the rule says that whenever there is a conflict between a local and a global variable, the local variable gets the priority. Moreover, the global variable is inaccessible when a local variable of the same name is available within the function. C++ allows you the flexibility of accessing both the variables. It achieves this through a scope resolution operator *::*.

Thus in the above example using *a* allows us an access to the local *a*, whereas, *::a* allows an access to the global *a*. The output proves that not only can we access a global variable and print its existing value, we can also reinitialize it to another value.

Let us try another program that further clarifies global scoping.

```
#include <iostream>
using namespace std ;

int i = 10 ;

int main( )
{
    int i = 20 ;
    cout << endl << i << " " << ::i ;
    {
        int i = 30 ;
        cout << endl << i << " " << ::i ;
    }
    cout << endl << i << " " << ::I << endl ;
    return 0 ;
}
```

Can you guess the output of this one? The first *cout* would of course print *20* and *10*. Then comes a block in which we have again defined *i*. This *i* has got nothing to do with the other two *i*'s already defined. In the second *cout*, *i* refers to the most local *i* (the one defined inside the block), hence prints out *30*; whereas, *::i* refers to the global *i* and not the one defined above the block and hence prints *10*. The last *cout* would output *20* and *10*. Here *i* refers to the local *i* since the moment control comes out of the block the *i* defined inside the block dies.

I hope you appreciate the apt name given to the :: operator. After all it resolves a dispute in scope when local and global variables exist with same names. The scope resolution operator is used in a number of more places. But that involves object-oriented features. So let's skip that for the moment. For the present let's take on another fundamental concept. Referencing.

References

A reference is like a pointer. But, there is a subtle difference between the two. This difference we would see later. Let us first write a program that uses a reference.

```
#include <iostream>
using namespace std ;

int main( )
{
    int i = 10 ;
    int &j = i ;
    cout << "i = " << i << "  j = " << j << endl ;
    j = 20 ;
    cout << "i = " << i << "  j = " << j << endl ;
    i = 30 ;
    cout << "i = " << i << "  j = " << j << endl ;
    i++ ;
    cout << "i = " << i << "  j = " << j << endl ;
    j++ ;
    cout << "i = " << i << "  j = " << j << endl ;
    cout << "address of i = " << &i << "address of j =" <<  &j << endl ;
    return 0 ;
}
```

And here is the output...

```
i = 10 j = 10
i = 20 j = 20
i = 30 j = 30
i = 31 j = 31
i = 32 j = 32
address of i = 61342 address of j = 61342
```

In this program *j* is called *reference* of *i*. A reference is indicated by using the & operator in the same way you use the * operator to indicate a pointer. A reference, as the name suggests, is like an alias. Call it by this name or that, it *refers* to the same entity. A variable and its reference are so tightly inter-locked, that a change in one necessarily results in a change in the other. So, whether you change the value of *i* or *j*, both the values will change concurrently. Cross check that with the output. Operators too work on reference variables similarly. Thus incrementing *i* increments *j* and vice-versa. The last line of the output very clearly brings out the fact that *i* and *j* refer to the same entity since their addresses are same.

A few points to note...

(a) A reference must always be initialised. Thus the following set of statements produce an error.

```
int i = 4 ;
int &j ; // error
j = i ;
```

(b) Once a reference variable has been defined to refer to a particular variable, it cannot refer to any other variable. That is, once the variable and the reference are linked they are tied together inseparably.

(c) The way we can create a reference to an *int*, or a *float* or a *char*, we can also create a reference to a pointer. The declaration of such a reference would look like this:

```
char *p = "Hello" ;
char *&q = p ;
```

(d) A variable can have multiple references. Changing the value of one of them effects a change in all others.

(e) Though an array of pointers is acceptable, an array of references is not.

What is the advantage of referencing? Referencing goes a long way in erasing untidiness in code, making it more readable, as the following program would justify.

```
# include <iostream>
using namespace std ;

// prototype declarations
void swapv ( int, int ) ;
void swapr ( int &, int & ) ;
void swapa ( int *, int * ) ;

int main( )
{
    int a =10, b = 20 ;

    swapv ( a, b ) ; // call by value
    cout << endl << a << "\t" << b ;

    swapa ( &a, &b ) ; // call by address
    cout << endl << a << "\t" << b ;

    swapr ( a, b ) ; // call by reference
    cout << endl << a << "\t" << b << endl ;
    return 0 ;
}

void swapv ( int i, int j )
{
    int t ;

    t = i ;
    i = j ;
```

```
    j = t ;
    cout << i << "\t" << j ;
}

void swapa ( int *i, int *j )
{
    int t ;

    t = *i ;
    *i = *j ;
    *j = t ;
}

void swapr ( int &i, int &j )
{
    int t ;

    t = i ;
    i = j ;
    j = t ;
}
```

In this program the call to *swapv( )* is the normal call by value. Interchanging the values of *i* and *j* in this function has no effect on the values of *a* and *b* in *main( )*. The *swapa( )* function demonstrates a call by address, whereby using pointers we change the values of *a* and *b* in the calling function. The *swapr( )* achieves the same purpose as *swapa( )*, the only difference being this function is called by reference. You would agree that the style of using references to swap values is more elegant and pleasant to the eye. Moreover, a pointer has to be de-referenced before you can access a value using it, while a reference need not be. A reference works more directly in that sense. The calling syntax of *swapr( )* too is much simpler as compared to that of *swapa( )*.

Thus *referencing* offers a clean, elegant and efficient way to pass parameters to functions that intend to change their values. Let's take another program and get the essence of references really clear.

```
#include <iostream>
#include <string>
using namespace std ;

struct employee
{
    char name[20] ;
    int age ;
    float salary ;
} ;

void modify_c ( employee * ) ;
void modify_cpp ( employee & ) ;

int main( )
{
    employee e1 = { "sanjay", 32, 3200.00 } ;
    employee e2 = { "sameer", 28, 1950.00 } ;

    modify_c ( &e1 ) ;
    cout << endl << e1.name << endl << e1.age << endl << e1.salary ;
    modify_cpp ( e2 ) ;
    cout << endl << e2.name << endl << e2.age << endl << e2.salary <<
    endl ;
    return 0 ;
}

void modify_c ( employee *e )
{
    strcpy ( e->name, "santosh" ) ;
    e->age = 37 ;
```

```
    e->salary = 3970.00 ;
}

void modify_cpp ( employee &e )
{
    strcpy ( e.name, "sanket" ) ;
    e.age = 31 ;
    e.salary = 2500.00 ;
}
```

This program has two functions *modify_c( )* and *modify_cpp( )*. Both are used to modify contents of structure variables. As their names suggest, the first uses C style (using a pointer) of modification, whereas the second uses C++ style (using a reference). You would agree that though both achieve the same purpose the C++ style is more elegant and doesn't involve the stars and spangles associated with the usage of a pointer.

This of course doesn't mean that wherever we use pointers we can substitute them by references. In certain situations pointers are just irreplaceable.

Returning By Reference

We have seen how we can pass a reference to a function as a parameter. We can also return a reference from a function. When a function returns a reference, the function call can exist in any context where a reference can exist, including on the receiving side of an assignment. The following example would clarify this.

```
#include <iostream>
using namespace std ;

struct emp
{
```

```
    char name[20] ;
    int age ;
    float sal ;
} ;

emp e1 = { "Amol", 21, 2345.00 } ;
emp e2 = { "Ajay", 23, 4500.75 } ;

emp &fun( ) ;

int main( )
{
    fun( ) = e2 ;
    cout << endl << e1.name << endl << e1.age << endl << e1.sal << endl ;
    return 0 ;
}

emp &fun( )
{
    cout << endl << e1.name << endl << e1.age << endl << e1.sal ;
    return e1 ;
}
```

Here we have declared a structure *emp* and initialized two global variables *e1* and *e2* to some values. In *fun( )*, having printed the values stored in *e1* we have returned it by reference. What is strange is the call to the function *fun( )*. It has been written on the left-hand side of the assignment operator:

```
fun( ) = e2 ;
```

The result is that the variable returned by the function is assigned the value on the right hand side of the = sign. The following output of the *cout* statement in *main( )* verifies that the assignment has indeed taken place.

```
Ajay
23
4500.75
```

A word of caution! Do not try to return a local variable by reference. This is because the local variable goes out of scope when the function returns. You would, therefore, be returning a reference for a variable that no longer exists, and the calling function would be referring to a variable that does not exist. Some C++ compilers issue a warning when they see code that returns references to automatic variables. If you ignore the warning, you get unpredictable results. Sometimes the program appears to work because the stack location where the automatic variable existed is intact when the reference is used. A program that appears to work in some cases can fail in others due to device or multitasking interrupts that use the stack.

The *const* Qualifier

The keyword *const* (for constant), if present, precedes the data type of a variable. It specifies that the value of the variable will not change throughout the program. Any attempt to alter the value of the variable defined with this qualifier will result into an error message from the compiler. *const* is usually used to replace #*define*d constants.

const qualifier ensures that your program does not inadvertently alter a variable that you intended to be a constant. It also reminds anybody reading the program listing that the variable is not intended to change. Variables with this qualifier are often named in all uppercase, as a reminder that they are constants. The following program shows the usage of *const*.

```
#include <iostream>
using namespace std ;

int main( )
{
    float r, a ;
    const float PI = 3.14f ;

    cin >> r ;
    a = PI * r * r ;
    cout << endl << "Area of circle = " << a << endl ;
    return 0 ;
}
```

const is a better idea as compared to *#define* because its scope of operation can be controlled by placing it appropriately either inside a function or outside all functions. If a *const* is placed inside a function its effect would be localised to that function, whereas, if it is placed outside all functions then its effect would be global. We cannot exercise such finer control while using a *#define*.

const Pointers

Look at the following program:

```
#include <iostream>
using namespace std ;

void xstrcpy ( char *, char * ) ;

int main( )
{
    char str1[ ] = "Nagpur" ;
    char str2[10] ;
```

```
    xstrcpy ( str2, str1 ) ;
    cout << endl << str2 << endl ;
    return 0 ;
}

void xstrcpy ( char *t, char *s )
{
    while ( *s != '\0' )
    {
        *t = *s ;
        t++ ;
        s++ ;
    }
    *t = '\0' ;
}
```

This program simply copies the contents of *str1[ ]* into *str2[ ]* using the function *xstrcpy( )*. What would happen if we add the following lines beyond the last statement of *xstrcpy( )*?.

```
s = s - 6 ;
*s = 'K' ;
```

This would change the source string to "Kagpur". Can we not ensure that the source string doesn't change even accidentally in *xstrcpy( )*? We can, by changing the prototype of the function to

```
void xstrcpy ( char *, const char * ) ;
```

Correspondingly the definition would change to:

```
void xstrcpy ( char *t, const char *s )
{
    // code
}
```

The following code fragment would help you to fix your ideas about *const* further.

```
char *p = "Hello" ; // pointer is variable, string is constant
*p = 'M' ; // error
p = "Bye" ; // works

const char *q = "Hello" ; // pointer is variable, string is constant
*q = 'M' ; // error
q = "Bye" ; // works

char const *s = "Hello" ; // pointer is variable, string is constant
*s = 'M' ; // error
s = "Bye" ; // works

char * const t = "Hello" ; // pointer is constant, so is string
*t = 'M' ; // works
t = "Bye" ; // error

const char * const u = "Hello" ; // string is fixed, so is pointer
*u = 'M' ; // error
u = "Bye" ; // error
```

const References

Earlier we saw that we can pass the reference of a variable to a function if we want to change the variable in the function without being required to use pointers. That is not the only use of passing by reference. If we pass the variable by value then it would be collected into another variable, thereby creating another variable. If several variables were passed by value then those many additional variables would get created. We can avoid creation of these variables by passing the variables by reference. This would improve the efficiency. However, now there is a possibility that the variables may accidentally get modified in the function. This can be prevented by declaring them as constant. This is shown below.

```
#include <iostream>
using namespace std ;

void change ( const int & ) ;

int main( )
{
    int i = 32 ;
    change ( i ) ;
    cout << endl << i ;
    return 0 ;
}
void change ( const int &j )
{
    j = 45 ;
}
```

Passing *i* by reference prevents a new variable from getting created. At the same time using the *const* qualifier prevents *j* (and in turn *i*) from getting modified. Our attempt to modify *j* is met with an error message 'Cannot modify a constant object'.

Let us now see a few examples that would further clarify the concept of the *const* qualifier and references.

```
#include <iostream>
using namespace std ;

int main( )
{
    const int i = 10 ;
    int &j = i ;
```

```
    cout << "i = " << i << " j = " << j ;
    j = 20 ;
    cout << "i = " << i << " j = " << j ;
    return 0 ;
}
```

Here we have tied *j* with *i*. So changing *j* should not change *i*, as we have declared *i* to be constant so it should not be possible to change it, even through its reference. So we should expect the following output from the program.

```
i = 10 j = 10
i = 10 j = 20
```

However, when we compile the program it reports an error saying 'cannot convert from *const int* to *int &* '. This error is reported because we have declared *j* to be a reference to an *int* and not to a *const int*.

Let us take another similar case where we keep the reference constant.

```
#include <iostream>
using namespace std ;

int main( )
{
    int i = 10 ;
    const int &j = i ;
    cout << i << j ;
    j = 20 ;
    cout << i << j ;
    return 0 ;
}
```

This program won't even clear the compilation hurdle. Obviously so, since we are going back on our word. We declared that *j* would remain constant and then we are attempting to change it through the statement *j = 20.*

Moral to be drawn from the above two programs is, once we declare a variable or a reference as constant we cannot change their values.

What do you think the following program would output?

```
#include <iostream>
using namespace std ;
int main( )
{
    int i = 10 ;
    const int &j = i ;
    i = 20 ;
    cout << endl << "i = " << i << " j = " << j << endl ;
    return 0 ;
}
```

The output would be:

```
i = 20 j = 20
```

What does that imply? The reference is dependent upon the variable it refers to. If we change the value of the variable, the value of the reference changes automatically, constant or otherwise.

The way we use referencing for integers can we do so with strings too? Of course. Here is how...

```
#include <iostream>
using namespace std ;
int main( )
{
    char *str1 = "Rain Rain Here Again " ;
    char * & str2 = str1 ;
    cout << endl << str1 << endl << str2 ;

    *str1 = 'M' ;
    cout << endl << str1 << endl << str2 ;

    *str2 = 'P' ;
    cout << endl << str1 << endl << str2 ;
    return 0 ;
}
```

Here *str1* is a pointer to a constant string "Rain Rain Here Again". And *str2* is a pointer that acts as reference to *str1*. Thus, both *str1* and *str2* point to the same string. Next we have attempted to change the constant string first through *str1* and through *str2* both result into a runtime error, as through them we are trying to change a string which is constant.

Returning *const* Values

A function can return a pointer to a constant string as shown below.

```
#include <iostream>
using namespace std ;

const char *fun( ) ;

int main( )
{
```

```
    const char *p ;
    p = fun( ) ;
    *p = 'A' ; // Error
    cout << p ;
    return 0 ;
}

const char *fun( )
{
    return "Rain" ;
}
```

Here since the function *fun( )* is returning a constant string, we cannot use the pointer *p* to modify it. Not only this, the following operations too would be invalid:

(a) *main( )* cannot assign the return value to a pointer to a *non-const* string.

(b) *main( )* cannot pass the return value to a function that is expecting a pointer to a non-*const* string.

const Member Functions

In C structures can contain only data types, whereas, in C++ they can contain functions too. Also, similar to structure, there is one more entity in C++ called class. It too can contain data members and member functions. *const* can be used to qualify member functions in a structure or a class. This usage of *const* would be discussed in Chapter 7.

Constructors For Intrinsic Data Types

If we are to initialize variables of intrinsic data types we do so through statements like,

```
int age = 23 ;
float salary = 4500.50 ;
```

C++ allows one more way to initialize the intrinsic data types. This is shown below.

```
int age ( 23 ) ;
float salary ( 4500.50 ) ;
```

This notation of initializing variables is known as a class constructor notation. You will learn about class constructors in Chapter 5.

The *bool* Data Type

This is a new addition to C++. The data type *bool* gets its name from George Boole, a 19th century English mathematician who inveneted the concept of using logical operators with true or false values. These values are often called boolean values.

This data type can take only two values *true* or *false*. It is most commonly used to hold the results of comparisons. For example,

```
bool x, y ;
int a = 10, b = 20, c = 30 ;
x = a < b ;
y = b >= c ;
```

Here *x* gets a value *true*, whereas, *y* gets value *false*.

By definition, *true* has a value *1* when converted to an integer and *false* has a value *0*. Conversely, integers can be implicitly converted to *bool* values: non-zero integers convert to *true* and *0* converts to *false*. *bool*s can be used in arithmetic and logical expressions. If so done they are converted to integers and integer arithmetic and logical operations are performed on these integers. The result of these operations can be converted back to *bool*; a *0* is converted to *false* and a non-zero value is converted to *true*. The following program and its output would help you to understand these conversions.

```
#include <iostream>
using namespace std ;

int main( )
{
    bool b = 32 ;
    int i = false ;
    cout << endl << b << endl << i ;

    int j = b + b ;
    bool k = b + b ;
    cout << endl << j << endl << k << endl ;
    return 0 ;
}
```

And here is the output

```
1
0
2
1
```

bool can also be used as a return type of a function, usually indicating the success or failure of the function to carry out the assigned job. Older C++ compilers including Turbo C++ 3.0 doesn't recognize the *bool* data type.

Exercise

[A] State True or False:

(a) In C++, a structure can contain data members, as well as functions that can operate upon the data members.

(b) In C++, a union can contain data members, as well as functions that can operate upon the data members.

(c) If the function is defined before calling it, there is no need to mention its prototype.

(d) It is possible to create an array references.

(e) Once a reference is tied with a variable it cannot be tied with another variable.

(f) A variable can be tied with several references.

(g) In a C++ program re-definitions are not allowed where as re-declarations are allowed.

(h) In C++ a function call can occur even on the left-hand side of an assignment operator.

(i) It is unsafe to return a local variable by reference.

(j) *cin* and *cout* are objects.

(k) C++ permits the use of anonymous structures.

(l) A pointer of another type can be assigned to a *void* pointer without the need for typecasting.

(m) The following two definitions are same:

```
enum grade g ;
grade g ;
```

(n) The following two statements perform the same job:

```
int a = 10 ;
int a ( 10 ) ;
```

(o) The following two statements perform the same job:

```
bool a ;
BOOL a ;
```

(p) The following three statements perform the same job:

```
cout << "\n" ;
cout << '\n' ;
cout << endl ;
```

[B] What will be the output of the following programs:

(a)
```
#include <iostream>
using namespace std ;

int main( )
{
    int i = 5 ;
    int &j = i ;
    int p = 10 ;

    j = p ;
    cout << endl << i << endl << j ;
    p = 20 ;
    cout << endl << i << endl << j ;
    return 0 ;
}
```

(b)
```
#include <iostream>
using namespace std ;

int main( )
```

```
{
    char *p = "hello" ;
    char *q = p ;
    cout << p << endl << q ;
    q = "Good Bye" ;
    cout << p << endl << q ;
    return 0 ;
}
```

(c)
```
#include <iostream>
using namespace std ;

int i = 20 ;

int main( )
{
    int i = 5 ;
    cout << i << endl << ::i ;
    return 0 ;
}
```

(d)
```
#include <iostream>
using namespace std ;

int i = 20 ;

int main( )
{
    int i = 5 ;
    cout << i << endl << ::i ;
    {
        int i = 10 ;
        cout << i << endl << ::i ;
    }
    return 0 ;
}
```

(e)
```
#include <iostream>
using namespace std ;

const int i = 10 ;

int main( )
{
    const int i = 20 ;
    cout << i << endl << ::i ;
    cout << &i << endl << &::i ;
    return 0 ;
}
```

(f)
```
#include <iostream>
using namespace std ;

int main( )
{
    int i ;
    cout << sizeof ( i ) << endl << sizeof ( 'i' ) ;
    return 0 ;
}
```

(g)
```
#include <iostream>
using namespace std ;

int main( )
{
    for ( int i = 1 ; i <= 10 ; i++ )
        cout << i << endl ;
    cout << i ;
    return 0 ;
}
```

[C] Point out the errors, if any, in the following programs.

(a)
```
#include <iostream>
```

```
using namespace std ;

int main( )
{
    int i = 5 ;
    int &j = i ;
    int &k = j ;
    int &l = i ;

    cout << i << j << k << l ;
    return 0 ;
}
```

(b)
```
#include <iostream>
using namespace std ;

int main( )
{
    int a = 10, b = 20 ;
    long int c ;
    c = a * long int ( b ) ;
    cout << c ;
    return 0 ;
}
```

(c)
```
#include <iostream>
using namespace std ;

const int i = 10 ;

int main( )
{
    const int i = 20 ;
    cout << &i << &::i ;
    return 0 ;
}
```

(d)
```
#include <iostream>
using namespace std ;

int main( )
{
    char *p = "Hello" ;
    p = "Hi" ;
    *p = 'G' ;
    cout << p ;
    return 0 ;
}
```

(e)
```
#include <iostream>
using namespace std ;

int main( )
{
    enum result { first, second, third } ;
    result a = first ;
        int b = a ;
        result c = 1 ;
        result d =  result ( 1 ) ;
    return 0 ;
}
```

(f)
```
const int a = 124 ;
const int *sample( ) ;
int main( )
{
    int *p ;
    p = sample( ) ;
    return 0 ;
}
const int *sample( )
{
    return ( &a ) ;
}
```

(g)
```
#include <iostream>
using namespace std ;

int a = 10 ;

int main( )
{
    int a = 20 ;
    {
        int a = 30 ;
        cout << a << ::a << ::::a ;
    }
    return 0 ;
}
```

(h)
```
#include <iostream>
using namespace std ;

struct emp
{
    char name[20] ;
    int age ;
    float sal ;
} ;
emp e1 = { "Amol", 21, 2345.00 } ;
emp e2 = { "Ajay", 19, 2300.00 } ;

emp &fun( ) ;

int main( )
{
    fun( ) = e2 ;
    cout << endl << e1.name << endl << e1.age << endl << e1.sal ;
    return 0 ;
}
```

```
emp &fun( )
{
    emp e3 = { "Aditya", 21, 3300.75 } ;
    return e3 ;
}
```

(i)
```
#include <iostream>
using namespace std ;

int main( )
{
    char t[ ] = "String functions are simple" ;
    int l = strlen ( t ) ;
    cout << l ;
    return 0 ;
}
```

[D] Answer the following:

(a) In the following program how would you define *q*, if the first *cout* is to output "Internet" twice, whereas, the second *cout* is to output "Intranet" twice.

```
#include <iostream>
using namespace std ;

int main( )
{
    char *p = "Internet" ;
    cout << p << q ;
    q = "Intranet" ;
    cout << p << q ;
    return 0 ;
}
```

(b) If *employee* is a structure, *REGS* is a *union* and *maritalstatus* is an *enum* then does there exist any other way in which the following definitions can be made:

```
struct employee e ;
union REGS i ;
enum maritalstatus m ;
```

(c) Can the following statements be written in any other way:

```
employee *p ;
p = ( employee * ) malloc ( sizeof ( e ) ) ;
float q ;
int a, b ;
q = ( float ) a / b ;
```

(d) Create four integers, four pointers to these integers and four references to them. Store these pointers and references in two arrays and print out the values of four integers using these arrays.

(e) Complete the following program by defining the function *swapb( )* and its prototype such that the output of the program is 20 10.

```
#include <iostream>
using namespace std ;

void swapa ( int &, int & ) ;

int main( )
{
    int a = 10, b = 20 ;

    swapa ( a, b ) ;
    cout << a << b ;
    return 0 ;
}
```

```
void swapa ( int &x, int &y )
{
    swapb ( x, y ) ;
}
```

(f) When should we make a call by reference?

(g) Why is using *const* a better idea than an equivalent *#define*?

(h) What are the advantages of *cout* and *cin* over *printf( )* and *scanf( )*?

(i) Is this a valid comment:

```
// This is an /* invalid */ comment
```

(j) What does the following prototype indicate:

```
const char *fun ( char const*, const char * ) ;
```

CHAPTER FOUR

Functions

The ways of supporting function has changed and improved in C++ as compared to C. Most of these changes are simple and straightforward. However, there are a few changes which require you to adopt a new way of thinking and organising your program's code. Many of these requirements were driven by object oriented facilities of C++. As we go along you would realise that these facilities were invented to make C++ programs *safer* and *more readable* than their C equivalents. Let us now see the various issues involved in C++ functions.

Function Prototypes

A function prototype is a declaration that defines both: the arguments passed to the function and the type of value returned by the function. If we were to call a function *fool( )* which receives a *float* and an *int* as arguments and returns a *double* value its prototype would look like this:

```
double fool ( float, int ) ;
```

The C++ compiler uses this prototype to ensure that the types of the arguments you pass in a function call are same as those mentioned in the prototype. If there is a mismatch the compiler points it out immediately. This is known as strong type checking; something which C lacks.

Without strong type checking, it is easier to pass illegal values to functions. For example, a non-prototyped function would allow you to pass an *int* to a pointer variable, or a *float* to a *long int*. The C++ compiler would immediately report such types of errors. In C++ prototypes do more than making sure that actual arguments (those used in calling function) and formal arguments (those used in called function) match in number, order and type. As we would see later, C++ internally generates names for functions, including the argument type information. This information is used when several functions have same names.

Remember that all functions in C++ must be prototyped. This means every function must have its argument list declared, and the actual definition of a function must exactly match its prototypes in the number, order and types of parameters.

Prototyping functions may mean a bit more work when you initially write a program, but prototypes can be invaluable tools in preventing hard-to-find errors. C++ was designed to prevent many of the problems caused by sloppy programmers passing the wrong data types to functions. If you really need to pass a *long* as an *int*, you can do so using a type cast. That way you have explicitly (rather than accidentally) passed a value of one type as an argument to a parameter of another type.

Let's now see the style of defining functions in C++. Though some C++ compilers still accept the K & R style (short for Kernighan & Ritchie) of defining functions it's possibly a better programming practice to use a prototype-like format. Both these formats are shown below:

```
// K & R style
double fool ( a, b )
int a ;  float b ;
{
    // some code
}

// prototype-like style
double fool ( int a, float b )
{
    // some code
}
```

Some of the C++ compilers don't accept the K & R style at all, whereas, some support both the styles. Sooner or later the K & R syntax may be dropped altogether.

Function Overloading

Another significant addition made to the capabilities of functions in C++ is that of *function overloading*. With this facility you can have multiple functions with the same name, unlike C, where all functions in a program must have unique names.

In C every function has to have a unique name. At times this becomes annoying. For example, in C there are several functions that return the absolute value of a numeric argument. Since a unique name is required, there is a separate function for each numeric data type. Thus, there are three different functions that return the absolute value of an argument:

```
int abs ( int i ) ;
long labs ( long l ) ;
double fabs ( double d ) ;
```

All these functions do the same thing, so it seems unnecessary to have three different function names. C++ overcomes this situation by allowing the programmer to create three different functions with the same name. This is called *function overloading*. The following program illustrates this.

```
#include <iostream>
using namespace std ;

int abs ( int ) ;
long abs ( long ) ;
double abs ( double ) ;
```

```
int main( )
{
    int i = -25, j ;
    long l = -100000L, m ;
    double d = -12.34, e ;

    j = abs ( i ) ;
    m = abs ( l ) ;
    e = abs ( d ) ;

    cout << endl << j << endl << m << endl << e << endl ;
    return 0 ;
}

int abs ( int ii )
{
    return ( ii > 0 ? ii : ii * -1 ) ;
}

long abs ( long ll )
{
    return ( ll > 0 ? ll : ll * -1 ) ;
}

double abs ( double dd )
{
    return ( dd > 0 ? dd : dd * -1 ) ;
}
```

How does the C++ compiler know which of the *abs( )s* should be called when a call is made? It decides that from the type of the argument being passed during the function call. For example, if an *int* is being passed the integer version of *abs( )* gets called, if a *double* is being passed then the double version of *abs( )* gets called and so on. That's quite logical, you would agree.

What if we make a call like,

ch = abs ('A') ;

We have not declared an *abs( )* function to handle a *char*. Hence the C++ compiler would report an error. If we want that this call should result into a call to the *int* version of *abs( )*, we must use typecasting during the call, as shown below:

ch = abs ((int) 'A') ;

Likewise, if we want to get the absolute value of a *float* then to ensure that the *double* version of *abs( )* gets called we must again use typecasting.

On similar lines as *abs( )* you can think of writing overloaded functions for converting an integer to a string (*itoa( )* in C) and a long to a string (*ltoa( )* in C).

Do you think the following program would work?

```
#include <iostream>
using namespace std ;

int asciitonumber ( char * ) ;
long int asciitonumber ( char * ) ;

int main( )
{
    int n1 ;
    int n2 ;

    char *ptr1 = "155" ;
    char *ptr2 = "400000" ;

    n1 = asciitonumber ( ptr1 ) ;
    n2 = asciitonumber ( ptr2 ) ;
    cout << n1 << endl << n2 ;
```

```
    return 0 ;
}
```

No, there is no need to even write the overloaded functions *asciitonumber( )*. Because howsoever we write them there would still be an ambiguity when we call these functions. The reason is that these functions would receive the same type of argument and would differ only in the value that they return. Moral is overloaded functions must at least differ in the type, number or order of parameters they accept. Don't rely on the return values to differentiate them.

Can we fool the C++ compiler into believing that two same data types are different by renaming one of them using *typedef*? No. A *typedef* merely gives another name for an existing type and does not constitute an original type of its own. Hence, the following program segment would give an error:

```
typedef INT int ;
void display ( int ) ;
void display ( INT ) ;
```

The example above would not compile correctly because the compiler has no way of differentiating between the two versions of the function *display( )*. An *INT* is just another name for an *int*.

It's a bad programming idea to create overloaded functions that perform different types of actions; functions with the same name should have the same general purpose. For example, if we write an *abs( )* function that returns the square root of a number, it would be both silly and confusing. We must use overloaded functions judiciously. Their purpose is to provide a common name for several similar but slightly divergent functions. Overusing overloaded functions can make a program unreadable.

Now that you have understood the concept of overloaded functions do you think the following overloaded functions would work? Think!

```
#include <iostream>
using namespace std ;

void display ( char * ) ;
void display ( const char * ) ;

int main( )
{
    char *ch1 = "Hello" ;
    const char *ch2 = "Bye" ;
    display ( ch1 ) ;
    display ( ch2 ) ;
    return 0 ;
}

void display ( char *p )
{
    cout << p << endl ;
}

void display ( const char *p )
{
    cout << p << endl ;
}
```

Let us now see a practical example where the concept of function overloading can be used. Suppose we wish to place an integer or float value on the screen at a specific location, using commas to separate hundreds and thousands. This is one situation where we can think of using function overloading. We would call this overloaded function as *newprintf( )*, and then call it to print an *int*, or a *float*, or a *char*, or even a *string*. Here is a program that implements this function.

```
# include <cctype>
# include <string>
# include <cstdlib>
# include <windows.h>
using namespace std ;

void newprintf ( int, int, long, char * ) ;
void newprintf ( int, int, double, char * ) ;
void newprintf ( int, int, char *, char * ) ;
void writechar ( char, int, int ) ;
void gotoxy (short, short) ;

int main( )
{
    int i = 22, j = 22222 ;
    long int l = 777777 ;
    float f = 0.77777f ;
    double d = 7777.5678 ;
    static char str[30] = " John O Hara! O Hara!! " ;

    system ( "cls" ) ;
    newprintf ( 14, 30, ( long ) i, "9,999" ) ;
    newprintf ( 15, 30, ( long ) j, "9,999" ) ;
    newprintf ( 16, 30, l, "99,99,999" ) ;
    newprintf ( 17, 30, ( double ) f, "nn,nnn.nn" ) ;
    newprintf ( 18, 30, d, "nn,nn,nnn.nnn" ) ;
    newprintf ( 19, 30, str, "!!!!!!!!!!!!!!!!" ) ;
    return 0 ;
}

// long version
void newprintf ( int r , int c, long val, char *format )
{
```

```
    char *p, str[20] ;
    int len, i, j, lstr ;

    len = strlen ( format ) ;

    _ltoa ( val, str, 10 ) ;
    lstr = strlen ( str ) ;
    p = str ;
    c += len ;
    p = str + lstr - 1 ;
    format = format + len - 1 ;

    for ( i = 0 ; i < lstr ; i++ )
    {
        if ( isdigit ( *p ) )
        {
            if ( *format == ',' )
            {
                writechar ( ',', r, c ) ;
                c-- ;
                format-- ;
            }
            writechar ( *p, r, c ) ;
            c-- ;
            format-- ;
            p-- ;
        }
    }
}

// double version
void newprintf ( int r , int c, double val, char *format )
{
    char *p, str[20] ;
    int len, i, j, lstr, dec = 0 ;

    len = strlen ( format ) ;
```

```
c += len ;
i = 0 ;
j = 0 ;
while ( *format != '\0' )
{
      if ( *format == '.' )
            dec = 1 ;
      else
      {
            if ( *format == 'n' )
            {
                  i++ ;
                  if ( dec == 1 )
                        j++ ;
            }
      }
      format++ ;
}

_gcvt ( val, i, str ) ;

p = str ;
lstr = strlen ( str ) ;
p = str + lstr - 1 ;

for ( i = 0 ; i < lstr ; i++ )
{
      if ( *format == ',' )
      {
            writechar ( ',', r, c ) ;
            c-- ;
            format-- ;
      }
      writechar ( *p, r, c ) ;
      c-- ;
      format-- ;
      p-- ;
```

```
    }
}

// string version
void newprintf ( int r , int c, char *val, char *format )
{
    int i, lstr ;

    lstr = strlen ( format ) ;

    for ( i = 0 ; i < lstr ; i++, format++, val++ )
    {
        if ( *format == '!' )
            *val = toupper ( *val ) ;
        else
        {
            if ( *format != 'x' && *format != 'a' )
                *val = *format ;
        }
        writechar ( *val, r, c + i ) ;
    }
}

void writechar ( char ch, int r, int c )
{
    gotoxy ( c, r ) ;
    putchar ( ch ) ;
}
void gotoxy ( short col, short row )
{
   HANDLE h = GetStdHandle ( STD_OUTPUT_HANDLE ) ;
   COORD position = { col, row } ;
   SetConsoleCursorPosition ( h, position ) ;
}
```

Note that in the three overloaded functions shown above, the type of the fourth parameter is all that differs. It is a *long,* a *double,* or a *char* pointer. If we call *newprintf( )* with a *long int* as the fourth argument then the *long int* version of *newprintf( )* gets called, if we call *newprintf( )* with a *double* as the fourth argument, then the *double* version of *newprintf( )* gets called, and so on. To print an *int*, it must be suitably typecasted to a *long int* to ensure that the *long int* version of *newprintf( )* gets called.

Let us now understand the working of the *newprintf( )* function. In each of the overloaded functions firstly the entity to be printed is converted to an ascii string using functions like *_ltoa( )* (in case of a *long int*) and *_gcvt( )* (in case of a *double*). (In the string version of *newprintf( )* there is no need for conversion since what is being passed to it is itself a string.) This string is then compared with the format string passed to *newprintf( )* on a character by character basis from right to left. If a number is being printed then, on encountering a comma in the format string the comma is printed as it is, whereas, on encountering a '9' a corresponding digit from the numeric string is printed. On similar lines, while printing a string if '!' is encountered then the corresponding character in the string to be printed is converted to upper case. Note that all *newprintf( )*s are intelligent enough to take into account the possibilities such as the format string specified being bigger than the length of the number/string to be printed or vice versa.

Default Values For Function Arguments

In C if a function is defined to receive 2 arguments, whenever we call this function we have to pass 2 values to this function. If we pass one value then some garbage value is assumed for the last argument. As against this, functions in C++ have an ability to define default values for arguments that are not passed when the function call is made. Let us understand this with an example program.

```
#include <iostream>
#include <windows.h>
using namespace std ;

void box ( int sr = 1, int sc = 1, int er = 24, int ec = 80 ) ;
void gotoxy ( short, short ) ;

int main( )
{
    system ( "cls" ) ;
    box ( 10, 20, 22, 70 ) ;
    box ( 10, 20, 15 ) ;
    box ( 5, 10 ) ;
    box( ) ;
    return 0 ;
}

void box ( int sr, int sc, int er, int ec )
{
    int r, c ;

    gotoxy ( sc, sr ) ;
    cout << ( char ) 218 ; // outputs a graphic character whose ascii
                           // value is 128
    gotoxy ( ec, sr ) ;
    cout << ( char ) 191 ;
    gotoxy ( sc, er ) ;
    cout << ( char ) 192 ;
    gotoxy ( ec, er ) ;
    cout << ( char ) 217 ;

    for ( r = sr + 1 ; r < er ; r++ )
    {
        gotoxy ( sc, r ) ;
        cout << ( char ) 179 ;
        gotoxy ( ec, r ) ;
```

```
        cout << ( char ) 179 ;
    }

    for ( c = sc + 1 ; c < ec ; c++ )
    {
        gotoxy ( c, sr ) ;
        cout << ( char ) 196 ;
        gotoxy ( c, er ) ;
        cout << ( char ) 196 ;
    }
}
void gotoxy ( short col, short row )
{
    HANDLE h = GetStdHandle ( STD_OUTPUT_HANDLE ) ;
    COORD position = { col, row } ;
    SetConsoleCursorPosition ( h, position ) ;
}
```

When we call the function *box( )* with 4 arguments the box is drawn with the arguments passed. However, when we call it with 3 arguments the default value mentioned in the prototype of *box( )* is used for the last argument. Likewise, when we call it with two arguments default values are used for the last two arguments, and finally when we call it without any arguments, a box gets drawn with all the four default values mentioned in the prototype. Thus, the default arguments are used if the calling function doesn't supply them when the function is called.

Note that if one argument is missing when the function is called, it is assumed to be the last argument. Thus, the missing arguments must be the trailing arguments (those at the end of the argument list). You can leave out last three arguments, but you cannot leave out the last but one and then put in the last. This is quite reasonable. After all, how would the compiler know which arguments you meant, if you left out some arguments in the middle. Not surprisingly, compiler will flag an error if you leave out some arguments for which the function you are calling doesn't provide default values.

The default arguments are given only in the function prototype and should not be repeated in the function definition. The compiler uses the prototype information to build a call, not the function definition.

Default arguments are useful in 2 cases:

(a) While making a function call if you don't want to take the trouble of writing arguments which almost always have the same value.

(b) They are also useful in such cases where, after having written a program we decide to increase the capability of a function by adding another argument. Using default arguments means that the existing function calls can continue to use old number of arguments, while new function calls can use more.

Remember that the default value for an argument can be a global constant, a global variable, or even a function call. For example, such a function prototype is perfectly acceptable:

```
int myfunc ( flag = display( ) ) ;
```

In this case if *myfunc( )* is called without an argument, a default value will be obtained by making a call to the function *display( )*.

Operator Overloading

Operator overloading is one of the most fascinating features of C++. It can transform complex, obscure program listings into intuitively obvious ones. By overloading operators we can give additional meaning to operators like +, *, -, <=, >=, etc. which by default are supposed to work only on standard data types like *int*s, *float*s etc. For example, if *str1* and *str2* are two character arrays holding strings "Bombay" and "Nagpur" in them then to store "BombayNagpur" in a third string *str3*, in C we need to perform the following operations:

```
char str1[20] = "Nagpur" ;
char str2[ ] = "Bombay" ;
char str3[20] ;
strcpy ( str3, str1 ) ;
strcat ( str3, str2 ) ;
```

No doubt this does the desired task but don't you think that the following form would have made more sense:

```
str3 = str1 + str2 ;
```

Such a form obviously would not work with C, since we are attempting to apply the + operator on non-standard data types (strings) for which addition operation is not defined. That's the place where C++ scores over C, because it permits the + operator to be overloaded such that it knows how to add two strings.

Let us take another example where operator overloading would make the programming logic more convenient to handle. Suppose we want to perform complex number arithmetic. As we know, a complex number consists of a real part and an imaginary part. Hence to handle these we must build a structure. The following program shows how we can tackle complex numbers in C.

```
# include <iostream>
using namespace std ;

struct complex
{
    double real, imag ;
} ;
```

```
complex complex_set ( double r, double i ) ;
complex complex_add ( complex, complex ) ;
void complex_print ( complex c ) ;

int main( )
{
    complex a, b, c ;

    a = complex_set ( 1.0, 1.0 ) ;
    b = complex_set ( 2.0, 2.0 ) ;
    c = complex_add ( a, b ) ;

    cout << "c = " ;
    complex_print ( c ) ;
    return 0 ;
}
complex complex_set ( double r, double i )
{
    complex temp ;
    temp.real = r ;
    temp.imag = i ;
    return temp ;
}
void complex_print ( complex t )
{
    cout << "( " << t.real << ', ' << t.imag << ")" << endl ;
}

complex complex_add ( complex c1, complex c2 )
{
    complex temp ;

    temp.real = c1.real + c2.real ;
    temp.imag = c1.imag + c2.imag ;
    return temp ;
```

```
}
```

Note that since the functions *complex_set( )* and *complex_add( )* return values of the type *complex* their prototypes are so defined.

Instead of adding two complex numbers by calling the function *complex_add( )* we can get the same thing done in C++ through an overloaded + operator. This program is shown below:

```
# include <iostream>
using namespace std ;

struct complex
{
    double real, imag ;
};

complex complex_set ( double r, double i ) ;
void complex_print ( complex c ) ;
complex operator + ( complex c1, complex c2 ) ;
complex operator - ( complex c1, complex c2 ) ;
int main( )
{
    complex a, b, c, d ;

    a = complex_set ( 1.0, 1.0 ) ;
    b = complex_set ( 2.0, 2.0 ) ;

    c = a + b ;
    d = b + c - a ;

    cout << endl << "c = " ;
    complex_print ( c ) ;
    cout << endl << "d = " ;
    complex_print ( d ) ;
    return 0 ;
```

```
}

complex complex_set ( double r, double i )
{
    complex temp ;

    temp.real = r ;
    temp.imag = i ;
    return temp ;
}

void complex_print ( complex t )
{
    cout << "( " << t.real << ', ' << t.imag << ")" << endl ;
}

complex operator + ( complex c1, complex c2 )
{
    complex temp ;

    temp.real = c1.real + c2.real ;
    temp.imag = c1.imag + c2.imag ;
    return temp ;
}

complex operator - ( complex c1, complex c2 )
{
    complex temp ;

    temp.real = c1.real - c2.real ;
    temp.imag = c1.imag - c2.imag ;
    return temp ;
}
```

Operator overloading really speaking teaches a normal C++ operator to act on a user-defined operand. In our case the operator

+ and - are taught to operate on a user-defined data type *complex*. This is achieved by declaring a function that defines the actions to be performed on the arguments passed to it. This function is declared using the keyword *operator* and the actual operator to be overloaded. For example, look at the following declaration,

```
complex operator - ( complex c1, complex c2 )
```

Here, *operator* is a keyword, and is followed by the operator (-) which is to be overloaded. The declaration also tells the compiler that arguments to be passed to this function should be of the type *complex* and on performing the necessary actions this function would return a value of the type *complex*.

Obviously the question comes how would the compiler be able to decide when to call this function, since a program may contain an operation like $x = y + z$ where *x*, *y* and *z* are ordinary integers. In this case naturally the overloaded operator function would not be called since + is operating upon integers. The overloaded operator function would be called only if the addition operation is being done on operands of the type *complex*.

In effect, operator overloading gives you the opportunity to redefine the C++ language. If you want to extend the reach of C++ operators you can always do so using operator overloading.

Let us now use operator overloading to carry out simple matrix operations like addition, subtraction and multiplication using overloaded +, - and * operators. You would agree that if we are to add two matrices *a* and *b* and store the result in another matrix *c*, instead of using a function call of the form,

```
c = matadd ( a, b ) ;
```

a more intuitive form would be,

```
c = a + b ;
```

The following program implements such a form of addition, subtraction and multiplication.

```
#include <iostream>
#include <iomanip>
using namespace std ;

const int MAXROW = 3, MAXCOL = 3 ;
struct matrix
{
    int arr[MAXROW][MAXCOL] ;
} ;

matrix operator + ( matrix a, matrix b ) ;
matrix operator - ( matrix a, matrix b ) ;
matrix operator * ( matrix a, matrix b ) ;
void mat_print ( matrix p ) ;

int main( )
{
    matrix a = {
                    1, 2, 3,
                    4, 5, 6,
                    7, 8, 9
                } ;

    matrix b = {
                    1, 2, 3,
                    4, 5, 6,
                    7, 8, 9
                } ;

    matrix c, d, e, f ;

    c = a + b ;
    d = a * b ;
```

```
    e = a + b * c ;
    f = a - b * c + d ;
    mat_print ( c ) ;
    mat_print ( d ) ;
    mat_print ( e ) ;
    mat_print ( f ) ;
    return 0 ;
}
matrix operator + ( matrix a, matrix b )
{
    matrix c ;
    int i, j ;

    for ( i = 0 ; i < MAXROW ; i++ )
    {
        for ( j = 0 ; j < MAXCOL ; j++ )
            c.arr[i][j] = a.arr[i][j] + b.arr[i][j] ;
    }
    return c ;
}

matrix operator - ( matrix a, matrix b )
{
    matrix c ;
    int i, j ;

    for ( i = 0 ; i < MAXROW ; i++ )
    {
        for ( j = 0 ; j < MAXCOL ; j++ )
            c.arr[i][j] = a.arr[i][j] - b.arr[i][j] ;
    }
    return c ;
}

matrix operator * ( matrix a, matrix b )
{
    matrix c ;
```

```
    int i, j, k ;

    for ( i = 0 ; i < MAXROW ; i++ )
    {
        for ( j = 0 ; j < MAXCOL ; j++ )
        {
            c.arr[i][j] = 0 ;
            for ( k = 0 ; k < MAXCOL ; k++ )
                c.arr[i][j] += a.arr[i][k] * b.arr[k][j] ;
        }
    }
    return c ;
}

void mat_print ( matrix p )
{
    int i, j ;

    cout << endl << endl ;
    for ( i = 0 ; i < MAXROW ; i++ )
    {
        cout << endl ;
        for ( j = 0 ; j < MAXCOL ; j++ )
            cout << setw ( 5 ) << p.arr[i][j] ;
    }
}
```

The program opens with a structure that contains a two-dimensional array. It is necessary to create this structure since after performing addition, subtraction or multiplication the structure can be conveniently returned and assigned to another structure variable. To keep the array size general two *const*s MAXROW and MAXCOL have been used to indicate the number of rows and columns in the matrix.

The limitation of the program is that it works correctly only for square size matrices. For a non-square matrix of say 3 rows and 4 columns the addition and subtraction would still work but not the multiplication. We have not performed any error checks to see whether multiplication of the two matrices is feasible or not. A more general program, which handles some of these issues, would be developed in Chapter 5.

Note the use of *setw( )* in the statement

```
cout << setw ( 3 ) << p.arr[i][j] ;
```

Here *setw( )* is a manipulator. It is being used to line up the numbers in each column properly one below the other. It causes the number that follows it in the output stream to be printed within 3 columns, right aligned. To use *setw( )* it is necessary to include the file 'iomanip.h'.

If we so desire we can display each element of the matrix left-aligned within 3 columns that are reserved for it using *setw( )*. Here is how it can be achieved.

```
cout << setw ( 3 ) << setiosflags ( ios::left ) << p.arr[i][j] ;
```

The word *ios* comes from input/output stream. It is the name of a predefined class. We would understand it in detail in Chapter 11. For the present just understand that it contains several formatting flags. They act as on/off switches that specify choices for various aspects of input and output format. For example, the flag *left* indicates that the output would be left aligned.

We could have obtained the same effect by exchanging positions of *setw( )* and *setiosflags( )* as shown below:

```
cout << setiosflags ( ios::left ) << setw ( 3 ) << p.arr[i][j] ;
```

Operator overloading really shines when we use it in conjunction with *classes* in C++... a topic that is the heart and soul of C++. We would discuss classes in the next chapter. Once we cover this I am sure you would be able to see the entire operator overloading concept in different light. Before we close let me answer three most frequently asked questions about operator overloading.

(a) Which operators cannot be overloaded?

The operators that cannot be overloaded are ., ::, ? and :.

If an operator has unary and binary forms (such as operators + or &), both can be overloaded.

(b) What is the precedence of operator functions?

The operator functions have the same precedence as the intrinsic operations that use the same operator. For example, the * operator always has a higher priority over the + operator. There is no way to change operator precedence.

(c) Is it possible to redefine intrinsic operators?

What you are really asking is, is it possible to create your own operator for adding a pair of *int*s? The answer is no. Allowing you to change the behavior of intrinsic operations would make any program virtually unreadable.

Inline Functions

One of the important advantages of using functions is that they help us save memory space. As all the calls to the function cause the same code to be executed; the function body need not be duplicated in memory.

Imagine a situation where a small function is getting called several times in a program. As you must be aware, there are certain overheads involved while calling a function. Time has to be spent on passing values, passing control, returning value and returning control. In such situations to save the execution time you may instruct the C++ compiler to put the code in the function body directly inside the code in the calling program. That is, at each place where there's a function call in the source file, the actual code from the function would be inserted, instead of a jump to the function. Such functions are called *inline* functions. The in-line nature of the individual copy of the function eliminates the function-calling overhead of a traditional function. The following program shows *inline* function at work.

```
#include <iostream>
using namespace std ;

inline void reporterror ( char *str )
{
    cout << endl << str ;
    exit ( 1 ) ;
}

int main( )
{
    // code to open source file
    if ( fileopeningfailed )
        reporterror ( "Unable to open source file" ) ;

    // code to open target file
    if ( fileopeningfailed )
        reporterror ( "Unable to open target file" ) ;

    // code to copy contents of source file into target file
    return 0 ;
}
```

Note that the function must be declared to be *inline* before calling it. On compilation the contents of the *reporterror( )* function would get inserted at two places within our program. These obviously are the places where *reporterror( )* is being called.

One question that should occur to you is why ask the compiler to insert the code of the function in line with the other program code when we can easily do so ourselves? The trouble with repeatedly inserting the same code is that you lose the benefits of program organization and clarity that come with using functions. The program may run faster and take less space, but the listing is longer and more complex. Instead, if we write the code in a *inline* function the source file remains well organized and easy to read, since the function is shown as a separate entity. However, when the program is compiled, the function body is actually inserted into the program wherever a function call occurs.

You should use the *inline* function qualifier only when the function code is small. If the functions are large you should prefer the normal functions since the savings in memory space is worth the comparatively small sacrifice in execution speed.

Note that when we define the function *inline* there is no guarantee that its code would get inserted at the place where the call is being made. This is because we are just making a request to the compiler. The C++ language does not define under what conditions the compiler may choose to ignore our request. Because of this ambiguity in the language specification, compiler builders have flexibility in how they interpret the requirements.

Inline functions are similar to *#define* macros. However, they provide better type checking and do not have the side effects so typically associated with macros. For example consider the following program:

```
#include <iostream>
using namespace std ;
```

```
#define SQUARE( x ) x * x
inline float square ( float y )
{
    return y * y ;
}

int main( )
{
    float a = 0.5, b = 0.5, c, d ;

    c = SQUARE ( ++a ) ;
    d = square ( ++b ) ;
    return 0 ;
}
```

During preprocessing the macro SQUARE gets expanded into

```
c = ++x * ++x ;
```

You can notice the undesirable side effect in this macro expansion: the variable is getting incremented twice even though we have used the incrementation operator only once. Such side effects would not occur in the *inline* function.

static, *virtual* And *friend* Functions

In C++ we can have three more types of functions: *static*, *virtual* and *friend*. However all of these are related with something called *classes*. Hence discussion of these cannot be taken up until you know classes. *static* functions have been explained in detail in Chapter 7, *virtual* functions in Chapter 10 and *friend* functions in Chapter 11.

With this much knowledge under our belt we have achieved enough competence to launch ourselves into the object-oriented world... which we would do in the next chapter.

Exercise

[A] State True or False:

(a) If the function is defined before calling it, there is no need to mention its prototype.

(b) Two functions can be overloaded if their arguments are similar but their return values are different.

(c) Two functions can be overloaded only if their arguments differ in number, order or type.

(d) If default values are mentioned for the four arguments in the function prototype, we can call this function and pass it the first and the fourth argument.

(e) A function can be overloaded any number of times.

(f) The assignment operator cannot be overloaded.

(g) When we define the function to be *inline* there is no guarantee that its code would get inserted at the place where the call is being made.

(h) The side effects of the macro definition get eliminated if we use *inline* functions.

[B] Point out the errors, if any, in the following programs.

(a)
```
int main( )
{
    int a = 30 ;
    f( ) ;
    return 0 ;
}
```

```
void f( )
{
    int b = 20 ;
}
```

(b)
```
#include <iostream>
using namespace std ;

void f( )
{
    cout << "Hello" ;
}

int main( )
{
    f( ) ;
    return 0 ;
}
```

(c)
```
#include <iostream>
using namespace std ;

int f ( int, int ) ;
int f ( int, int ) ;

int main( )
{
    int a ;
    a = f ( 10, 30 ) ;
    cout << a ;
    return 0 ;
}

void f ( int x, int y )
{
    return x + y ;
```

```
}
```

(d)
```
#include <iostream>
using namespace std ;

int main( )
{
    void fun1 ( void ) ;
    void fun2 ( void ) ;
    fun1( ) ;
    return 0 ;
}

void fun1 ( void )
{
    fun2( ) ;
    cout << endl << "Hi...Hello" ;
}

void fun2 ( void )
{
    cout << endl << "to you" ;
}
```

(e)
```
#include <iostream>
using namespace std ;

void f ( int, float ) ;

int main( )
{
    f( ) ;
    return 0 ;
}

void f ( int i = 10, float a = 3.14 )
{
```

```
    cout << i << a ;
}
```

(f)
```
#include <iostream>
using namespace std ;

void f ( int = 10, int = 20, int = 30 ) ;
void f ( int, int ) ;

int main( )
{
    f ( 1, 2 ) ;
    return 0 ;
}

void f ( int x, int y, int z )
{
    cout << endl << x << endl << y << endl << z ;
}

void f ( int x, int y )
{
    cout << endl << x << endl << y ;
}
```

[C] Answer the following:

(a) Write a program which calls a function called *cls( )*. This function should be capable of clearing a part of the screen. If the function is called without any arguments then it should clear the entire screen.

(b) Write a program which contains a *writestring( )* function which displays a string at a given row and column on a given VDU page, in a given color. If the page number and the color are not passed the page number zero and color number 7 should be used.

(c) Suppose there is a function with the following prototype:

```
void f ( int = 10, int = 20, int = 30, int = 40 )
```

If this function is called by passing 2 arguments to it, how can we make sure that these arguments are treated as first and third, whereas, the second and the fourth are taken as defaults.

(d) Write overloaded functions to convert an *int* to an ascii string and to convert a *float* to an ascii string.

(e) Write overloaded functions to convert an ascii string to an *int* and to convert an ascii string to a *float*.

(f) Write function prototypes for the following:

- A function which receives an *int* and a *float* and returns a *double*.
- A function that receives an *int* pointer and *float* reference and returns an *int* pointer.
- A function which doesn't receive anything and doesn't return anything.
- A function that receives an array of *int*s, and a *float* reference and doesn't return anything.

(g) Which operators cannot be overloaded?

(h) Can we change the hierarchy of operators by overloading them?

CHAPTER FIVE

Classes In C++

Having familiarised ourselves with the non-object oriented extensions of C++ like default values in functions, overloaded functions, overloaded operators, call by reference, the *const* qualifier etc., it's time to look at the object oriented features of C++. Let us begin with structures and classes.

A structure in C is a collection of similar or dissimilar data types. C++ extends the reach of structures by allowing the inclusion of even functions within structures. The functions defined within a structure have a special relationship with the structure elements present within the structure. Placing data and functions (that work upon the data) together into a single entity is the central idea in object oriented programming.

There is another entity in C++ called *class* that too can hold data and functions. There is almost no difference in the syntax of a structure and a class, hence at least in principle they can be used interchangeably. But most C++ programmers use structures to exclusively hold data and classes to hold both data and functions.

To begin with, let us take a program that demonstrates the syntax and general features of classes in C++. The program contains a class and three objects. Here's the listing of the program.

```
#include <iostream>
using namespace std ;

class rectangle
{
    private :

        int len, br ;

    public :

        void getdata( )
```

```
        {
            cout << endl << "Enter length and breadth " ;
            cin >> len >> br ;
        }

        void setdata ( int l, int b )
        {
            len = l ;
            br = b ;
        }

        void displaydata( )
        {
            cout << endl << "length = " << len ;
            cout << endl << "breadth = " << br ;
        }

        void area_peri ( )
        {
            int a, p ;
            a = len * br ;
            p = 2 * ( len + br ) ;
            cout << endl << "area = " << a ;
            cout << endl << "perimeter = " << p << endl ;
        }
} ;

int main( )
{
    rectangle r1, r2, r3 ; // define three objects of class rectangle

    r1.setdata ( 10, 20 ) ; // set data in elements of the object
    r1.displaydata( ) ;     // display the data set by setdata( )
    r1.area_peri( ) ;       // calculate and print area and perimeter

    r2.setdata ( 5, 8 ) ;
    r2.displaydata( ) ;
```

```
    r2.area_peri( ) ;

    r3.getdata( ) ; // receive data from keyboard
    r3.displaydata( ) ;
    r3.area_peri( ) ;
    return 0 ;
}
```

The class *rectangle* specified in this program contains two data items length and breadth and four functions *setdata( )*, *getdata( )*, *displaydata( )* and *area_peri( )*. As their names suggest, the first function sets the data items (length and breadth) to given values, the second function receives the values of data items, the third displays these values, whereas the fourth calculates and prints the area and perimeter. Let us now understand the meaning of the terms *object* and *class*.

An object is an *instance* of a class, and the process of creating an object is called *instantiation*. In our program we have defined three objects *r1*, *r2* and *r3* which are instances of the class *rectangle*. Hence *r1*, *r2* and *r3* are often known as instance variables. To draw a parallel, look at the following declarations:

```
int i ;
rectangle r1 ;
```

In simplest terms a class is like a data type (*int* in the above declaration), whereas an object is like a variable of that data type. Look at the class definition in our program. The word *class* is a keyword and is followed by *rectangle*, which is called class name. Like a structure, the body of a class is delimited by braces and terminated by a semicolon. The body of the class contains two unfamiliar keywords: *private* and *public*. They are used in C++ to implement a concept called *data hiding*. It means that data is concealed within a class, so that it cannot be accessed by functions outside the class even by mistake. The mechanism used to hide data is to put it in a class and make it *private*. *private* data and functions can be accessed from within the class. *public* data and functions on the other hand, are accessible from outside the class. In the class the data items *len* and *br* follow the keyword *private*, so they can be accessed from within the class, but not from outside it.

Don't confuse data hiding with the security techniques used to protect computer data. Security techniques prevent illegal users from accessing data. Data hiding, on the other hand, is used to protect well-intentioned users from honest mistakes. Programmers who really want to, have a way to access *private* data, but they will be doing it with intention, not by accident.

A function declared within the definition of a class is called a 'member function' or 'method'. These two terms are interchangeable; member function is a C++ term and method is a general object-oriented programming term. The member functions provide controlled access to the data members of class. The *rectangle* class has four member functions *getdata( )*, *setdata( )*, *displaydata( )* and *area_peri( )*.

Usually the data within a class is *private* and the functions are *public*. This is a result of how classes are used. The data is hidden so it will be safe from accidental manipulation, while the functions that operate on the data are *public* so they can be accessed from outside the class. However, there is no rule that data must be *private* and functions *public*. In fact in some cases you may be required to use *private* functions and *public* data.

Now that the class is specified, let us see how *main( )* makes use of it. The first statement in *main( )*,

```
rectangle r1, r2, r3 ;
```

defines three objects, *r1*, *r2* and *r3* of class *rectangle*. Remember that the specification of the class does not create any objects. It only describes how the objects will look like when they are created. It is the definition that actually creates objects, which can then be used by the program. Thus, defining an object is similar to defining a variable of any data type: space is set aside for it in memory.

The next two statements in *main( )* call the member function *setdata( )*:

```
r1.setdata ( 10, 20 ) ;
```

This statement doesn't look like a normal function call. Why is the object name *r1* connected to the function using a '.'? This syntax is used to call a member function that is associated with the specific object. Since *setdata( )* is a member function of the *rectangle* class, it must always be called in connection with an object of this class. It won't make much sense if we say,

```
setdata ( 10, 20 ) ;
```

This is because a member function is always called to act on a specific object, not on the class in general. Not only does this statement not make much sense, but the compiler would also flash an error message if you use it. Moral is, member functions of a class can be accessed only by an object of that class.

To use a member function, the dot operator connects the object name and the member function. The syntax is similar to the way we refer structure elements, but the parentheses signal that we are accessing a member function rather than a data item. The dot operator is also called `class member access operator'.

The first call to *setdata( )*,

```
r1.setdata ( 10, 20 ) ;
```

executes the *setdata( )* member function of the *r1* object. This function sets the variables *len* and *br* to values *10* and *20* respectively. Likewise, the second call to *setdata( )* sets the values for variables in the second object.

Calls to other functions like *displaydata( )*, *area_peri( )* are similar. Some languages refer to calls to member functions as *messages*. Thus the call

```
r1.setdata ( 10, 20 ) ;
```

can be thought of as sending a message to *r1* telling it to set up values in variables. The term *message* is not a formal part of C++, but is a useful idea to keep in mind when we discuss member functions.

Classes And Constructors

In the last section we had our first tryst with classes in C++. Just to reiterate, a class is a collection of data and functions that operate upon this data. Both data and functions can be *private* or *public*, which essentially decides the access to the data and functions within the class. Let us now move one step further. Observe the following program carefully.

```
#include <iostream>
using namespace std ;

class integer
{
    private :

        int i ;

    public :
```

```
        void getdata( )
        {
            cout << endl << "Enter any integer " ;
            cin >> i ;
        }

        void setdata ( int j )
        {
            i = j ;
        }

        integer( ) // zero argument constructor
        {
        }

        integer ( int j ) // one argument constructor
        {
            i = j ;
        }

        void displaydata( )
        {
            cout << endl << "value of i = " << i << endl ;
        }
};

int main( )
{
    integer i1 ( 100 ), i2, i3 ;

    i1.displaydata( ) ;
    i2.setdata ( 200 ) ;
    i2.displaydata( ) ;
    i3.getdata( ) ;
    i3.displaydata( ) ;
    return 0 ;
}
```

This program shows three ways in which we can give values to data items in an object. One is through the member function *setdata( )* to whom we pass the value to be set up. Another way is by receiving values through keyboard as shown in function *getdata( )*. That brings us to the third method, which uses an entity called 'constructor'. The constructor is a special member function that allows us to set up values while defining the object, without the need to make a separate call to a member function. Thus, constructor is a member function that is executed automatically whenever an object is created.

There are some unusual aspects to constructor functions. First, it is no accident that they have exactly the same name as the class of which they are members. In fact it's a rule that the class and the constructor function within it must have same names. This is how the compiler knows that the member function is a constructor.

Secondly, no return type is used for constructors. Why not? Since the constructor is called automatically when an object is created, returning a value would not make sense.

In our program the statement

```
integer i1 ( 100 ), i2, i3 ;
```

creates three objects of the type *integer*. As each is created, its constructor, *integer( )*, is executed. So the effect of this single statement is to not only create three objects but also to initialize their *i* variables.

If you notice carefully, you would find that there are two constructors with the same name *integer( )*. Hence we call these constructors as *overloaded constructors*. Which of the two constructors gets called when an object is created depends on how many arguments are used in the definition of the object.

```
integer i2 ; // calls zero-argument constructor
integer i1 ( 100 ) ; // calls one-argument constructor
```

The overloaded constructors are useful when we want some objects to be initialised during definition and some not to be initialised.

What would happen if we declare an object of a particular class type and the class doesn't have a constructor? Nothing. Because when no constructor is present in a class the compiler builds an implicit constructor. Note that once we declare a one-argument constructor it is necessary to define the implicit constructor as well. The zero-argument constructor in our program is this implicit constructor.

Destructors

We've seen that a special member function—the constructor—is called automatically when an object is first created. Similarly, when an object is destroyed a function called destructor automatically gets called. A destructor has the same name as the constructor (which is same as the class name) but is preceded by a tilde. The following program shows destructor at work.

```
#include <iostream>
using namespace std ;

class example
{
    prlvate :

        int data ;

    public :
```

```
        example( ) // contstuctor (same name as class)
        {
            cout << endl << "Inside the constructor" ;
        }

        ~example( ) // destructor (same name with tilde)
        {
            cout << endl << "Inside the destructor" << endl ;
        }
};

int main( )
{
    example e ;
    return 0 ;
}
```

When the object *e* gets created the constructor gets called. When control goes outside *main( )* the object *e* gets destroyed. This invokes the destructor function. Like constructors, destructors do not have a return value. They also take no arguments (the assumption being that there's only one way to destroy an object).

The most common use of destructors is to deallocate memory that was allocated for the object by the constructor. We'll investigate this issue further in a later section of this chapter.

A Complex Class

As we know, a complex number consists of a real part and an imaginary part. The following program puts the concept of constructor to a practical stint by developing a class to implement complex numbers.

```
#include <iostream>
```

```
using namespace std ;

class complex
{
    private :

        float real, imag ;

    public :

    complex( )
    {
    }

    complex ( float r, float i )
    {
        real = r ;
        imag = i ;
    }

    void getdata( )
    {
        float r, i ;
        cout << endl << "Enter real and imaginary part " ;
        cin >> r >> i ;
        real = r ;
        imag = i ;
    }

    void setdata ( float r, float i )
    {
        real = r ;
        imag = i ;
    }

    void displaydata( )
    {
```

```
        cout << endl << "real= " << real ;
        cout << endl << "imaginary= " << imag << endl ;
    }

    void add_complex ( complex c1, complex c2 )
    {
        real = c1.real + c2.real ;
        imag = c1.imag + c2.imag ;
    }

    complex mul_complex ( complex c2 )
    {
        complex t ;

        t.real = real * c2.real - imag * c2.imag ;
        t.imag = real * c2.imag + c2.real * imag ;
        return ( t ) ;
    }
} ;

int main( )
{
    complex c1, c2 ( 1.5, -2.5 ), c3, c4 ;

    c1.setdata ( 2.0, 2.0 ) ;  // set data in var. in the object
    c3.add_complex ( c1, c2 ) ;
    c3.displaydata( ) ;

    c4.getdata( ) ;
    complex c5 ( 2.5, 3.0 ), c6 ;
    c6 = c4.mul_complex ( c5 ) ;
    c6.displaydata( ) ;

    complex c7 ;
    c7.add_complex ( c1, c2.mul_complex ( c3 ) ) ;
    c7.displaydata( ) ;
    return 0 ;
```

```
}
```

In this program we have once again used overloaded constructors and functions *getdata( )* and *setdata( )* to set up values of data items in different objects. To add two complex numbers we have called the member function *add_complex( )* through the statement,

```
c3.add_complex ( c1, c2 ) ;
```

The two complex numbers to be added are supplied as arguments to *add_complex( )*. The syntax for arguments that are objects is the same as that for arguments that are simple data types like *int*s or *float*s.

In our program which objects can the member function *add_complex( )* access? It can access *c1* and *c2*, because they are supplied as arguments. *add_complex( )* can also access *c3* because it is a member function of *c3*. You might think of *c3* as a sort of phantom argument: the member function always has an access to it. The mechanism through which this access becomes possible is discussed later in this chapter under the section 'The *this* Pointer'.

Look at the calls to *add_complex( )* and *mul_complex( )* functions:

```
c3.add_complex ( c1, c2 ) ;
c6 = c4.mul_complex ( c5 ) ;
```

In the call to *add_complex( )* the result of addition of *c1* and *c2* gets stored in *c3*, so there is no need to return any value. As against this, in the call to *mul_complex( )* the result of multiplication of *c4* and *c5* is returned and collected in *c6*.

Ideally both the calls should have looked similar since addition and multiplication both are binary operations. The reason why we have implemented the two functions differently is just to bring to your notice the two different ways in which we can implement such functions.

We could have easily implemented these functions in a manner shown below:

```
complex add_complex ( complex c2 )
{
    complex t ;
    t.real = real + c2.real ;
    t.imag = imag + c2.imag ;
    return t ;
}

void mul_complex ( complex c1, complex c2 )
{
    real = c1.real * c2.real – c1.imag * c2.imag ;
    imag = c1.real * c2.imag + c2.real * c1.imag ;
}
```

If we implement the functions in this fashion the way they are called would also change. The calls would now look like this:

```
c3 = c1.add_complex ( c2 ) ;
c6.mul_complex ( c4, c5 ) ;
```

Can we use both the forms of *add_complex( )* and *mul_complex( )* in the same class? Of course, you can. They would then be treated as overloaded functions. In such a case you would have the flexibility of calling them in any of the two ways shown above.

Overloaded Operators Revisited

We had our first tryst with overloaded operators in the last chapter. Let us now examine the same concept in relation with classes. We would once again take the example of complex numbers to understand overloading in classes. Here is the program which implements complex number addition and multiplication using overloaded operators rather than through member functions like *add_complex( )* and *mul_complex( )*.

```
#include <iostream>
using namespace std ;

class complex
{
    private :

        float real, imag ;

    public :

        complex( )
        {
        }

        complex ( float r, float i )
        {
            real = r ;
            imag = i ;
        }

        void getdata( )
        {
            float r, i ;
            cout << endl << "Enter real and imaginary part " ;
            cin >> r >> i ;
            real = r ;
            imag = i ;
        }
```

```
        void setdata ( float r, float i )
        {
            real = r ;
            imag = i ;
        }

        void displaydata( )
        {
            cout << endl << "real= " << real ;
            cout << endl << "imaginary= " << imag << endl ;
        }

        complex operator + ( complex c )
        {
            complex t ;
            t.real = real + c.real ;
            t.imag = imag + c.imag ;
            return t ;
        }

        complex operator * ( complex c )
        {
            complex t ;

            t.real = real * c.real - imag * c.imag ;
            t.imag = real * c.imag + c.real * imag ;
            return t ;
        }
} ;

int main( )
{
    complex c1, c2 ( 1.5, -2.5 ), c3, c4 ;

    c1.setdata ( 2.0, 2.0 ) ;
    c3 = c1 + c2 ;
    c3.displaydata( ) ;
```

```
    c4.getdata( ) ;
    complex c5 ( 2.5, 3.0 ), c6 ;
    c6 = c4 * c5 ;
    c6.displaydata( ) ;

    complex c7 ;
    c7 = c1 + c2 * c3 ;
    c7.displaydata( ) ;
    return 0 ;
}
```

You would agree that the statement

```
c7 = c1 + c2 * c3 ;
```

is more intuitive than the statement

```
c7.add_complex ( c1, c2.mul_complex ( c3 ) ) ;
```

In the statement *c7 = c1 + c2 * c3* the multiplication operator function is called before the addition operator function. As you may recall, the hierarchy of operators remains same even when they are overloaded.

Let us examine the call and the definition of the overloaded '+' operator more closely.

```
// definition
complex operator + ( complex c )
{
    complex t ;
    t.real = real + c.real ;
    t.imag = imag + c.imag ;
    return t ;
}
```

```
// call
c3 = c1 + c2 ;
```

When the *operator +( )* function is called, the object *c2* is passed to it and is collected in the object *c*. As against this, the object *c1* gets passed to it automatically. This becomes possible because the statement *c3 = c1 + c2* is internally treated by the compiler as

```
c3 = c1.operator + ( c2 ) ;
```

That should give you an idea why the first operand in case of a overloaded binary operator function becomes available automatically, whereas, the second operand needs to be passed explicitly.

In the definition of the overloaded + operator function when we use the statement

```
t.real = real + c.real ;
```

real refers to the one that belongs to the object using which the operator function has been called. That is, if the function has been called through the statement,

```
c3 = c1 + c2 ;
```

then *real* represents *c1*'s *real*, since the statement *c3 = c1 + c2* is internally treated as *c3 = c1.operator + (c2)*. That should be an acceptable explanation for the time being. The real mechanism that makes this possible is a pointer called *this* pointer. It is time to understand the *this* pointer.

The *this* Pointer

The member functions of every object have access to a pointer named *this*, which points to the object itself. When we call a member function, it comes into existence with the value of *this* set to the address of the object for which it was called. The *this* pointer can be treated like any other pointer to an object.

Using a *this* pointer any member function can find out the address of the object of which it is a member. It can also be used to access the data in the object it points to. The following program shows the working of the *this* pointer.

```
#include <iostream>
using namespace std ;

class example
{
    private :

        int i ;

    public :

        void setdata ( int ii )
        {
            i = ii ;  // one way to set data
            cout << endl << "my object's address is " << this ;
            this->i = ii ;  // another way to set data
        }

        void showdata( )
        {
            cout << i ; // one way to display data
            cout << endl << "my object's address is " << this << endl ;
            cout << this->i << endl ;  // another way to display data
        }
} ;

int main( )
{
```

```
    example e1 ;
    e1.setdata ( 10 ) ;
    e1.showdata( ) ;
    return 0 ;
}
```

Here is the output of the program…

```
my object's address is 0012FF6010
my object's address is 0012FF60
10
```

From the output we can confirm that each time the address of the same object *e1* got printed. Since the *this* pointer contains the address of the object, using it we can reach the data member of the *example* class through statements like:

```
this->i = ii ;  // another way to set data
cout << this->i ;  // another way to display data
```

Let us now get back to our overloaded *operator +( )* function of the last section. In it we had a statement,

```
t.real = real + c.real ;
```

This statement internally is treated as:

```
t.real = this->real + c.real ;
```

When the *operator +( )* function is called through the statement

```
c3 = c1.operator + ( c2 ) ;
```

the *this* pointer would contain the *c1* object's address. As a result, *this->real* would refer to *c1*'s *real*.

A more practical use of *this* is in returning values from member functions and overloaded operators. Let us now understand this utility of the *this* pointer. Consider the following program.

```
#include <iostream>
using namespace std ;

class circle
{
    private :

        int radius ;
        float x, y ;

    public :
        circle( )
        {
        }

        circle ( int rr, float xx, float yy )
        {
            radius = rr ;
            x = xx ;
            y = yy ;
        }

        circle operator = ( circle& c )
        {
            cout << endl << "Assignment operator invoked" ;
            radius = c.radius ;
            x = c.x ;
            y = c.y ;
            return circle ( radius, x, y ) ;
        }

        void showdata( )
```

```
        {
            cout << endl << "\nRadius = " << radius ;
            cout << endl << "X-Coordinate = " << x ;
            cout << endl << "Y-Coordinate = " << y << endl ;
        }
} ;

int main( )
{
    circle c1 ( 10, 2.5, 2.5 ) ;
    circle c2, c3 ;
    c3 = c2 = c1 ;
    c1.showdata( ) ;
    c2.showdata( ) ;
    c3.showdata( ) ;
    return 0 ;
}
```

Most of the program is straightforward. What is important here is the function *operator = ( )*, which overloads the = operator. The overloaded operator function gets called when the statement *c3 = c2 = c1 ;* gets executed. The overloaded = operator does the copying of the member data from one object to another. It also prints the 'Assignment operator invoked' message so that we can keep track of when it executes.

We have passed the argument to overloaded operator function by reference. Though not absolutely necessary, this is often desirable. Had the argument been passed by value it would have generated a copy of itself in the function. In our program it would not have mattered much, but in case of large objects this would lead to considerable wastage of memory.

The *operator = ( )* function in our program returns a value by creating a temporary *circle* object and initialising it using the three-argument constructor. Note that the value returned is a copy of the object of which the overloaded = operator is a member. Returning a value makes it possible to chain = operators in *c4 = c2 = c1*.

However, returning by value creates an extra copy of the object, which means wastage of memory space. We know that when an object is returned by reference, no new object is created.

Then can we not return the value from the overloaded operator function by reference using a declaration like

```
circle& operator = ( circle & c )
```

Unfortunately, we can't use reference returns on variables that are local to a function since the local variables are destroyed when the function returns. This problem can be overcome using a *this* pointer as shown below:

```
circle& operator = ( circle& c )
{
    cout << endl << "Assignment operator invoked" ;
    radius = c.radius ;
    x = c.x ;
    y = c.y ;
    return *this ;
}
```

Since *this* is a pointer to the object of which the above function is a member, **this* naturally is that object itself. The statement

```
return *this
```

returns this object by reference.

Overloading Unary Operators

As you know, an unary operators acts on only one operand. Examples of unary operators are the increment and decrement operators ++ and --, and the unary minus, as in -45. Let us now implement an overloaded unary operator for a class called *index*. Here is the program…

```
#include <iostream>
using namespace std ;

class index
{
    private :

        int count ;

    public :

        index( )
        {
            count = 0 ;
        }

        index ( int i )
        {
            count = i ;
        }

        void operator ++ ( )
        {
            ++count ;
        }

        void showdata( )
```

```
        {
                cout << count ;
        }
};

int main( )
{
    index c ;

    cout << endl << "c = " ;
    c.showdata( ) ;

    ++c ;
    cout << endl << "c = " ;
    c.showdata( ) ;

    ++c ;
    cout << endl << "c = " ;
    c.showdata( ) ;
    return 0 ;
}
```

In this program the *count* of object *c* is initially set to *0*. On encountering the expression *++c* it is incremented by *1*. The program output looks like this:

```
c = 0
c = 1
c = 2
```

Internally, the expression *++c* is treated as:

```
c.operator ++ ( ) ;
```

While calling this function no value is passed to it and no value is returned from it. The compiler can easily distinguish between the expression *++c* and an expression, say *++j*, where *j* might be an integer variable. It can make this distinction by looking at the data type of the operands. If the operand is a basic type like an *int*, as in *++j* then the compiler will use its built-in routine to increment an *int*. But if the operand is an *index* variable, then the compiler will now use our *operator++()* function instead.

Can you guess in which situation our *operator ++( )* function flop? Suppose we you use a statement like this in *main ()*:

```
d = ++c ;
```

The compiler will complain. Why? Because we have defined the ++ operator to have a return type of *void* in the *operator ++( )* function, while in the assignment statement it is being asked to return a variable of type *index*. That is, the compiler is being asked to return whatever value *c* has after being operated on by the ++ operator, and assign this value to *d*. So, in its existing form we can't use ++ to increment *index* objects in assignments. Of course the normal ++ operator, applied to basic data types like *int*, would not have this problem.

To make it possible to use our *operator ++ ( )* in assignment expressions, we must provide a way for it to return a value. The next program shows how this can be achieved.

```
#include <iostream>
using namespace std ;

class index
{
    private :

        int count ;

    public :
```

```
        index( )
        {
            count = 0 ;
        }

        index operator ++ ( )
        {
            ++count ;
            index temp ;
            temp.count = count ;
            return temp ;
        }

        void showdata( )
        {
            cout << count ;
        }
};

int main( )
{
    index c, d ;

    cout << endl << "c = " ;
    c.showdata( ) ;

    ++c ;
    cout << endl << "c = " ;
    c.showdata( ) ;

    d = ++c ;
    cout << endl << "c = " ;
    c.showdata( ) ;
    cout << endl << "d = " ;
    d.showdata( ) ;
    return 0 ;
```

```
}
```

Here the *operator ++( )* function increments the *count* in its own object as before, then creates the new *temp* object and assigns *count* in the new object the same value as in its own object. Finally it returns the *temp* object. This has the desired effect. Expressions like *++c* now return a value, so they can be used in other expressions, such as

```
d = ++c ;
```

In this case the value returned from *++c* is assigned to *d.* Program's output would now look like this:

```
c = 0
c = 1
c = 2
d = 2
```

In our program we created a temporary object called *temp*. Its sole purpose was to provide a return value for the ++ operator. We could have achieved the same effect using the following the approach:

```
#include <iostream>
using namespace std ;

class index
{
    private :

        int count ;

    public :

        index( )
```

```
        {
            count = 0 ;
        }

        index ( int i )
        {
            count = i ;
        }

        index operator ++ ( )
        {
            ++count ;
            return index ( count ) ;
        }

        void showdata( )
        {
            cout << count ;
        }
} ;

int main( )
{
    index c, d ;
    cout << endl << "c = " ;
    c.showdata( ) ;

    ++c ;
    cout << endl << "c = " ;
    c.showdata( ) ;

    d = ++c ;
    cout << endl << "c = " ;
    c.showdata( ) ;
    cout << endl << "d = " ;
    d.showdata( ) ;
    return 0 ;
```

```
}
```

Note that the *operator ++( )* function has changed now. In this function the statement,

```
return index ( count ) ;
```

creates an object of type *index*. This object has no name. It won't need one since it is anyway going to die soon. This unnamed object is initialized to the value provided by the argument *count*.

But to carry out this initialisation don't we need a one-argument constructor? We certainly do. And if you observe the program carefully you would notice that now we have provided one in our program.

Once the unnamed object is initialized to the value of *count*, it can then be returned. The output of this program would be same as that of the previous one.

The approaches in both the programs involve making a copy of the original object (the object of which the function is a member), and then returning the copy. Instead of making the copy we can return the value of the original object using the *this* pointer as shown below:

```
index operator ++ ( )
{
    ++count ;
    return *this ;
}
```

Postfix Notation

So far we've used the overloaded increment operator in its prefix form:

```
++c ;
d = ++c ;
```

What about postfix, where the variable is incremented after its value is used in the expression, as in

```
c++ ;
d = c++ ;
```

To make both versions of the increment operator work, we must define two overloaded ++ operators, as shown in the following program:

```
#include <iostream>
using namespace std ;

class index
{
    private :

        int count ;

    public :

        index( )
        {
            count = 0 ;
        }
```

```
        index ( int i )
        {
            count = i ;
        }

        index operator ++ ( )
        {
            return index ( ++count ) ;
        }

        index operator ++ ( int )
        {
            return index ( count++ ) ;
        }

        void showdata( )
        {
            cout << count ;
        }
} ;

int main( )
{
    index c, d, e, f ;
    e = ++c ;
    cout << endl << "c = " ;
    c.showdata( ) ;
    cout << endl << "e = " ;
    e.showdata( ) ;

    f = d++ ;
    cout << endl << "d = " ;
    d.showdata( ) ;
    cout << endl << "f = " ;
    f.showdata( ) ;
    return 0 ;
```

```
}
```

Now there are two different functions for overloading the ++ operator. The one we've seen before, for prefix notation, is

```
index operator ++ ( )
{
    return index ( ++count ) ;
}
```

The new one, for postfix notations, is

```
index operator ++ ( int )
{
    return index ( ++count ) ;
}
```

The only difference is the *int* in the parentheses. This *int* isn't really an argument, and it doesn't mean integer. It's simply a signal to the compiler to create the postfix version of the operator. Here's the output from the program:

```
c = 1
e = 1
d = 1
f = 0
```

The last two lines of the output show the result of the statement

```
f = d++ ;
```

Here *d* is incremented to *1*, but *f* is assigned the value of *d* before it is incremented, so *f* contains the value *0*.

On similar lines we can implement the pre and post decrement operators as well.

Function Definition Outside The Class

In all classes that we have declared so far we defined the member functions inside the class declaration. This need not always be the case. If we so desire we can keep the declaration of the member function inside the class, whereas, its definition can be done outside the class. The following program illustrates this point.

```
#include <iostream>
#include <string>
using namespace std ;

class employee
{
    private :

        char name[20] ;
        int age ;

    public :

        employee( ) ;
        employee ( char *n, int a ) ;
        void getdata( ) ;
        void showdata( ) ;
} ;

employee::employee( )
{
    strcpy ( name, "" ) ;
    age = 0 ;
}
```

```
employee::employee ( char *n, int a )
{
    strcpy ( name, n ) ;
    age = a ;
}

void employee::getdata( )
{
    cout << endl << "Enter name and age" << endl ;
    cin >> name >> age ;
}

void employee::showdata( )
{
    cout << "name = " << name << endl
         << "age = " << age << endl ;
}

int main( )
{
    employee e1 ( "sanjay", 34 ) ;
    e1.showdata( ) ;
    employee e2 ;
    e2.getdata( ) ;
    e2.showdata( ) ;
    return 0 ;
}
```

In this program the declarations of the two constructors and the *getdata( )* and *showdata( )* functions have been done inside the class. Let us take the declaration of the *showdata( )* function:

```
void showdata ( ) ;
```

This tells the compiler that this function is a member of the class but it will be defined outside the class declaration, at some other place in the program. We have defined this function after the class declaration.

The definition of this function uses an unfamiliar syntax. The function name, *showdata( )* is preceded by the class name, *employee*, and the scope resolution operator. It is a way of specifying to what class does *showdata( )* belong.

new And *delete* Operators

While doing dynamic memory allocation in C the memory is allocated from *heap*. Thus heap is a pool of memory from which standard library C functions like *malloc( )* and *calloc( )* allocate memory. The memory allocated from system heap using *malloc( )*, *calloc( )* and *realloc( )* is vacated (deallocated) using the function *free( )*.

C++ offers a better way to accomplish the same job through the use of the *new* and *delete* operators. The *new* operator allocates memory from free store (in the C++ lexicon, heap is called *free store*)., whereas, the *delete* operator returns the allocated memory back to the free store. Thus the *new* and *delete* operators perform the job of *malloc( )* and *free( )*. These operators associate the allocation of memory with the way we use it.

The *new* operator, when used with the pointer to a data type, a structure, or an array, allocates memory for the item and assigns the address of that memory to the pointer. The *delete* operator does the reverse. It returns to the free store the memory owned by the object.

The following code snippet shows the *new* and *delete* operators at work.

```
int *p1 ;
struct employee
{
    char name[20] ;
    int age ;
    float sal ;
} *p2 ;

p1 = new int ;            // allocates 4 bytes
p2 = new employee ;  // allocates 28 bytes

int *p3 ;
p3 = new int[30] ;  // allocates memory for storing 30 integers

// some code

delete p1 ;
delete p2 ;
delete [ ] p3 ;
```

Note the last usage of the *delete* operator:

```
delete [ ] p3 ;
```

It indicates that we are not deleting a *thing* but an array of *thing*s (*thing*s being integers in this case) pointed to by the pointer *p3*. Would a simple

```
delete p3 ;
```

not work in this case? The compiler may not flag an error, but whether it would work successfully or not would vary from compiler to compiler. In some compilers the heap may get corrupted, in some others only the first object in the array would get deleted. In short, you would be better off if you use *delete [ ]* whenever you allocate memory using *new [ ]*. Otherwise be prepared for a disaster.

Instead of using the *new* operator to allocate memory had we used *malloc( )* the allocation statements would have looked like this:

```
p1 = ( int * ) malloc ( sizeof ( int ) ) ;
p2 = ( stuct employee * ) malloc ( sizeof ( struct employee ) ) ;
p3 = ( int * ) malloc ( sizeof ( int ) * 30 ) ;
```

Note that since *malloc( )* returns a *void* pointer it is necessary to typecast it into an appropriate type depending on the type of pointer we have on the left hand side of the assignment operator. This gets completely avoided when we are using the *new* operator.

Look at the last allocation done using *new*. Here the *new* operator accepts a data type with an array dimension. The dimension that we gave was a constant 30, representing the number of integers. You can, however, supply a variable dimension, and the *new* operator allocates the correct amount of memory as shown below:

```
int n ;
cin >> n ;
int *p = new int[n] ;

// some code

delete [ ] p ;
```

When you run this code you type in the size of the array. The *new* operator uses the value that you enter to establish the size of memory to be allocated. The program builds the array by using the *new* operator and deletes the array by using the *delete* operator.

Can we *free( )* the memory allocated with *new* or *delete* the pointers allocated with *malloc( )*? No. They are incompatible with one another. Memory allocated using *new* should be freed only using *delete*. Similarly, memory allocated using *malloc( )* should be freed only using *free( )*.

The advantages of *new* and *delete* over the C functions *malloc( )* and *free( )* are not immediately obvious. They appear to do the same job. However, *new* and *delete* provide a more readable syntax than *malloc( )* and *free( )*. When you read the section after the next you would be able to appreciate their advantages over traditional memory allocation used in C.

Using *new* And *delete*

The following program shows how to allocate a dynamically dimensioned array of pointers to structures using the *new* operator.

```
#include <iostream>
#include <string>
using namespace std ;

struct employee
{
    char name[20] ;
    int age ;
    float sal ;
} ;

int sort_func ( const void *a, const void *b ) ;

int main( )
{
    int num, i ;
    employee *ptr_to_record ;

    cout << "Enter number of records " ;
    cin >> num ;
```

```
employee **ptr_to_array_of_ptrs = new employee *[num] ;
for ( i = 0 ; i < num ; i++ )
{
    ptr_to_record = new employee ;
    cout << endl << "Enter a record " ;
    cin >> ptr_to_record-> name
        >> ptr_to_record->age
        >> ptr_to_record->sal ;
    ptr_to_array_of_ptrs[i] = ptr_to_record ;
}

cout << "You entered the following records" << endl ;

for ( i = 0 ; i < num ; i++ )
{
    ptr_to_record = ptr_to_array_of_ptrs[i] ;
    cout << endl << ptr_to_record-> name << '\t'
                 << ptr_to_record->age << '\t'
                 << ptr_to_record->sal ;
}

qsort ( ptr_to_array_of_ptrs, num,
        sizeof ( ptr_to_array_of_ptrs[0] ), sort_func ) ;

cout << endl << "The sorted records are" << endl ;

for ( i = 0 ; i < num ; i++ )
{
    ptr_to_record = ptr_to_array_of_ptrs[i] ;
    cout << endl << ptr_to_record-> name << '\t'
                 << ptr_to_record->age << '\t'
                 << ptr_to_record->sal ;
}

for ( i = 0 ; i < num ; i++ )
    delete ptr_to_array_of_ptrs[i] ;
```

```
    delete [ ] ptr_to_array_of_ptrs ;
    return 0 ;
}

int sort_func ( const void *a, const void *b )
{
    employee *aa, *bb ;
    aa = *( ( employee ** ) a ) ;
    bb = *( ( employee ** ) b ) ;
    return ( strcmp ( aa->name, bb->name ) ) ;
}
```

The program begins by asking you to enter the maximum number of records. From this value, the program allocates an array of structure pointers through the statement:

```
employee **ptr_to_array_of_ptrs = new employee *[num] ;
```

Here we are allocating an array of *num* pointers, where each element of the array would be a pointer to a structure *employee*.

Once this allocation is done, you begin entering each record. For each record the program allocates a new structure and stores the address of this structure in the array pointed to by *ptr_to_array_of_ptrs*. Once all records are entered the library function *qsort( )* is called to sort the records in alphabetical order by names. Observe carefully the typecasting done in the function *sort_func( )*. This is necessary since the prototype of *qsort( )* functions suggests that the comparison function (*sort_func( )* in our case) collects two *const void* pointers.

Finally the sorted records are printed. Once the printing is over the memory occupied by each record as well as by the array of pointers to records is deleted using the *delete* operator. Note, once again that to delete the array we have used the form *delete [ ]* for reasons discussed earlier.

malloc( )/free( ) Versus *new/delete*

The programs that we have written in the last few sections may have given you an impression that the only advantages of using *new/delete* over *malloc( )/free( )* are their easier syntax and ability to work with variety of data types without being required to do some clumsy typecasting. However, there is more to *new* and *delete* than meets the eye. Consider the following program to understand this.

```
#include <iostream>
#include <string>
using namespace std ;

class employee
{
    private :

        char name[20] ;
        int age ;
        float sal ;

    public :

        employee( )
        {
            cout << endl << "reached zero-argument constructor" ;
            strcpy ( name, "" ) ;
            age = 0 ;
            sal = 0.0 ;
        }

        employee ( char *n, int a, float s )
        {
            cout << endl << "reached three-argument constructor" ;
            strcpy ( name, n ) ;
```

```
        age = a ;
        sal = s ;
    }

    void setdata ( char *n, int a, float s )
    {
        strcpy ( name, n ) ;
        age = a ;
        sal = s ;
    }

    void showdata( )
    {
        cout << endl << name << "\t"
                      << age << "\t"
                      << sal ;
    }

    ~employee( )
    {
        cout << endl << "reached destructor" << endl ;
    }
} ;

int main( )
{
    employee *p ;
    p = new employee ;
    p -> setdata ( "sanjay", 23, 4500.50 ) ;

    employee *q ;
    q = new employee ( "ajay", 24, 3400.50 ) ;

    p -> showdata( ) ;
    q -> showdata( ) ;

    delete p ;
```

```
    delete q ;
    return 0 ;
}
```

The output of the program looks like this...

```
reached one-argument constructor
reached three-argument constructor
sanjay   23  4500.5
ajay     24  3400.5
reached destructor

reached destructor
```

From the output it is obvious that when we allocated memory for objects pointed to by *p* and *q* not only the memory allocation took place but the zero-argument and the three-argument constructors also got called. Similarly, on using *delete* not only did the memory got deallocated but the destructor of the class also got called. Thus *new* and *delete* create and destroy objects. In contrast *malloc( )* and *free( )* merely allocate and deallocate memory.

The Matrix Class

We have already learnt how to develop elementary classes, overload operators and use *new* and *delete* to construct/destroy objects. However we learnt these as isolated concepts. Their real utility comes when they are combined to work together. For example, we can think of developing a matrix class that can handle integer matrices of different dimensions. Not only this, within the matrix class we can have overloaded operators to carry out the addition, multiplication and comparison of two matrices. The following program implements this class.

```
#include <iostream>
#include <iomanip>
using namespace std ;

class matrix
{

    private :

        int maxrow, maxcol ;
        int *ptr ;

    public :

        matrix ( int r, int c )
        {
            maxrow = r ; maxcol = c ;
            ptr = new int [ r * c ] ;
        }

    void getmat( )
    {
        int i, j, mat_off ;

        cout << endl << "Enter elements matrix:" << endl ;
        for ( i = 0 ; i < maxrow ; i++ )
        {
            for ( j = 0 ; j < maxcol ; j++ )
            {
                mat_off = i * maxcol + j ;
                cin >> ptr[mat_off] ;
            }
        }
    }

    void printmat( )
```

```
{
    int i, j, mat_off ;

    for ( i = 0 ; i < maxrow ; i++ )
    {
        cout << endl ;
        for ( j = 0 ; j < maxcol ; j++ )
        {
            mat_off = i * maxcol + j ;
            cout << setw ( 3 ) << ptr[mat_off] ;
        }
    }
}

int detmat( )
{
    matrix q ( maxrow - 1, maxcol - 1 ) ;
    int sign = 1, sum = 0, i, j, k, count ;
    int newpos, pos, order ;

    order = maxrow ;
    if ( order == 1 )
        return ( ptr[0] ) ;

    for ( i = 0 ; i < order ; i++, sign *= -1 )
    {
        for ( j = 1 ; j < order ; j++ )
        {
            for ( k = 0, count = 0 ; k < order ; k++ )
            {
                if ( k == i )
                    continue ;

                pos = j * order + k ;
                newpos = ( j - 1 ) * ( order - 1 ) + count ;
                q.ptr[newpos] = ptr[pos] ;
                count++ ;
```

```
                }
            }
            sum = sum + ptr[i] * sign * q.detmat( ) ;
        }
        return ( sum ) ;
    }

    matrix operator + ( matrix b )
    {
        matrix c ( maxrow, maxcol ) ;
        int i, j, mat_off ;

        for ( i = 0 ; i < maxrow ; i++ )
        {
            for ( j = 0 ; j < maxcol ; j++ )
            {
                mat_off = i * maxcol + j ;
                c.ptr[mat_off] = ptr[mat_off] + b.ptr[mat_off] ;
            }
        }
        return ( c ) ;
    }

    matrix operator * ( matrix b )
    {
        matrix c ( b.maxcol, maxrow ) ;
        int i, j, k, mat_off1, mat_off2, mat_off3 ;

        for ( i = 0 ; i < c.maxrow ; i++ )
        {
            for ( j = 0 ; j < c.maxcol ; j++ )
            {
                mat_off3 = i * c.maxcol + j ;
                c.ptr[mat_off3] = 0 ;
                for ( k = 0 ; k < b.maxrow ; k++ )
                {
                    mat_off2 = k * b.maxcol + j ;
```

```
                    mat_off1 = i * maxcol + k ;
                    c.ptr[mat_off3] += ptr[mat_off1] * b.ptr[mat_off2] ;
                }
            }
        }
        return ( c ) ;
    }

    int operator == ( matrix b )
    {
        int i, j, mat_off ;

        if ( maxrow != b.maxrow || maxcol != b.maxcol )
            return ( 0 ) ;

        for ( i = 0 ; i < maxrow ; i++ )
        {
            for ( j = 0 ; j < maxcol ; j++ )
            {
                mat_off = i * maxcol + j ;
                if ( ptr[mat_off] != b.ptr[mat_off] )
                    return ( 0 ) ;
            }
        }
        return ( 1 ) ;
    }
} ;

int main( )
{
    int rowa, cola, rowb, colb ;

    cout << endl << "Enter dimensions of matrix A " ;
    cin >> rowa >> cola ;
    matrix a ( rowa, cola ) ;
    a.getmat( ) ;
```

```
    cout << endl << "Enter dimensions of matrix B " ;
    cin >> rowb >> colb ;
    matrix b ( rowb, colb ) ;
    b.getmat( ) ;

    matrix c ( rowa, cola ) ;
    c = a + b ;
    cout << endl << "The sum of two matrices = " ;
    c.printmat( ) ;

    matrix d ( rowa, colb ) ;
    d = a * b ;
    cout << endl << "The product of two matrices = " ;
    d.printmat( ) ;

    cout << endl << "Determinant of matrix a = " << a.detmat( ) ;
    if ( a == b )
        cout << endl << "a & b are equal" << endl ;
    else
        cout << endl << "a & b are unequal" << endl ;
    return 0 ;
}
```

In the class we have declared three *private* data members: two integers to signify the dimensions of the matrix and an integer pointer to point to the memory that is allocated for holding the matrix. When we declare an object of the type *matrix* the constructor allocates the necessary memory using the *new* operator. Then a call to *getmat( )* fills the user-supplied data into this allocated memory.

The most important part of the class is the overloaded binary operators. The operator functions get called on encountering the expressions like

```
c = a + b ;
d = a * b ;
```

When the compiler sees such expressions the overloaded + or * operator functions get called. As we know, while calling these functions the argument on the left of the + (or *) operator (*a* in our case) is available to the operator function since *a* is the object of which the operator is a member function. The object to the right of + or * (*b* in our case) must be furnished as an argument to the operator function. In the operator function, the left operand is accessed directly (since this is the object of which the function is a member) using expressions like *ptr[mat_off]*. The right operand is accessed as function's argument, as *b.ptr[mat_off]*. Here *mat_off* represents the offset within the memory allocated for the matrix. It is calculated using the formula:

```
mat_off = i * maxcol + j ;
```

where *i* and *j* stand for the row number and column number of the element which we are trying to access, whereas *maxcol* is the number of columns present in the matrix.

Classes, Objects And Memory

If an object is similar to a variable can we find out the number of bytes occupied by it in memory. Yes, using the good old *sizeof* operator that we use for standard data types. The following program illustrates this.

```
#include <iostream>
using namespace std ;

class sample
{
    private :
```

```
        int i ;
        float a ;
        char ch ;

    public :

        sample( )
        {
        }

        sample ( int ii, float aa, char chch )
        {
            i = ii ;
            a = aa ;
            ch = chch ;
        }

        void display( )
        {
            cout << endl << i << a << ch ;
        }

} ;

int main( )
{
    sample s1 ( 10, 3.14f, 'A' ) ;
    sample s2 ( 20, 6.28f, 'B' ) ;
    cout << endl << sizeof ( s1 ) ;
    cout << endl << sizeof ( s2 ) << endl ;
    return 0 ;
}
```

The program reports the size of the objects *s1* and *s2* as 12 bytes, which is the sum of sizes of *i*, *a* and *ch*. This means the size of any object is sum of sizes of its data members. This leads to an important question: do functions have no role to play in the size of an object? The answer is no, since all the objects in a given class use the same member functions.

The member functions are created and placed in memory only once—when they are defined in the class declaration. As against this, the data members are placed in memory when each object is defined, as there is a separate set of data for each object.

This makes sense, as there's no point in duplicating all the member functions in a class every time you create another object of that class (as the functions for each object are identical). The data members, however, will hold different values, so there must be a separate set of data members for each object.

In our program there are two objects of type *sample*, so there are two instances of *i*, *a* and *ch* in memory. However, there is only one instance of the two constructor functions and the *display( )* function. All the objects of the class share these functions. This does not lead to conflict of any type since only one function is executed at a time.

While programming rarely are you required to bother about whether there is a separate copy of a member function for each object or are all objects sharing a single copy. However, knowing what is happening behind the scenes has never harmed anybody.

Structures And Classes

In programs that we have written so far when it was time to collect dissimilar data we used structures, whereas, to group data and functions we used classes. In fact, you can use structures in almost exactly the same way that you use classes. The only formal difference between a class and a structure is that in a class the members are *private* by default, while in a structure they are *public* by default.

So far we have been using the following format for the classes.

```
class sample
{
    private :

        int data ;

    public :

        void fun( )
        {
            // some code
        }
} ;
```

Since in a class all members (data and functions) are *private* by default we may as well drop the keyword *private* from the above class declaration. In the interest of clarity however, you are advised to use the keyword *private* explicitly.

The work carried out by the *sample* class declaration can also be accomplished using a structure as shown below:

```
struct sample
{
    private :

        int data ;

    public :
```

```
        void fun( )
        {
            // some code
        }
};
```

In a structure all members are by default *public*. Still here we can't afford to drop the keyword *public*. On doing so the *private* clause would become applicable even to the function *fun( )*. If we are still keen on dropping the keyword *public* we will have to define the function before the data members as shown below:

```
struct sample
{
        void fun( )
        {
            // some code
        }

    private :

        int data ;
};
```

Though in principle we can use a structure at every place where a class is used, in most situations programmers prefer to use structures to group data, and classes to group both data and functions.

Exercise

[A] State True or False:

(a) By default members of a structure are *public* and that of a class are *private*.

(b) Nested classes are legal.

(c) In a class data members are always *private*, whereas, member functions are always *public*.

(d) It is necessary that a constructor in a class should always be *public*.

(e) If a class contains a 3-argument constructor then it is necessary to define explicitly a zero-argument, a 1-argument and a 2-argument constructor.

(f) Member functions of a class have to be called explicitly, whereas, the constructor gets called automatically.

(g) A constructor gets called whenever an object gets instantiated.

(h) Constructors can be overloaded.

(i) A constructor never returns a value.

(j) Static memory allocation takes place during compilation, whereas, dynamic memory allocation takes place during execution.

(k) Size of an object is equal to sum of sizes of data members and member functions within the class.

(l) If the ++ operator has been overloaded then the expressions *j++* and *++j* would call the same overloaded function.

(m) When an object goes out of scope its destructor gets called automatically.

(n) If the binary + operator is overloaded inside a class then while calling it only one argument needs to be passed.

(o) The *this* pointer always contains the address of the object using which the member function/data is being accessed.

(p) The *this* pointer can be used even outside the class.

(q) If member functions of a class are defined outside the class it is necessary to declare them inside the class.

[B] Point out the errors, if any, in the following programs.

(a)
```
#include <string>
using namespace std ;

class address
{
    private :
        char name[10] ;
        char city[10] ;
    public :
        address ( char *p, char *q )
        {
            strcpy ( name, p ) ;
            strcpy ( city, q ) ;
        }
}

// main follows here
int main( )
```

```
{
    address my ( "Mac", "London" ) ;
    return 0 ;
}
```

(b)
```
class date
{
    private :
        int day, month, year ;
        date( )
        {
            day = 7 ;
            month = 9 ;
            year = 1997 ;
        }
} ;

int main( )
{
    date today ;
    return 0 ;
}
```

(c)
```
#include <iostream>
using namespace std ;

class value
{
    private :
        int i ;
        float f ;

    public :
        val( )
        {
            i = 0 ;
            f = 0.0 ;
```

```
                return 1 ;
            }
    } ;

    int main( )
    {
        val v1 ;
        return 0 ;
    }
```

(d)
```
#include <iostream>
using namespace std ;

class triplets
{
    private :
        int t1, t2, t3 ;

    public :
        triplets ( int x, int y, int z )
        {
            t1 = x ;
            t2 = y ;
            t3 = z ;
        }
        void display( )
        {
            cout << endl << t1 << t2 << t3 ;
        }
} ;

int main( )
{
    triplets r ( 2, 3, 4 ), s ;
    r.display( ) ;
    s.display( ) ;
    return 0 ;
```

```
}
```

(e)
```
#include <iostream>
using namespace std ;

class sample
{
    private :
        int data1 ;
        float data2 ;
    public :
        void sample( ) ;
        void displaydata( ) ;
} ;

int main( )
{
    sample s ;
    s.showdata( ) ;
    return 0 ;
}
sample::void sample( )
{
    data1 = 10 ;
    data2 = 20 ;
}
sample::void showdata( )
{
    cout << endl << data1 << data2 ;
}
```

(f)
```
#include <iostream>
using namespace std ;

class list
{
    private :
```

```
        class node
        {
            int data ;
            node *link ;
        } *p ;
    public :
        void create( )
        {
            p = new node ;
            p.data = 10 ;
            p->data = 10 ;
        }
};

int main( )
{
    list l1 ;
    l1.create( ) ;
    return 0 ;
}
```

[C] What would be the output of the following programs:

(a)
```
#include <iostream>
using namespace std ;

class user
{
    private :
        int i ;
        float f ;
        char c ;
    public :
        void displaydata( )
        {
            cout << endl << i << '\n' << f << "\n" << c ;
        }
```

```
};

int main( )
{
    cout << sizeof ( user ) ;
    user u1 ;
    cout << endl << sizeof ( u1 ) ;
    u1.displaydata( ) ;
    return 0 ;
}
```

(b)
```
#include <iostream>
using namespace std ;

class date
{
    private :
        int dd, mm, yy ;
    public :
        date( )
        {
            cout << endl << "Reached here" ;
        }
};

int main( )
{
    date today ;
    date *p = &today ;
    cout << endl << p ;
    return 0 ;
}
```

(c)
```
#include <iostream>
using namespace std ;

class student_rec
```

```
{
    private :
        int m1, m2, m3 ;
        float percentage ;
    public :
        student_rec( )
        {
            m1 = m2 = m3 = 0 ;
            percentage = 0.0 ;
        }
        void calc_perc ( int x, int y , int z )
        {
            m1 = x ; m2 = y ; m3 = z ;
            percentage = ( m1 + m2 + m3 ) / 3.0 ;
            display_perc( ) ;
        }
        void display_perc( )
        {
            cout << endl << "Percentage = " << percentage << "%" ;
        }
} ;

int main( )
{
    student_rec s1 ;
    s1.display_perc( ) ;
    s1.calc_perc( 35, 35, 35 ) ;
    s1.display_perc( ) ;
    return 0 ;
}
```

(d)

```
#include <iostream>
using namespace std ;

class control
{
    public :
```

```
        control( )
        {
            calculate( ) ;
            cout << endl << "Constructor" ;
        }
        void calculate( )
        {
            display( ) ;
            cout << endl << "Calculator" ;
        }
        void display( )
        {
            cout << endl << "displayed" ;
        }
};

int main( )
{
    control c1 ;
    return 0 ;
}
```

(e)

```
#include <iostream>
#include <dos>
using namespace std ;

void set_position ( int, int ) ;

class string
{
    private :
        char *p ;
    public :
        string ( char *temp )
        {
            p = temp ;
            display ;
```

```
        }
        void dispiay( )
        {
            set_position ( 10, 30 ) ;
            cout << p ;
        }
};

int main( )
{
    string s1 = "abcd" ;
    return 0 ;
}

void set_position ( int row, int col )
{
    union REGS i ;
    i.h.ah = 0x02 ;
    i.h.bh = 0 ;
    i.h.dh = row ;
    i. h. dl = col ;
    int86 ( 0x10, &i, &i ) ;
}
```

[D] Answer the following:

(a) Modify the class *rectangle* discussed in the text of this chapter such that a statement,

```
rectangle r1 = 3 ;
```

assigns a value *3* to *len* as well as *br*.

(b) Can we increase or decrease the size of an array during execution?

(c) Point out the reasons why using *new* is a better idea than using *malloc( )*?

(d) What is the difference in the following two statements?

```
delete a ;
delete [ ] a ;
```

(e) What does the *delete* operator do in addition to deallocating the memory used by the object?

(f) If there are four objects used in a program how many *this* pointers would exist for these objects and why?

CHAPTER SIX

The C++ Free Store

We used the *new* and *delete* operators in the last chapter in their simplest forms. However, there are several more issues involved in using them. Before we look at these issues let us reiterate a few things that we learnt about *new* and *delete* in the last chapter.

(a) In addition to allocating memory *new* also creates an object by calling the object's constructor.

(b) In addition to deallocating memory *delete* also destroys the object by calling the object's destructor.

(c) While allocating memory using *new* it is allocated from the heap. In C++ lexicon heap is known as a *free store*.

(d) Memory allocated using *new [ ]* must be deallocated using *delete [ ]*. If not done the best you can hope for is disaster.

Before we cover any fresh material here are a few subtleties of *new* and *delete* which would help you to understand them better.

(a) An object created using *new* exists until it is explicitly destroyed using *delete*.

(b) The *delete* operator may be applied only to a pointer returned by *new* or to zero. Applying *delete* to *0* has no effect. In other words passing a NULL pointer to *delete* is safe and is guaranteed to do nothing. This simplifies the code that uses *delete* by allowing such code to *delete* a pointer that may be NULL without being required to use a special *if*.

(c) The expression *delete p* doesn't delete the pointer. It deletes the object being pointed to by *p*. So ideally the name of the keyword should have been *deletethethingpointedtoby* rather than *delete*. Any takers?

(d) Parallel to *realloc( )* function of C there is no *renew* operator in C++. Never use *realloc( )* on user-defined objects. When *realloc( )* needs to move data during the reallocation it does a bitwise copying which is disastrous for many user-defined classes. C++ objects know how to copy themselves using the copy constructors and assignment operators (these you would learn in Chapter 7).

(e) The *new* operator is better than *malloc( )* on three counts: Firstly it creates an object, whereas *malloc( )* merely allocates memory. Secondly, it is type safe. It returns a pointer of appropriate type, whereas, *malloc( )* returns a *void* pointer which needs to be typecasted explicitly. Lastly *new* can be overloaded on a class-by-class basis, whereas, *malloc( )* cannot be.

(f) Never delete a pointer twice. Suppose you have a pointer variable *p*. The first time you delete *p*, the object **p* is safely destructed, and the memory pointed to by *p* is safely returned to the heap. The second time you pass the same pointer to *delete* the remains of what used to be an object at **p* are passed to the destructor (which could be disastrous), and the memory pointed to by *p* is handed back to the heap a second time. This may corrupt the heap.

(g) Not deleting an object is not an error as far as the language is concerned. However, it is a bad practice. If the program is going to run for a long time then it is all the more important that we delete the object once its purpose is over.

Free Store Exhaustion

So far we did not consider the possibility of what to do if the free store has been exhausted when we use the *new* operator. Instead, we assumed that there is always ample memory available and the free store is never exhausted. Obviously, this is not the best approach to follow. In C the function *malloc( )* returns a NULL pointer if memory allocation fails, and programs that call *malloc( )* usually test whether NULL is returned, and if so, then they do something meaningful about it.

We can carry out a similar job in C++ by simply testing each use of the *new* operator for a NULL return; *new* returns a null pointer if it is unable to allocate memory. There is a better way, however. C++ includes an internal function pointer named *_new_handler*. Usually, this pointer contains NULL, and when *new* fails to allocate memory, *new* returns NULL. But if the *_new_handler* function pointer contains a non-null value, then when *new* fails to allocate memory it transfers the control to the function being pointed to by the *_new_handler* pointer. There exists a function named *set_new_handler( )* that lets you set the *_new_handler* function pointer. When the *new* operator can't allocate memory the function being pointed to by *_new_handler* gets called. The following program shows how this can be achieved.

```
#include <iostream>
#include <cstdlib>
#include <new>
using namespace std ;

void memwarning( ) ;

int main( )
{
    set_new_handler ( memwarning ) ;

    char *p = new char[100] ;
    cout << endl << "First allocation: p = " << hex << long ( p ) ;
    p = new char[0x7FFFFFFF] ;
    set_new_handler ( 0 ) ; // return to default
    return 0 ;
```

```
}

void memwarning( )
{
    cout << endl << "Free store has now gone empty" << endl ;
    exit ( 1 ) ;
}
```

Here the program first allocates memory from the free store for an array of 100 *chars*. Next it attempts to allocate memory for a much bigger character array. Since *new* is unable to allocate memory for this array it transfers control to the function *memwarning( )* which sends an error message to the screen and exits. Ideally *memwarning( )* should free up some memory and return. *new* would then be able to satisfy the request and the program can continue. However, if *memwarning( )* can't free memory for *new* it should terminate the program by calling *exit( )*.

Custom *new* And *delete* Operators

The compiler provides global *new* and *delete* operators which get called whenever we allocate or free memory. This includes calls from compiler's library functions and startup code. Most programmers rarely find it necessary to replace the global *new* and *delete* operator functions. However at times when we may want a finer control over what happens when a *new* operator executes we may decide to overload the normal *new* operator. The following program shows how this overloading can be carried out to roll out our own *new* and *delete* operators.

```
#include <iostream>
#include <cstdlib>
#include <new>
using namespace std ;
```

```
void memwarning( ) ;
void * operator new ( size_t, int ) ;
void operator delete ( void * ) ;

int main( )
{
    char *p = new ( '$' ) char[100] ;
    cout << endl << "First allocation: p = " << hex << long ( p ) << endl ;
    for ( int i = 0 ; i < 100 ; i++ )
        cout << p[i] ;

    cout << endl ;

    delete p ;

    p = new ( '*' ) char[64000u] ;
    delete p ;
    return 0 ;
}

void memwarning( )
{
    cout << endl << "Free store has now gone empty" ;
    exit ( 1 ) ;
}

void * operator new ( size_t sz, int setvalue )
{
    void *p ;

    p = malloc ( sz ) ;
    if ( p == NULL )
        memwarning( ) ;

    memset ( p, setvalue, sz ) ;
    return ( p ) ;
}
```

```
void operator delete ( void *pp )
{
    free ( pp ) ;
}
```

Observe carefully how the *new* operator has been overloaded. The first parameter for an overloaded *new* operator must always be of the type *size_t*. It contains the size of the object for whom the space is being allocated. In case of the default *new* function provided by the compiler this is the only parameter. However, to enhance the capability of our *new* operator we have accepted one more parameter in *new*. It represents the value that should be set in the allocated memory.

Since here we are providing the memory allocator we are in a position to decide the strategy for memory exhaustion. Under this strategy we have decided to call the function *memwarning( )* from the *new* operator function whenever the memory is exhausted.

In the above program what would happen if we decide to allocate memory for an integer array through the statement,

```
int *q = new int[64000u] ;
```

Once again the memory allocation would fail since we are demanding a huge chunk of memory. However, this time the *memwarning( )* function would not get called since the allocation was attempted using the global *new( )* function and not through our *new( )* function. If we want that in this case too, the *memwarning( )* function should get called then we must once again use the *set_new_handler( )* function as shown below.

```
#include <iostream>
#include <cstdlib>
#include <new>
```

```
using namespace std ;

void memwarning( ) ;
void * operator new ( size_t, int ) ;
void operator delete ( void * ) ;

int main( )
{
    set_new_handler ( memwarning ) ;

    char *p = new ( '$' ) char[100] ;
    cout << endl << "First allocation: p = " << hex << long ( p ) << endl ;
    for ( int i = 0 ; i < 100 ; i++ )
        cout << p[i] ;

    cout << endl ;

    delete p ;

    int *q = new int[64000u] ;

    p = new ( '*' ) char[64000u] ;
    delete p ;

    return 0 ;
}
void memwarning( )
{
    cout << endl << "Free store has now gone empty" ;
    exit ( 1 ) ;
}

void * operator new ( size_t sz, int setvalue )
{
    void *p ;

    p = malloc ( sz ) ;
```

```
    if ( p == NULL )
        memwarning( ) ;

    memset ( p, setvalue, sz ) ;
    return ( p ) ;
}

void operator delete ( void *pp )
{
    free ( pp ) ;
}
```

Overloading *new/delete* In Classes

As said earlier, we can overload *new* on a class-by-class basis. Let us see an example that does this.

```
#include <iostream>
#include <cstdlib>
#include <string>
#include <new>
using namespace std ;

const int MAX = 5 ;
const int FREE = 0 ;
const int OCCUPIED = 1 ;
void memwarning( ) ;

void memwarning( )
{
    cout << endl << "Free store has now gone empty" ;
    exit ( 1 ) ;
}

class employee
```

```
{
    private :

        char name[20] ;
        int age ;
        float sal ;

    public :

        void * operator new ( size_t bytes ) ;
        void operator delete ( void *q ) ;
        void setdata ( char *n, int a, float s ) ;
        void showdata( ) ;
        ~employee( ) ;
} ;

struct pool
{
    employee obj ;
    int status ;
} ;

struct pool *p = NULL ;

int flag = 0 ;

void * employee::operator new ( size_t sz )
{
    int i ;

    if ( flag == 0 )
    {
        p = ( pool * ) malloc ( sz * MAX ) ;
        if ( p == NULL )
            memwarning( ) ;

        for ( i = 0 ; i < MAX ; i++ )
```

```
                p[i].status = FREE ;

            flag = 1 ;
            p[0].status = OCCUPIED ;
            return &p[0].obj ;
        }
        else
        {
            for ( i = 0 ; i < MAX ; i++ )
            {
                if ( p[i].status == FREE )
                {
                    p[i].status = OCCUPIED ;
                    return &p[i].obj ;
                }
            }
            memwarning( ) ;
        }
}

void employee::operator delete ( void *q )
{
    if ( q == NULL )
        return ;

    for ( int i = 0 ; i < MAX ; i++ )
    {
        if ( q == &p[i].obj )
        {
            p[i].status = FREE ;
            strcpy ( p[i].obj.name, "" ) ;
            p[i].obj.age = 0 ;
            p[i].obj.sal = 0.0 ;
        }
    }
}
```

```
void employee::setdata ( char *n, int a, float s )
{
    strcpy ( name, n ) ;
    age = a ;
    sal = s ;
}

void employee::showdata( )
{
    cout << endl << name << "\t" << age << "\t" << sal ;
}

employee::~employee( )
{
    cout << "reached destructor" << endl ;
}

int main( )
{
    set_new_handler ( memwarning ) ;

    employee *e1, *e2, *e3, *e4, *e5, *e6 ;

    e1 = new employee ;
    e1->setdata ( "ajay", 23, 4500.50 ) ;

    e2 = new employee ;
    e2->setdata ( "amol", 25, 5500.50 ) ;

    e3 = new employee ;
    e3->setdata ( "anil", 26, 3500.50 ) ;

    e4 = new employee ;
    e4->setdata ( "anuj", 30, 6500.50 ) ;

    e5 = new employee ;
    e5->setdata ( "atul", 23, 4200.50 ) ;
```

```
    e1->showdata( ) ;
    e2->showdata( ) ;
    e3->showdata( ) ;
    e4->showdata( ) ;
    e5->showdata( ) ;

    delete e4 ;
    delete e5 ;
    e4->showdata( ) ;
    e5->showdata( ) ;

    e4 = new employee ;
    e5 = new employee ;

    // now exhaust the store
    e6 = new employee ;
    cout << endl << "Done!!" ;
    return 0 ;
}
```

Here is the output of the program…

```
ajay    23  4500.5
amol    25  5500.5
anil    26  3500.5
anuj    30  6500.5
atul    23  4200.5
        0   0
        0   0
Free store has now gone empty
```

Replacing the global *new* and *delete* operators is not a job of weak hearted programmer. After all someone else might rely on some aspect of the default behaviour of *new* and *delete* or might even have supplied other versions of these functions. A more selective, and often better, approach is to implement these operators for a specific class. The above program takes this approach and implements memory management of class *employee* using operator *new* and operator *delete* functions. This feature is usually used to gain some performance benefit. For example, if we know in advance that at one time we are never going to need more than MAX *employee* objects then we can speed up execution by overriding the default *new* and *delete* operators. Such class-specific knowledge about the memory requirements of a class can avoid overheads involved in using the global *new* and *delete* operators. In the class-specific *new* operator, we can allocate the necessary memory for all instances of that class at one shot and then manage this memory using the *new* and *delete* operators defined within the class.

The *employee* class in our program has four member functions. Their purposes are shown in Figure 6.1.

Function	**Purpose**
new( )	Allocates memory only when it is invoked for the first time. During subsequent invocations just manages the memory that was allocated during the first invocation
delete( )	Marks the allocated memory as free and resets the values present there
setdata( )	Sets the values in *private* data members of the object
showdata( )	Displays the *private* data members of the object

Figure 6.1

Almost all memory managers store additional information on each allocated memory block. One common method for doing this is by using a 'wrapper' structure. In our program we have used the structure *pool* for this purpose. This structure consists of an object and a variable *status* that indicates whether a block is *free* or *occupied.*

The allocation strategy of our program is simple. When the *employee::new* operator is invoked for the first time we have allocated space for an array of 5 objects. Subsequent times *new* is invoked, we simply assign an empty slot from this array (provided there is one) and return its address. If none of the slots are empty we report that the store has exhausted.

The *operator new* always has the first argument of type *size_t* and it returns a *void* *. Thus the prototype of *operator new* is:

```
void * employee::operator new ( size_t sz ) ;
```

where *sz* contains the size of the object being allocated. In our case this value would be *sizeof (employee).*

When the *employee::delete* operator is invoked it is passed the address of the object being deleted. This address is then matched against the addresses of the allocated objects. When the match is met, the slot is marked as FREE and the values present there are reset to null or 0. The FREE slot can then get reassigned during subsequent calls to *new*.

If we try to allocate space for the sixth object then the 'Free store has now gone empty' message is flashed by the function *memwarning( )*. Since the program execution is terminated in memwarning( ) the 'Done!!' message in the last *cout* statement of *main( )* doesn't get printed at all. If we are making a specific call to *memwarning( )* from *employee::new( )* then what is the need to set the handler using *set_new_handler ( )*? This has been done to take care of the possibility of memory allocation failure when the global *new( )* function is called. When the global *new* function would be called is discussed in the following pages.

Now a few important things that you should note:

(a) The *this* pointer is not passed to the class-specific *new* function because it gets called before the constructor. This makes sense as the *new* function allocates memory for the object prior to its initialization.

(b) When allocating an array of *employee* objects, the global operator will be used even if the *new* operator has been defined in the *employee* class.

(c) Only one operator *delete( )* per class can be used. We cannot overload *delete( )*.

(d) We can now understand why never to mix *malloc( )* and *new* or *free( )* and *delete*. Since *new* and *delete* operators use 'wrapper' structure for management, they store different block information than *malloc( )* and *free( )*.

Understanding The Sequence

Overloaded *new* and *delete* functions within a class definition are always *static* (*static* functions are discussed in Chapter 7) and have no *this* pointer associated with the object being created or deleted. This is because the compiler calls the *new* function before it calls the class's constructor function, and it calls the *delete* function after it calls the destructor. The following program demonstrates this sequence of calling the constructor, destructor, and overloaded *new* and *delete* operator functions.

```
#include <iostream>
```

```
#include <cstdlib>
#include <string>
#include <new>
using namespace std ;

class employee
{
    private :

        char name[20] ;
        int age ;
        float sal ;

    public :

        void * operator new ( size_t bytes ) ;
        void operator delete ( void *q ) ;
        employee( ) ;
        ~employee( ) ;
} ;

char pool[ sizeof ( employee ) ] ;

employee::employee( )
{
    cout << endl << "Reached constructor" ;
}

employee::~employee( )
{
    cout << endl << "Reached destructor" ;
}

void * employee::operator new ( size_t sz )
{
    cout << endl << "Reached employee::new" ;
    return pool ;
```

```
}

void employee::operator delete ( void *q )
{
    cout << endl << "Reached employee::delete" << endl ;
}

int main( )
{
    employee *e1 ;
    e1 = new employee ;
    delete e1 ;
    return 0 ;
}
```

The program does nothing within the class except display the following messages as the various functions execute.

```
Reached employee::new
Reached constructor
Reached destructor
Reached employee::delete
```

As you can see, the *new* function executes before the constructor function. The *new* function may not access any of the class's members because no memory exists for them until *new* allocates it and because the constructor function has not yet performed any other class-specific initializations. Likewise, because the delete operator executes after the destructor function, the *delete* operator may not have access to the class members.

Construction At Predetermined Location

When we construct objects using *new* we have no control over where they get created in memory. Can we create objects at predetermined locations? Yes, using the placement syntax of the *new* operator. For example, suppose we want to place an object of class *sample* at a specific address. Also while constructing this object we would like to pass the values (10, 20) as arguments to the *sample* constructor. This can be accomplished through the following statements:

```
char *buf = new char [ sizeof ( sample ) ] ;
sample *p = new ( buf ) sample ( 10, 20 ) ;
p -> fun( ) ;
```

Obviously the storage pointed to by *address* must be large enough to hold a *sample* object. The returned pointer *p* will be numerically the same as *address*, but it will be a *sample** rather than a *void**. Using pointer *p* we can then call the functon *fun( )* defined in the *sample* class.

The objects created by placement *new* are destroyed using placement destruction. For example, if *p* is a *sample** that was returned from placement *new*, **p* can be destroyed through the statement:

```
p -> ~sample( ) ;
```

We can reclaim the memory like this:

```
delete[ ] buf ;
```

What we have used here is called the scalar version of placement new. It takes a user-supplied address on which it constructs a single object. Unlike the ordinary version of the *new* operator, placement new doesn't allocate storage for the object; it merely constructs the object on the memory address you provide.

In programming environments for Mobile devices and other embedded systems you may be required to use placement *new* allocation for arrays.

Allocating arrays with placement new follows the same steps more or less, but you have to pay attention to additional nuances. Here is how you can do it...

```
#include <iostream>
using namespace std ;
const int MAX = 15 ;

class sample
{
    private :

        int i ;

    public :

        sample ( )
        {
        }
        ~sample( )
        {
        }

        void fun( )
        {
            cout << "Reached fun" << endl ;
        }
} ;
```

```
int main( )
{
    int i ;
    char *buf ;
    sample *p ;

    buf = new char [ sizeof ( sample ) * MAX ] ;
    p = new ( buf ) sample [ MAX ] ;

    for ( i = 0 ; i < MAX ; i++ )
        p[i].fun() ;

    for ( i = 0 ; i < MAX ; i++ )
        p[i].~sample();

    delete[ ] buf;

    return 0 ;
}
```

Here we have firstly allocated a buffer large enough to hold an array of sample objects using the statements:

```
const int MAX = 15;
char *buf = new [ sizeof ( sample ) * MAX ] ;
```

Then we have constructed an array of MAX objects on the buffer using placement new[ ] through the statement:

```
sample * p = new ( buf ) sample [ MAX ] ;
```

Then we have used the allocated array as usual through the statements:

```
for ( int i = 0 ; i < MAX ; i++ )
```

```
    p[i].fun( ) ;
```

It is important to ensure that our target class - sample in this example - has a public zero-argument constructor. Without it, it would be impossible to create array of sample objects.

Finally, to destroy the array allocated using placement new we need to call the destructor for each element explicitly as shown below:

```
i = MAX ;
while ( i )
    sample[--i].~sample( ) ;
```

The *while* loop uses a descending order to preserve the canonical destruction order of C++— the object that was constructed last, must be destroyed first. To comply with this requirement, the element with the highest index is destroyed first.

Finally, we have released the raw memory where the array was created by calling *delete* as shown below:

```
delete[ ] buf ;
```

Note that with placement new there's no danger of allocation failure since the memory has already been allocated. Also, constructing an object on a pre-allocated buffer takes less time. The placement new technique is useful when building a memory pool, or a garbage collector or simply when performance and exception safety are of paramount importance.

A word of caution! Do not use placement destruction on an object that will later be automatically destroyed, such as an object on the stack, or an object on the heap that will be *delete*d. Use placement destruction only when you are in total control of the storage allocation and lifetime of the object. In other words, use it only with objects initialized by the placement new syntax.

One question that remains unanswered is when would we like to create objects at predetermined locations? We would do so in a case where the hardware uses a piece of storage as a way of communicating with the software.

One Last Issue

Imagine a case where we have a pointer member within a class. In this case we should call *delete* on this pointer member in the destructor of the class. This pointer would usually get initialised in the constructor of the class. If we forget this initialisation you would be able to locate this mistake fairly quickly when you compile and execute the program. However, if we forget to *delete* the pointer in the destructor no obvious symptoms are exhibited. Such memory leaks often go undetected for long. So form a habit of performing a *delete* on the pointer in the destructor function.

Note, that deleting a null pointer (i.e., one with value 0) is always safe (it does nothing). Thus, if you write the constructors, assignment operators, and other member functions such that each pointer member of the class is always either pointing to valid memory or is NULL, you can delete them in the destructor without regards for whether you ever actually called *new* for the pointer in question.

Exercise

[A] State True or False:

(a) If memory is allocated using *new [ ]* it must be deallocated using *delete [ ]*.

(b) *new* not only allocates memory but also calls the object's constructor.

(c) Heap and free store are two different things.

(d) *delete*ing a NULL pointer is safe and is guaranteed to do nothing.

(e) In C++ to reallocate memory we should use the *renew* operator.

(f) The *new* operator always returns a pointer of appropriate type, whereas, *malloc( )* returns a *void* pointer which needs to be typecasted explicitly.

(g) Like other operators the *new* operator can also be overloaded.

(h) We should never *delete* a pointer twice.

(i) _*new*_handler is a pointer to a function provided by C++ for managing free store exhaustion.

(j) We can overload the *new* and *delete* operators on a global basis as well as on a class by class basis.

(k) In one class the *delete* operator can be overload only once.

(l) It is unsafe to deallocate the memory using *delete* if it has been allocated using *malloc( )*.

[B] Answer the following:

(a) Does the expression *delete p* delete the pointer or the object being pointed to by *p*?

(b) Write a program that will allocate memory for a 1-D, 2-D and a 3-D array of integers. Store some values in these arrays and then print them out. We must be able to access elements of these arrays using forms *a[i]*, *b[i][j]* and *c[i][j][k]*.

(c) How many bytes would be allocated by the following code?

```
#define MAXROW 3
#define MAXCOL 4

int main( )
{
    int ( *p )[MAXCOL] ;
    p = new int[MAXROW][MAXCOL] ;
    return 0 ;
}
```

(d) What will be the output of the following program?

```
#include <iostream>
#define MAXROW 3
#define MAXCOL 4
using namespace std ;

int main( )
{
    int ( *p )[MAXCOL] ;
    p = new int[ MAXROW ][ MAXCOL ] ;
    cout << endl << sizeof ( p ) << endl << sizeof ( *p ) ;
```

```
    return 0 ;
}
```

(e) Point out the errors, if any, in the following program.

```
#include <iostream>
#include <stdlib>
#include <new>
using namespace std ;

void memwarning( ) ;

int main( )
{
    _new_handler = warning ;

    char *p ;
    p = new char[64000u] ;
    return 0 ;
}

void warning( )
{
    cout << endl << "Free store has now gone empty" ;
    exit ( 1 ) ;
}
```

(f) Point out the logical error, if any, in the following program.

```
#include <iostream>
using namespace std ;

class sample
{
    private :
        int *p ;
    public :
```

```
        sample( )
        {
            p = new int ;
        }
};

int main( )
{
    sample s ;
    return 0 ;
}
```

(g) Replace the following code using the *new* operator.

```
#include <alloc>
#define MAXROW  3
#define MAXCOL  4
using namespace std ;

int main( )
{
    int ( *p )[ MAXCOL ] ;
    p = ( int ( * ) [ MAXCOL ] ) malloc ( MAXROW * sizeof ( *p ) ) ;
    return 0 ;
}
```

(h) Replace the following code using the *new* operator.

```
#include <alloc>
#define MAXROW  3
#define MAXCOL  4
using namespace std ;

int main( )
{
    int ( *p )[ MAXCOL ][ MAXROW ] ;
    p = ( int ( * ) [ MAXROW ][ MAXCOL ] ) malloc ( sizeof ( *p ) ) ;
    return 0 ;
```

```
}
```

(i) Replace the following code using the *new* operator.

```
#include <alloc>
#define MAXROW 3
#define MAXCOL 4
using namespace std ;

int main( )
{
    int **p, i ;
    p = ( int ** ) malloc ( MAXROW * sizeof ( int * ) ) ;
    for ( i = 0 ; i < MAXROW ; i++ )
        p[i] = ( int * ) malloc ( MAXCOL * sizeof ( int ) ) ;
    return 0 ;
}
```

(j) Replace the following code using the *new* operator.

```
#include <alloc>
#define MAXROW 3
#define MAXCOL 4
using namespace std ;

int main( )
{
    int **p, i, j ;
    p = ( int ** ) malloc ( MAXROW * sizeof ( int * ) ) ;
    p[0] = ( int * ) malloc ( MAXROW * MAXCOL * sizeof ( int ) ) ;

    for ( i = 0 ; i < MAXROW ; i++ )
        p[i] = p[0] + i * MAXCOL ;
    return 0 ;
}
```

CHAPTER SEVEN

Miscellaneous Class Issues

Having spent enough time with classes and objects it is time for a few subtleties that would add more polish to your classes. Let us begin with the *static* class data.

Static Class Data

We know that each object contains its own separate data members, whereas, the member functions are shared amongst all objects. However, there is an exception to this rule. If a data member of a class is declared as *static*, then only one such item is created for the entire class, irrespective of the number of objects created from that class. A *static* data member is useful when all objects of the same class must share a common item of information. A *static* data member is available only within the class, but it continues to live till the time program execution doesn't come to an end. In that sense a *static* data member is similar to the ordinary *static* variable. However, their utility is different. While a normal *static* variable is used to retain information between calls to a function, *static* data members of a class are used to share information among the objects of a class. The following program shows *static* data member at work.

```
#include <iostream>
using namespace std ;

class sample
{
    private :

        static int index ; // declaration of index
        int count ;

    public:

        sample( )
```

```
        {
            index++ ;
            count++ ;
        }

        void showdata( )
        {
            cout << endl << "index = " << index ;
            cout << endl << "count = " << count ;
        }
};

int sample::index = 0 ; // definition of index

int main( )
{
    sample s1, s2, s3 ;

    s1.showdata( ) ;
    s2.showdata( ) ;
    s3.showdata( ) ;
    return 0 ;
}
```

The class *sample* has two data members, *index*, which is of the type *static int*, and *count*, which is a normal *int*. The constructor for this class causes each of them to be incremented. In *main( )* we have defined three objects of class *sample*. Each time an object is created the constructor gets called. Hence, *index* and *count* would get incremented thrice. Another member function, *showdata( )*, displays the current values of *index* and *count*. Here is the output of the program.

```
index = 3
count = -29312
```

```
index = 3
count = 645
index = 3
count = -2012
```

As we expected, the value of *index* is reported as *3* for each object, whereas, the value of *count* is reported as *–29312*, *645* and *–2012*. This is so because *index* is being shared amongst the three objects, whereas, each object enjoys its own *count*. Since *count* has not been specifically initialised its value is being reported as garbage.

If you observe carefully you would find that *static* data members require an unusual format. Ordinary variables like *count* are declared (the compiler is told about their name and type) and defined (the compiler sets aside memory to hold the variable) in the same statement. *static* data members like *index*, on the other hand, requires two separate statements. The variable's declaration appears in the class declaration, but the variable is actually defined outside the class.

Why such an approach is used for *static* data members? If *static* data members were defined inside the class declaration it would violate the idea that a class declaration is only a blueprint and does not set aside any memory. Defining the *static* member data outside the class also emphasizes two facts:

(a) The memory space for such data is allocated only once, before the program starts executing.

(b) There is only one *static* member variable for the entire class; each object does not have its own version of the variable.

A word of caution! If you include the declaration of a *static* variable but forget its definition, the compiler would pass it, whereas, the linker would tell you that you're trying to reference an undeclared external variable. This happens even if you include the definition, but forget the class name (the *sample::* in the program above).

Lastly, the most important question: when would we be required to use *static* member data? Imagine a situation where an object is required to know how many other objects of its class are in existence. In this case a *static* variable *index* can be included as a member of the class. Being *static*, this variable would be shared by all the objects.

Static Member Functions

The way we can have *static* data members in a class we can have *static* member functions as well. The following program shows how they can be used.

```
#include <iostream>
using namespace std ;

class sample
{
    private :

        static int count ;

    public :

        sample( )
        {
            count++ ;
        }

        static void showcount( )
        {
```

```
        cout << endl << "count = " << count ;
    }
} ;

int sample::count = 0 ;

int main( )
{
    sample s1 ;
    sample::showcount( ) ;
    sample s2 ;
    sample::showcount( ) ;
    sample s3 ;
    sample::showcount( ) ;
    return 0 ;
}
```

In this program there is a *static* data member, *count*, in the class *sample*. It keeps track of how many objects of the class there are. It is incremented every time an object is constructed. We have created a function *showcount( )* to display the current value of *count*. Problem is how to access this function? We can do so in two ways:

```
sample s1 ;
s1.showcount( ) ;
sample::showcount( ) ;
```

The first way is a little clumsy. We shouldn't need to refer to a specific object when we're doing something that relates to the entire class. The second way is more elegant:

```
sample ::showcount( ) ;
```

It's more reasonable to use the name of the class itself with the scope resolution operator. However, for this form to work it is necessary to define *showcount( )* as a *static* member function.

const And Classes

So far we have used *const* in two cases:

(a) On normal variables to prevent them from being modified.

(b) On function arguments to keep a function from modifying a variable passed to it by value or by reference.

We are allowed to use *const* in three more situations:

(a) On member functions of a class
(b) On member function arguments
(c) On objects

Let us now examine how *const* can be used in the above ways.

const Member Functions

A *const* member function guarantees that it will never modify any of its class's member data. The following program shows this.

```
#include <iostream>
using namespace std ;

class sample
{
    private :

        int data ;
```

```
    public :

        sample( )
        {
            data = 0 ;
        }

        void changedata( )
        {
            data = 10 ;
        }

        void modifydata( ) const
        {
            data = 20 ; // error
        }

        void showdata( )
        {
            cout << endl << "data = " << data ;
        }
} ;

int main( )
{
    sample s1 ;

    s1.showdata( ) ;
    s1.changedata( ) ;
    s1.showdata( ) ;
    s1.changedata( ) ;
    s1.showdata( ) ;
    return 0 ;
}
```

In this program the non-*const* function *changedata( )* can modify *data*, but the constant function *modifydata( )* can't. If it tries to, a compiler error 'Cannot modify a const object' results.

Note that to make *modifydata( )* constant the keyword *const* is placed after the declarator but before the function body. If the function is declared inside the class but defined outside it then it is necessary to use *const* in declaration as well as definition. Member functions that do nothing but acquire data from an object are obvious candidates for being made *const*. In our program one such function was *showdata( )*, which too could have been made a constant function.

const Member Function Arguments

In Chapter 3 we saw that if we want that an argument passed to an ordinary function by reference should not get modified then the argument should be made *const* in the function declaration (and definition). This holds good for member functions as well.

```
#include <iostream>
using namespace std ;

class sample
{
    private :

        int data ;

    public :

        sample( )
        {
            data = 0 ;
        }
```

```
    void changedata( )
    {
        data = 10 ;
    }

    void showdata( ) const
    {
        cout << endl << "data = " << data << endl ;
    }

    void add ( sample const &s, sample const &t )
    {
        data = s.data + t.data ;
    }

    void getdata( )
    {
        cin >> data ;
    }
} ;

int main( )
{
    sample s1 ;
    s1.changedata( ) ;

    sample s2 ;
    s2.changedata( ) ;

    sample s3 ;
    s3.add ( s1, s2 ) ;
    s3.showdata( ) ;
    return 0 ;
}
```

In this program the arguments to the function *add( )* are passed by reference, and we want to make sure that *add( )* won't modify these arguments. To ensure this we have declared the arguments as *const*.

const Objects

We know that we can apply *const* to variables of basic types like *int* to keep them from being modified. In a similar way we can apply *const* to objects of classes. When an object is declared as *const*, you can't modify it. Thus in the above program had we added the following statements in *main( )* it would have resulted into a warning from the compiler.

```
const int a ;
a.getdata( ) ;
```

It follows that you can use only *const* member functions with *const* objects, because they're the only ones that guarantee not to modify the object.

Overloaded Assignment Operator And Copy Constructor

The C++ compiler is a fatherly old chap who doesn't nag you with small little details. It understands the pulls and pressures that the C++ programmer has to contend with and does things on your behalf. It carries out several small little tasks in its own way unless you order to do it some other way. Two important examples of this process are the *assignment operator* and the *copy constructor*.

Consider the following statements:

```
circle c1, c2 ;
c1 = c2 ;
circle c3 = c2 ;
```

Here *c1* and *c2* are objects of the type *circle* which is a predefined class. The statement

```
c1 = c2 ;
```

will cause the compiler to copy the data from *c2*, member-by-member, into *c1*. This is what the *assignment* operator does by default.

In the next statement we have initialised one object with another object during declaration. This statement causes a similar action. The compiler creates a new object *c3* and copies the data from *c2* member-by-member, into *c3*. This is what the *copy constructor* does by default. The difference between the two is that the copy constructor also creates a new object, whereas, the assignment operator doesn't.

The compiler carries out both these activities by default. However, should you want that the assignment operator or the copy constructor should do something more complex, then you can always override these default actions. Before we see when it would be necessary to override these default actions let us first confirm through a program that these actions really take place.

```
#include <iostream>
using namespace std ;

class circle
{
    private :

        int radius ;
```

```
        float x, y ;

    public :

        circle( )
        {
        }

        circle ( int rr, float xx, float yy )
        {
            radius = rr ;
            x = xx ;
            y = yy ;
        }

        circle operator = ( circle& c )
        {
            cout << endl << "Assignment operator invoked" ;
            radius = c.radius ;
            x = c.x ;
            y = c.y ;
            return circle ( radius, x, y ) ;
        }

        circle ( circle& c )
        {
            cout << endl << "Copy constructor invoked" ;
            radius = c.radius ;
            x = c.x ;
            y = c.y ;
        }

        void showdata( )
        {
            cout << endl << endl << "Radius = " << radius ;
            cout << endl << "X-Coordinate = " << x ;
            cout << endl << "Y-Coordinate = " << y << endl ;
```

```
        }
};

int main( )
{
    circle c1 ( 10, 2.5, 2.5 ) ;
    circle c2, c4 ;
    c4 = c2 = c1 ;
    circle c3 = c1 ;

    c1.showdata( ) ;
    c2.showdata( ) ;
    c3.showdata( ) ;
    c4.showdata( ) ;
    return 0 ;
}
```

Most of the program is straightforward. What is important here is the function *operator = ( )*, which overloads the = operator, and the copy constructor. The overloaded operator function gets called when the statement *c4 = c2 = c1* gets executed. As against this, when the statement *circle c3 = c1* gets executed the overloaded copy constructor gets called.

That is why the assignment operator is executed twice, whereas, the copy constructor is called only once.

The overloaded = operator does the copying of the member data from one object to another. The function also prints the "Assignment operator invoked" message so that we can keep track of when it executes.

Note that we have passed the argument to overloaded operator function by reference. This is often desirable, though not absolutely necessary. Had the argument been passed by value it would have created another local object in the function. In our program it would not have mattered much, but in case of large objects this would lead to considerable wastage of memory.

The *operator = ( )* function in our program returns a value by creating a temporary *circle* object and initialising it using the three-argument constructor. Note that the value returned is a copy of the object of which the overloaded = operator is a member. Returning a value makes it possible to chain = operators in *c4 = c2 = c1*. However, returning by value creates an extra copy of the object which means wastage of memory space. We know that when an object is returned by reference, no new object is created. Then can we not return the value from the overloaded operator function by reference using a declaration like

```
circle& operator = ( circle & c )
```

Unfortunately, we can't use reference returns on variables that are local to a function since the local variables are destroyed when the function returns. This problem can be overcome using the *this* pointer that we learnt in Chapter 5. Here is the modified version of the overloaded assignment operator which uses the *this* pointer.

```
circle& operator = ( circle& c )
{
    cout << endl << "Assignment operator invoked" ;
    radius = c.radius ;
    x = c.x ;
    y = c.y ;
    return *this ;
}
```

Consider the statement,

```
c4 = c2 = c1 ;
```

As we know, during execution firstly *c2 = c1* will get executed. This internally becomes,

```
c2.operator = ( c1 ) ;
```

The argument *c1* passed to the assignment operator gets collected in the object *c*. Now data of c is copied into *c2's* data members through the statements,

```
radius = c.radius ;
x = c.x ;
y = c.y ;
```

At this stage the *this* pointer contains *c2*'s address. Hence on returning **this* we are simply returning *c2*. Since this is not a local object we can safely return it by reference.

Let us now turn our attention to the copy constructor. The copy constructor takes one argument, an object of the type *circle*, passed by reference. Here's its prototype:

```
circle ( circle & )
```

Is it necessary for us to use a reference in the argument to the copy constructor? Can we not pass a value instead? No. Because, if we pass the argument by value, its copy is constructed using the copy constructor. This means the copy constructor would call itself to make this copy. This process would go on and on until the compiler runs out of memory. Hence in the copy constructor the argument must always be passed by reference.

A copy constructor also gets invoked when objects are passed by value to functions and when objects are returned from functions. When an object is passed by value the copy that the function operates on is created using a copy constructor. If we pass the address or reference of the object the copy constructor would of course not be invoked, since in these cases the copies of the objects are not to be created.

When an object is returned from a function the copy constructor is invoked to create a copy of the value returned by the function.

Data Conversion

We are already aware that the = operator assigns a value from one variable to another in statements like

```
int a, b ;
a = b ;
```

We have also used the = operator in context of user-defined data types. Here, = assigns the value of one user-defined object to another, provided they are of the same type, in statements like

```
matrix3 = matrix1 + matrix2 ;
```

where the result of the addition is of the type *matrix*, and this result is assigned to another object *matrix3* of type *matrix*. Normally, when we assign the value of one object to another object of the same type, the values of all the data members are copied into the corresponding data members of the new object. The compiler doesn't need any special instructions to use = for the assignment of user-defined objects such as *matrix* objects.

Thus assignments between types, whether they are basic or user-defined, are handled by the compiler with no effort on our part, provided that the same data type is used on both sides of the assignment operator.

What if the variables on the two sides of the = are of different types? This is going to be a slightly complicated issue. Let us first see how the compiler handles the conversion of basic types, which it does automatically.

When we write a statement like

```
a = b ;
```

where *a* is of type *int* and *b* is of type *float*, the compiler calls a special routine to convert the value of *b*, which is expressed in floating-point format, to an integer format so that it can be assigned to *a*. There are many other such conversions possible: from *float* to *double*, *char* to *float*, and so on. Each such conversion has its own routine built into the compiler. These routines and called when the data types on either side of the assignment operator are different. These conversions are often known as implicit conversions since these conversions are not apparent in the listing of the program.

At times we may want to force the compiler to convert one type of data to another. This can be achieved by using typecasting. For instance, to convert a *float* to a *double* we can say

```
double a ;
float b = 3.14 ;
a = double ( b ) ;
```

Typecasting provides an explicit conversion. That is, in the listing it can be obviously seen that the *double( )* conversion function will convert *b* from *float* to a *double*. However, such explicit conversions use the same built-in routines as implicit conversions.

When we want to convert between user-defined data types and basic types, we can't rely on built-in conversion routines, since the compiler doesn't know anything about user-defined types besides what we tell it. Instead, we must write these conversion routines ourselves.

The following program shows how to convert between a basic type and a user-defined type and vice versa. In this program the user-defined type is a *string* class and the basic type is *int*. The program shows conversion from *string* to *int* and from *int* to *string*. Here's the program...

```
// conversions: string to int, int to string
#include <iostream>
#include <cstdlib>
#include <string>
using namespace std ;
class mystring
{
    private :

        char str[20] ;
    public :

        mystring( )
        {
            str[0] = '\0' ;
        }

        mystring ( char *s )
        {
            strcpy ( str, s ) ;
        }

        mystring ( int a )
        {
            itoa ( a, str, 10 );
        }

        operator int( )
        {
            int i = 0, l, ss = 0, k = 1 ;

            l = strlen ( str ) - 1 ;
            while ( l >= 0 )
```

```
            {
                ss = ss + ( str[l] - 48 ) * k ;
                l-- ;
                k *= 10 ;
            }

            return ( ss ) ;
        }

        void displaydata( )
        {
            cout << str ;
        }
} ;

int main( )
{
    mystring s1 = 123 ;
    cout << endl << "s1 = " ;
    s1.displaydata( ) ;

    s1 = 150 ;
    cout << endl << "s1 = " ;
    s1.displaydata( ) ;

    mystring s2 ( "123" ) ;
    int i = int ( s2 ) ;
    cout << endl << "i = " << i ;

    mystring s3 ( "456" ) ;
    i = s3 ;
    cout << endl << "i = " << i << endl ;
    return 0 ;
}
```

Here, to convert an *int* to a user-defined type *string* we have used a constructor with one argument. It is called when an object of type *string* is created with a single argument. The function assumes that this argument represents an *int* which it converts to a *string* and assigns it to *str* using the *itoa( )* function. Thus the conversion from *int* to *string* is carried out when we create an object in the statement

```
string s1 = 123 ;
```

A similar conversion is carried out when the statement

```
s1 = 150 ;
```

is executed. Here we are converting an *int* to a *string*, but we are not creating a new object. The one argument constructor is called even in this case. When the compiler comes across a statement that needs a conversion, it looks for any tool that can carry out this work for it. In our program it finds a constructor that converts an *int* to a *string*, so it uses it in the assignment statement by first creating an unnamed temporary object with it's *str* holding the value corresponding to the integer *150* and then assigns this object to *s1*. Thus if the compiler doesn't find an overloaded = operator it looks for a constructor to do the same job.

To convert a *string* to an *int* the overloaded cast operator is used. This is often called a conversion function. This operator takes the value of the *string* object of which it is a member, converts this value to an *int* value and then returns this *int* value. This operator gets called in two cases:

```
i = int ( s2 ) ;
```

and

```
i = s3 ;
```

In the second assignment the compiler first searches for an overloaded assignment operator. Since this search fails the compiler uses the conversion function to do the job of conversion.

One might think that it would not be a sound programming practice to routinely convert from one type to another. However, the flexibility provided by allowing conversions often outweighs the dangers of making mistakes by allowing mixing of data types.

Data Conversion Between Objects Of Different Classes

In the last section we saw how data conversion takes place from user-defined objects to intrinsic data types and vice versa. Let us now see how do we go about converting data between objects of different user-defined classes? The same two methods used for conversion between basic types and user-defined types apply to conversions between two user-defined types. That is, we can use a one-argument constructor, or we can use a conversion function. The choice depends on where we want to put the conversion routine: in the class declaration of the source object or of the destination object. We propose to examine both the cases here.

Conversion Routine In Source Object

When the conversion routine is in the source class, it is commonly implemented as a conversion function as shown in the following program. The two classes used in the program are *date* and *dmy*. Both classes are built to handle dates, the difference being the *date* class handles it as a string, whereas the *dmy* class handles it as three integers representing day, month and year. Here is the listing of the program…

```
#include <iostream>
#include <stdlib>
#include <string>
using namespace std ;
```

```
class date
{
    private :

        char dt[9] ;

    public :

        date( )
        {
            dt[0] = '\0' ;
        }

        date ( char *s )
        {
            strcpy ( dt, s ) ;
        }

        void displaydata( )
        {
            cout << dt ;
        }
} ;

class dmy
{
    private :

        int day, mth, yr ;

    public :

        dmy( )
        {
            day = mth = yr = 0 ;
        }
```

```
        dmy ( int d, int m, int y )
        {
            day = d ;
            mth = m ;
            yr = y ;
        }

        operator date( )
        {
            char temp[3], str[9] ;

            itoa ( day, str, 10 ) ;
            strcat ( str, "/" ) ;
            itoa ( mth, temp, 10 ) ;
            strcat ( str, temp ) ;
            strcat ( str, "/" ) ;
            itoa ( yr, temp, 10 ) ;
            strcat ( str, temp ) ;

            return ( date ( str ) ) ;
        }

        void displaydata( )
        {
            cout << day << "\t" << mth << "\t" << yr << endl ;
        }
} ;

int main( )
{
    date d1 ;
    dmy d2 ( 17, 11, 94 ) ;

    d1 = d2 ;

    cout << endl << "d1 = " ;
    d1.displaydata( ) ;
```

```
    cout << endl << "d2 = " ;
    d2.displaydata( ) ;
    return 0 ;
}
```

In *main( )* we have defined an object *d1* of the type *date*, which is not initialized. We have also defined an object *d2* of the type *dmy*, which has been initialised. Next an assignment is carried out through the statement *d1 = d2*.

Since *d1* and *d2* are objects of different classes, the assignment involves a conversion, and as we specified, in this program the conversion function *date( )* is a member of the *dmy* class. This function transforms the object of which it is a member to a *date* object, and returns this object, which *main( )* then assigns to *d1*.

Conversion Routine In Destination Object

Let's now see how the same conversion is carried out when the conversion routine is present in the destination class. In such cases usually a one-argument constructor is used. However, things are complicated by the fact that the constructor in the destination class must be able to access the data in the source class to perform the conversion. That is, since the data *day*, *mth* and *yr* in the *dmy* class is *private* we must provide special functions like *getday( )*, *getmth( )* and *getyr( )* to allow direct access to it. Here's a program that implements this.

```
#include <iostream>
#include <stdlib>
#include <string>
using namespace std ;

class dmy
{
```

```
private :

    int day, mth, yr ;

public :

    dmy( )
    {
        day = mth = yr = 0 ;
    }

    dmy ( int d, int m, int y )
    {
        day = d ;
        mth = m ;
        yr = y ;
    }

    int getday( )
    {
        return ( day ) ;
    }

    int getmth( )
    {
        return ( mth ) ;
    }

    int getyr( )
    {
        return ( yr ) ;
    }

    void displaydata( )
    {
        cout << day << "\t" << mth << "\t" << yr << endl ;
    }
```

```
};

class date
{
    private :

        char dt[9] ;

    public :

        date( )
        {
            dt[0] = '\0' ;
        }

        date ( char *s )
        {
            strcpy ( dt, s ) ;
        }

        void displaydata( )
        {
            cout << dt ;
        }

        date ( dmy t )
        {
            int d = t.getday( ) ;
            int m = t.getmth( ) ;
            int y = t.getyr( ) ;

            char temp[3] ;
            itoa ( d, dt, 10 ) ;
            strcat ( dt, "/" ) ;
            itoa ( m, temp, 10 ) ;
            strcat ( dt, temp ) ;
            strcat ( dt, "/" ) ;
```

```
            itoa ( y, temp, 10 ) ;
            strcat ( dt, temp ) ;
        }
};

int main( )
{
    date d1 ;
    dmy d2 ( 17, 11, 94 ) ;

    d1 = d2 ;

    cout << endl << "d1 = " ;
    d1.displaydata( ) ;
    cout << endl << "d2 = " ;
    d2.displaydata( ) ;
    return 0 ;
}
```

When we execute the statement *d1 = d2* the one-argument constructor in the *date* class (whose argument is a *dmy* object) gets called. This constructor function gets the access to the data of *d2* by calling the *getday( )*, *getmth( )* and *getyr( )* functions. Finally it converts this data into a string. The output of this program is similar to the earlier one. The difference is behind the scenes. Here a constructor in the destination object, rather than a conversion function in the source object, handles the conversion.

That brings us to the important question: when should we use a one-argument constructor in the destination class, and when should we use a conversion function in the source class? Often this choice is simple. If you have a library of classes, you may not have access to its source code. If you use an object of such a class as the source in a conversion, then you'll have access only to the destination class, and you'll need to use a one-argument constructor. Or, if the library class object is the destination, then you must use a conversion function in the source. What if we use a conversion function as well as a one-argument constructor? The compiler would of course flash an error since this becomes an ambiguous situation.

Exercise

[A] State True or False:

(a) A *static* data member is useful when all objects of the same class must share a common item of information.

(b) If a class has a *static* data member and three objects are created from this class, then each object would have its own *static* data member.

(c) A class can have *static* data members as well as *static* member functions.

(d) A *static* data member's definition appears in the class declaration, but the variable is actually declared outside the class.

(e) If *display( )* is a *static* member function of a class called *sample* then it can be called in the following way:

```
sample s1 ;
s1.display( ) ;
```

(f) If *display( )* is a *static* member function of a class called *sample* then it can be called in the following way:

```
sample::display( ) ;
```

(g) The *const* can be used on member functions of a class as well as on member function arguments.

(h) A *const* member function prevents modification of any of its class's member data.

(i) If a member function of a class is to be *const* then it is necessary to use *const* in declaration as well as definition of the member function.

(j) You can use only *const* member functions with *const* objects.

(k) If we don't provide an assignment operator in a class declaration then the compiler automatically adds one to our class.

(l) If we don't provide a copy constructor in a class declaration then the compiler automatically adds one.

(m) The following two set of statements are same:

```
sample s1 ;
s1 = s2
```

and

```
sample s1 = s2 ;
```

(n) It is not possible to return a local object by reference.

(o) When an object is passed to a function or returned from a function the copy constructor gets called.

(p) To carry out conversion from an object to a basic type or vice versa it is necessary to provide the conversion functions.

(q) To carry out conversion from object of one type to another it is necessary to provide the conversion functions.

[B] Point out the errors, if any, in the following programs.

(a)
```
#include <iostream>
using namespace std ;

class sample
```

```
{
    private :
        static int count ;
    public:
        sample( )
        {
            count = 10 ;
        }

        void display( ) const
        {
            cout << endl << "count = " << count ;
        }
} ;

int main( )
{
    sample s1, s2, s3 ;
    s1. display ( ) ;
    s2. display ( ) ;
    s3. display ( ) ;
    return 0 ;
}
```

(b)
```
#include <iostream>
using namespace std ;

class example
{
    private :
        int data ;
    public:
        example( ) ;
        void display( ) const ;
} ;
example::example( )
{
```

```
    data = 0 ;
}
example::display( )
{
    cout << endl << "count = " << count ;
}

int main( )
{
    example d ;
    d.display( ) ;
    return 0 ;
}
```

[C] Answer the following:

(a) In which of the following cases can we use *const* :

- On normal variables
- On function arguments
- On member functions of a class
- On member function arguments
- On objects

(b) If we wish to provide an assignment operator and a copy constructor within a class called *rectangle* what would be their prototypes?

(c) Write a program that consists of two classes *time12* and *time24*. The first one maintains time on a 12-hour basis, whereas the other one maintains it on a 24-hour basis. Provide conversion functions to carry out the conversion from object of one type to another.

(d) Write a program that implements a *date* class containing data members *day*, *month* and *year*. Implement assignment operator and copy constructor in this class.

CHAPTER

EIGHT

Data Structure Through C++

Having familiarised ourselves with objects and classes let us now put them to work in implementing standard data structures like stacks, queues, linked lists and binary trees. Let us begin with stacks and queues.

Stacks And Queues

Stacks and queues are two very common and popular data structures. A stack is a data structure in which addition of new element or deletion of existing element always takes place at the same end. This end is often known as *top* of stack. This situation can be compared to a stack of plates in a cafeteria where every new plate added to the stack is added at the *top*. Similarly, every new plate taken off the stack is also from the *top* of the stack. The two changes that can be made to a stack are given special names. When an item is added to a stack, the operation is called *push*, and when an item is removed from the stack the operation is called *pop*. There are several applications where stack can be put to use. For example, recursion, keeping track of function calls, evaluation of expressions etc.

Unlike a stack, in a queue the addition of new element takes place at the end (called *rear* of queue), whereas, deletion takes place at the other end (called *front* of queue). Figure 8.1 shows these two data structures. Application of queues are even more common than applications of stacks, since in performing tasks by computer, it is often necessary to wait one's turn before having access to something. Within a computer system there may be queues of tasks waiting for the line printer, for access to disk storage, or in a time-sharing system, for use of the CPU. Within a single program, there may be multiple requests to be kept in a queue, or one task may create other tasks, which must be done in turn by keeping them in a queue.

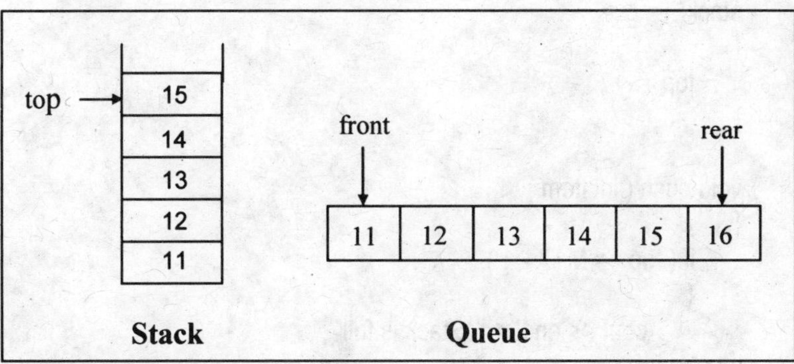

Figure 8.1

Since the last item added to the stack is the first one to get removed, a stack is often called a Last-In-First-Out (LIFO) structure. Similarly, a queue is called a First-In-First-Out (FIFO) structure, as the first item added to the queue is the first one to get deleted.

The following programs show how these data structures can be implemented using classes and objects.

```
// implementation of stack
#include <iostream>
using namespace std ;

#define MAX 10

class stack
{
    private :

        int arr[MAX] ;
        int top ;

    public :
```

```
        stack( )
        {
            top = -1 ;
        }

        void push ( int item )
        {
            if ( top == MAX - 1 )
            {
                cout << endl << "Stack is full" ;
                return ;
            }

            top++ ;
            arr[top] = item ;
        }

        int pop( )
        {
            if ( top == -1 )
            {
                cout << endl << "Stack is empty" ;
                return NULL ;
            }

            int data = arr[top] ;
            top-- ;

            return data ;
        }
} ;

int main( )
{
    stack s ;

    s.push ( 11 ) ;
```

```
    s.push ( 12 ) ;
    s.push ( 13 ) ;
    s.push ( 14 ) ;
    s.push ( 15 ) ;
    s.push ( 16 ) ;
    s.push ( 17 ) ;
    s.push ( 18 ) ;
    s.push ( 19 ) ;
    s.push ( 20 ) ;
    s.push ( 21 ) ;

    int i = s.pop( ) ;
    cout << endl << "Item popped = " << i ;

    i = s.pop( ) ;
    cout << endl << "Item popped = " << i ;

    i = s.pop( ) ;
    cout << endl << "Item popped = " << i ;

    i = s.pop( ) ;
    cout << endl << "Item popped = " << i << endl ;
    return 0 ;
}
```

Here, to begin with we have defined a class called *stack* containing member functions *push( )* and *pop( )*. These functions respectively add and delete items from the top of stack. The actual storage is done in an array *arr*, and the data member *top* is an index into this array. It contains a value where the addition or deletion is going to take place in the array, and thereby in the stack. To indicate that to begin with the stack is empty the variable *top* is set with a value -1. Every time an element is added to the stack it is verified whether such an addition is possible at all. If it is not then the message 'Stack is full' is reported.

Let us now switch over to the implementation of the queue. As we did for stacks, we can use an array to hold the items in the queue. We must keep track of both the front and the rear of the queue. One method would be to keep the front of the queue always in the first location of the array. Then an item could be added to the queue simply by increasing the counter showing the rear, in exactly the same way as we added an item to a stack. To delete an item from the queue, however, would be very expensive indeed, since after the first item is removed, all the remaining items would have to be moved one position up the queue to fill in the vacancy. With a long queue, this process would be prohibitively slow. Although this method of storage closely models a queue of people waiting to be served, it is a poor choice for use in computers.

For efficient processing of queues, we shall therefore need two indices so that we can keep track of both the front and the rear of the queue without moving any items. To add an item to the queue, we simply increase the rear by one and put the item in that position. To remove an item, we take it from the position at the front and then increase the front by one. Here is the program that implements these ideas…

```
#include <iostream>
using namespace std ;

#define MAX 10

class queue
{
    private :

        int arr[MAX] ;
        int front, rear ;

    public :
```

```
queue( )
{
    front = -1 ;
    rear = -1 ;
}

void addq ( int item )
{
    if ( rear == MAX - 1 )
    {
        cout << endl << "Queue is full" ;
        return ;
    }

    rear++ ;
    arr[rear] = item ;

    if ( front == -1 )
        front = 0 ;
}

int delq( )
{
    int data ;

    if ( front == -1 )
    {
        cout << endl << "Queue is Empty" ;
        return NULL ;
    }

    data = arr[front] ;
    if ( front == rear )
        front = rear = -1 ;
    else
        front++ ;
```

```
            return data ;
        }
};

int main( )
{
    queue a ;

    a.addq ( 11 ) ;
    a.addq ( 12 ) ;
    a.addq ( 13 ) ;
    a.addq ( 14 ) ;
    a.addq ( 15 ) ;
    a.addq ( 16 ) ;
    a.addq ( 17 ) ;
    a.addq ( 18 ) ;
    a.addq ( 19 ) ;
    a.addq ( 20 ) ;
    a.addq ( 21 ) ;

    int i = a.delq( ) ;
    cout << endl << "Item deleted = " << i ;

    i = a.delq( ) ;
    cout << endl << "Item deleted = " << i ;

    i = a.delq( ) ;
    cout << endl << "Item deleted = " << i << endl ;
    return 0 ;
}
```

Since addition of new element to the queue takes place at the rear end and deletion of an element from the queue takes place from the front, in the class we have two data members *front* and *rear* to monitor the two ends. When the queue is empty their values are set to *-1*. To carry out the addition and deletion operations on the queue we have implemented two functions within the queue class, namely, *addq( )* and *delq( )*. Let us understand these functions. Here is the first one.

```
void addq ( int item )
{
    if ( rear == MAX - 1 )
    {
        cout << endl << "Queue is full";
        return ;
    }

    rear++ ;
    arr[rear] = item ;

    if ( front == -1 )
        front = 0 ;
}
```

While adding a new element to the queue, first it is ascertained whether such an addition is possible or not. Since the array indexing begins with *0* the maximum number of elements that can be stored in the queue are *MAX - 1*. If these many elements are already present in the queue then it is reported to be full. If the element can be added to the queue then the value of the variable *rear* is incremented and the new item is stored in the array. If the item is being added to the queue for the first time (i.e. if the variable *front* has a value *-1*) then as soon as the item is added to the queue front is set to *0* indicating that the queue is no longer empty.

Let us now look at the *delq( )* function.

```
int delq( )
```

```
{
    int data ;

    if ( front == -1 )
    {
        cout << endl << "Queue is Empty" ;
        return NULL ;
    }

    data = arr[front] ;
    if ( front == rear )
        front = rear = -1 ;
    else
        front++ ;

    return  data ;
}
```

Before deleting an element from the queue it is first ascertained whether there are any elements available for deletion. If not then the queue is reported as empty. Otherwise, an element is deleted from *arr[front]*.

Imagine a case where we add 5 elements to the queue. Value of *rear* would now be *4*. Suppose we have not deleted any elements from the queue, then at this stage the value of *front* would be *0*. Now suppose we go on deleting elements from the queue. When the fifth element is deleted the queue would fall empty. To make sure that another attempt to delete should me met with an 'empty queue' message, in such a case *front* and *rear* both are reset to *-1* to indicate emptiness of the queue.

Can you imagine the limitation of our implementation of the queue? Suppose we go on adding elements to the queue till the entire array gets filled. At this stage the value of *rear* would be *MAX – 1*. Now if we delete 5 elements from the queue, at the end of these deletions the value of *front* would be 5. If we now attempt to add a new element to the queue then it would be reported as full even though in reality the first five slots of the queue are empty. To overcome this situation we can implement a queue as a circular queue. That is, during addition if we reach the end of the array and if slots at the beginning of the queue are empty (as a result of a few deletions) then new elements would get added at the beginning of the array. The following program implements a circular queue. I would leave it for you to figure out its working.

```
// circular queue implementation

#include <iostream>
using namespace std ;

#define MAX 10

class queue
{
    private :

        int arr[MAX] ;
        int front, rear ;

    public :

        queue( )
        {
            front = -1 ;
            rear = -1 ;
        }

        void addq ( int item )
        {
            if ( ( rear == MAX - 1 && front == 0 ) || ( rear + 1 == front ) )
            {
```

```
            cout << endl << "Queue is full" ;
            return ;
        }

        if ( rear == MAX - 1 )
            rear = 0 ;
        else
            rear = rear + 1 ;

        arr[rear] = item ;
        if ( front == -1 )
            front = 0 ;
    }

    int delq( )
    {
        int data ;

        if ( front == -1 )
        {
            cout << endl << "Queue is Empty" ;
            return NULL ;
        }
        else
        {
            data = arr[front] ;

            if ( front == rear )
            {
                front = -1 ;
                rear = -1 ;
            }
            else
            {
                if ( front == MAX - 1 )
                    front = 0 ;
                else
```

```
                    front = front + 1 ;
                }

                return data ;
            }
        }
};

int main( )
{
    queue a ;

    a.addq ( 11 ) ;
    a.addq ( 12 ) ;
    a.addq ( 13 ) ;
    a.addq ( 14 ) ;
    a.addq ( 15 ) ;
    a.addq ( 16 ) ;
    a.addq ( 17 ) ;
    a.addq ( 18 ) ;
    a.addq ( 19 ) ;
    a.addq ( 20 ) ;
    a.addq ( 21 ) ;

    int i = a.delq( ) ;
    cout << endl << "Item deleted = " << i ;

    i = a.delq( ) ;
    cout << endl << "Item deleted = " << i ;

    i = a.delq( ) ;
    cout << endl << "Item deleted = " << i << endl ;
    return 0 ;
}
```

The Linked List

What is a linked list? It's a way to store data. You can imagine numerous examples of data stored in arrays. While implementing stacks and queues we have assumed that all items of data are kept within arrays. These arrays were declared to have size MAX, which is fixed once the program is written, and it cannot be changed while the program is running. Thus while writing a program, we had to decide on the maximum amount of memory that would be needed for our arrays and we set this much memory aside in the declarations. If the number of elements stored in the stack/queue is small, then much of this space will never be used. However, if we decide to store a large number of items in the stack/queue, then we may exhaust the space set aside and encounter overflow, even when the computer memory itself is not fully used, simply because our original bounds on the array were too small.

Thus arrays suffer from the necessity to declare the size of the array before running the program. If we are to overcome this limitation we need to use a data structure called *Linked List*. A linked list provides a more flexible storage system in that it doesn't use arrays at all. The idea of a linked list is simple. For every item in the list it associates a pointer that would give the location of the next item in the list. This idea is illustrated in Figure 8.2.

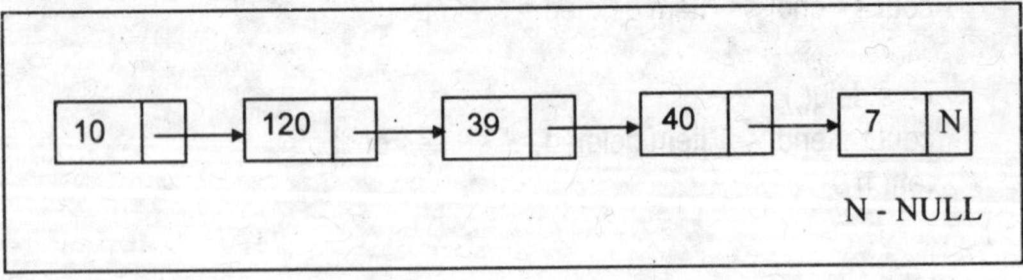

Figure 8.2

As you can see from the figure, a linked list is simple in concept. It uses the same idea as the children's treasure hunt, where each clue that is found tells where to find the next one.

Instead of allocating space for each item during compilation, in a linked list space for each data item is obtained as and when needed (during execution), and each item is connected, or *linked*, to the next data item using a pointer. As can be seen from Figure 8.2, unlike the array elements, the individual items of the linked list don't need to be located in adjacent memory locations. They may be scattered anywhere in memory.

The following program implements a linked list as a class.

```
// Program to maintain a linked list
#include <iostream>
using namespace std ;

class linklist
{
	private :

		struct node
		{
			int data ;
			node *link ;
		} *p ;

	public :

		linklist( ) ;
		void append ( int num ) ;
		void addatbeg ( int num ) ;
		void addafter ( int c, int num ) ;
		void del ( int num ) ;
		void display( ) ;
```

```
        int count( ) ;
        ~linklist( ) ;
} ;

linklist::linklist( )
{
    p = NULL ;
}

// adds a new node at the end of the linked list
void linklist::append ( int num )
{
    node *q, *t ;

    // if the list is empty
    if ( p == NULL )
    {
        // create first node
        p = new node ;
        p -> data = num ;
        p -> link = NULL ;
    }
    else
    {
        // go to the last node
        q = p ;
        while ( q -> link != NULL )
            q = q->link ;

        // add node at the end
        t = new node ;
        t->data = num ;
        t->link = NULL ;
        q->link = t ;
    }
}
```

```
// adds a new node at the beginning of the linked list
void linklist::addatbeg ( int num )
{
    node *q ;

    // add new node
    q = new node ;
    q->data = num ;
    q->link = p ;
    p = q ;
}

// adds a new node after the specified number of nodes
void linklist::addafter ( int c, int num )
{
    node *q, *t ; int i ;

    // skip to the desired portion
    for ( i = 0, q = p ; i < c ; i++ )
    {
        q = q->link ;

        // if end of linked list is encountered
        if ( q == NULL )
        {
            cout << endl << "There are less than " << c
                << " elements." ;
            return ;
        }
    }

    // insert new node
    t = new node ;
    t->data = num ;
    t->link = q->link ;
    q->link = t ;
}
```

```
// deletes the specified node from the linked list
void linklist::del ( int num )
{
    node *q, *r ;

    q = p ;

    // if node to be deleted is first node
    if ( q->data == num )
    {
        p = q->link ;
        delete q ;
        return ;
    }

    // traverse list till the last but one node is reached
    r = q ;
    while ( q != NULL )
    {
        if ( q->data == num )
        {
            r->link = q->link ;
            // free the memory occupied by the node
            delete q ;
            return ;
        }

        r = q ;
        q = q->link ;
    }

    cout << endl << "Element " << num << " not found" ;
}

// displays the contents of the linked list
void linklist::display( )
```

```
{
    node *q ;

    cout << endl ;

    // traverse the entire linked list
    for ( q = p ; q != NULL ; q = q->link )
        cout << endl << q->data ;
}

// counts number of nodes present in the linked list
int linklist::count( )
{
    node *q ; int c = 0 ;

    // traverse the entire linked list
    for ( q = p ; q != NULL ; q = q->link )
        c++ ;

    return ( c ) ;
}

// destroys the linked list object
linklist::~linklist( )
{
    node *q ;

    if ( p == NULL )
        return ;

    while ( p != NULL )
    {
        q = p->link ;
        delete p ;
        p = q ;
    }
}
```

```
int main( )
{
    linklist ll ;

    cout << endl << "No. of elements in Linked List = " << ll.count( ) ;
    ll.append ( 11 ) ;
    ll.append ( 22 ) ;
    ll.append ( 33 ) ;
    ll.append ( 44 ) ;
    ll.append ( 55 ) ;
    ll.append ( 66 ) ;

    ll.addatbeg ( 100 ) ;
    ll.addatbeg ( 200 ) ;
    ll.addatbeg ( 300 ) ;

    ll.addafter ( 3, 333 ) ;
    ll.addafter ( 6, 444 ) ;

    ll.display( ) ;
    cout << endl << "No. of elements in linked list = " << ll.count( ) ;

    ll.del ( 300 ) ;
    ll.del ( 66 ) ;
    ll.del ( 0 ) ;

    ll.display( ) ;
    cout << endl << "No. of elements in linked list = " << ll.count( ) << endl ;
    return 0 ;
}
```

The following points would help you to understand the program better.

(a) The individual data items and links are represented by structures of type *node*. Each such node contains an integer and a pointer to the next node in the linked list.

(b) The structure pointer *p* always points to the first node in the linked list. When the list is empty *p* contains NULL.

(c) In addition to the constructor and destructor there are six more member functions in the class. Their names and purposes are as under.

Function	**Purpose**
append ( )	Adds a new node beyond the last node in the linked list
addatbeg ( )	Adds a new node at the beginning of the linked list
addafter ( )	Inserts a new node after a specific node in the linked list
display( )	Displays the data present in each node in the linked list
count( )	Counts the number of nodes present in the linked list
del( )	Deletes a specified node from the linked list

(d) In *append( )* before adding the node it is first ascertained whether the linked list is empty or not. This is necessary because if the list is empty and we create the first node then *p* should start pointing to it. And if the list is not empty then a link should be established between the existing last node and the new node that has been added, keeping *p* undisturbed.

(e) In *addatbeg( )* once the new node is added it is necessary to make *p* point to this node, since we have decided that *p* would always point to the first node in the list.

(f) In *addafter( )* after creating a new node it is necessary to carry out readjustments of links as shown in the Figure 8.3.

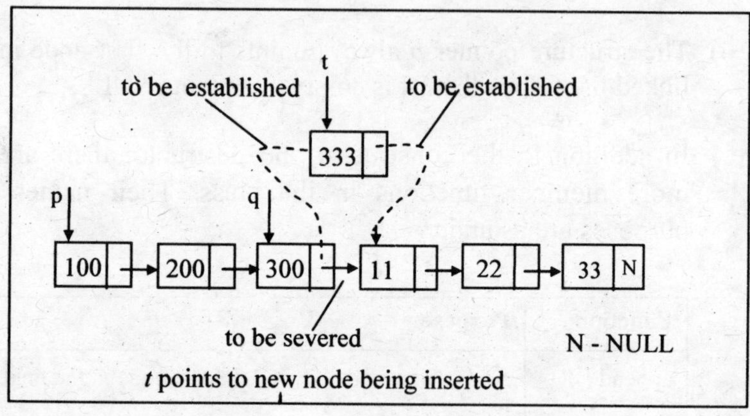

Figure 8.3

(g) In *display( )* as well as *count( )* the entire linked list is traversed without disturbing *p* which continues to point to the first node in the list. As the list is traversed one displays the contents of the node, whereas the other counts them.

(h) In del( ) the deletion of the node is done using the operator *delete*. Deletion calls for readjustments of links as shown in Figure 8.4.

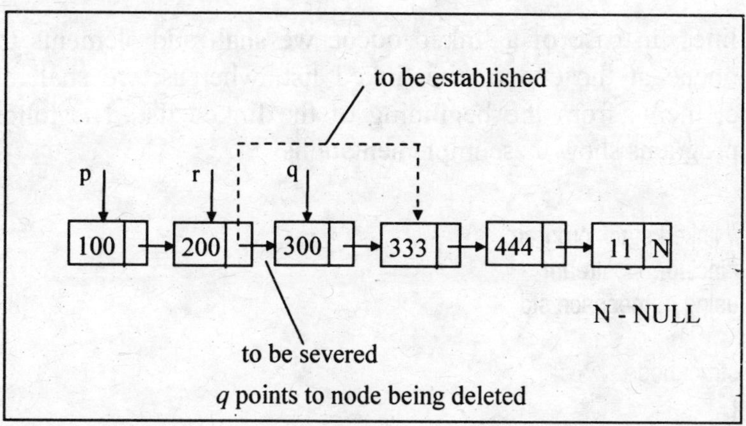

Figure 8.4

(i) When the *linklist* object *ll* goes our of scope the destructor gets called which deletes the entire linked list.

With some practice in their use, you will find that linked lists are as easy to work with as compared to lists implemented using arrays. You can make the *linklist* class more foolproof by considering the possibility that when a new node is being added the memory allocation fails.

Stacks And Queues Revisited

In the earlier section we had used arrays to store the elements that get added to the stack or the queue. However, when implemented as an array these data structures suffer from the basic limitation of an array: that its size cannot be increased or decreased once it is declared. As a result, one ends up reserving either too much space or too less space for an array and in turn for a stack or a queue. This difficulty is eliminated when we implement these data structures using linked lists. In case of a linked stack we shali push and pop nodes from one end of a linked stack. On similar lines, in case of a linked queue we shall add elements to the queue at the end of the linked list, whereas, we shall delete elements from the beginning of the linked list. The following programs show these implementations.

```
// linked stack program
#include <iostream>
using namespace std ;

struct node
{
    int data ;
    node *link ;
} ;

class stack
{
    private :

        node *top ;

    public :

        stack( )
        {
            top = NULL ;
        }

        void push ( int item )
        {
            node *temp ;

            temp = new node ;
            if ( temp == NULL )
                cout << endl << "Stack is full" ;
```

```
        temp -> data = item ;
        temp -> link = top ;
        top = temp ;
    }

    int pop( )
    {
        if ( top == NULL )
        {
            cout << endl << "Stack is empty" ;
            return NULL ;
        }

        node *temp ;
        int item ;

        temp = top ;
        item = temp -> data ;
        top = top -> link ;
        delete temp ;
        return item ;
    }

    ~stack( )
    {
        if ( top == NULL )
            return ;

        node *temp ;

        while ( top != NULL )
        {
            temp = top ;
            top = top -> link ;
            delete temp ;
        }
    }
```

```
};

int main( )
{
    stack s ;

    s.push ( 11 ) ;
    s.push ( 12 ) ;
    s.push ( 13 ) ;
    s.push ( 14 ) ;
    s.push ( 15 ) ;
    s.push ( 16 ) ;

    int i = s.pop( ) ;
    cout << endl << "Item popped = " << i ;

    i = s.pop( ) ;
    cout << endl << "Item popped = " << i ;

    i = s.pop( ) ;
    cout << endl << "Item popped = " << i << endl ;
    return 0 ;
}
```

Following is the implementation of the queue implemented as a linked list.

```
// linked queue program
#include <iostream>
using namespace std ;

struct node
{
    int data ;
    node *link ;
};
```

```
class queue
{
    private :

        node *front, *rear ;

    public :

        queue( )
        {
            front = rear = NULL ;
        }

        void addq ( int item )
        {
            node *temp ;

            temp = new node ;
            if ( temp == NULL )
                cout << endl << "Queue is full" ;

            temp -> data = item ;
            temp -> link = NULL ;

            if ( front == NULL )
            {
                rear = front = temp ;
                return ;
            }

            rear -> link = temp ;
            rear = rear -> link ;
        }

        int delq( )
        {
```

```
        if ( front == NULL )
        {
            cout << endl << "Queue is empty" ;
            return NULL ;
        }

        node *temp ;
        int item ;

        item = front  -> data ;
        temp = front ;
        front = front -> link ;
        delete temp ;
        return item ;
    }

    ~queue( )
    {
        if ( front == NULL )
        return ;
        node *temp ;
        while ( front != NULL )
        {
            temp = front ;
            front = front -> link ;
            delete temp ;
        }
    }
} ;

int main( )
{
    queue a ;

    a.addq ( 11 ) ;
    a.addq ( 12 ) ;
    a.addq ( 13 ) ;
```

```
    a.addq ( 14 ) ;
    a.addq ( 15 ) ;
    a.addq ( 16 ) ;
    a.addq ( 17 ) ;

    int i = a.delq( ) ;
    cout << "\nItem extracted = " << i ;

    i = a.delq( ) ;
    cout << "\nItem extracted = " << i ;

    i = a.delq( ) ;
    cout << "\nItem extracted = " << i << endl ;
    return 0 ;
}
```

Trees

The data structures that we have seen so far (linked lists, stacks, queues) were linear data structures. As against this, trees are non-linear data structures. Trees are encountered frequently in everyday life. In a linked list each node has a link which points to another node. In a tree structure, however, each node may point to several other nodes (which may then point to several other nodes, etc.). Thus a tree is a very flexible and powerful data structure that can be used for a wide variety of applications. For example, suppose we wish to use a data structure to represent a person and all of his or her descendants. Assume that the person's name is *Rahul* and that he has 3 children, *Sanjay*, *Sameer* and *Nisha*. Also suppose that *Sameer* has 3 children, *Abhay*, *Ajit* & *Madhu* and *Nisha* has one child *Neha*. We can represent *Rahul* and his descendants quite naturally with the tree structure shown in Figure 8.5.

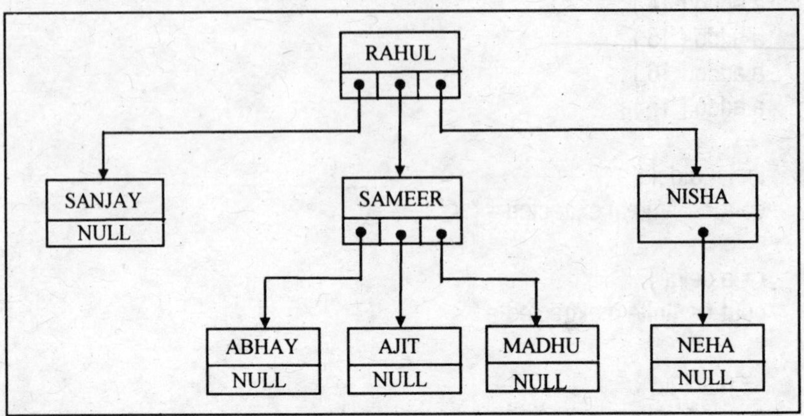

Figure 8.5

Notice that each tree node contains a name for data and one or more pointers to the other tree nodes. Although the nodes in a general tree may contain any number of pointers to the other tree nodes, a large number of data structures have at the most two pointers to the other tree nodes. This type of a tree is called a *binary tree*. In this chapter we would restrict our discussion of trees to only binary trees.

Binary Trees

Let us begin our study of binary trees by discussing some basic concepts and terminology. A simple binary tree is shown in Figure 8.6.

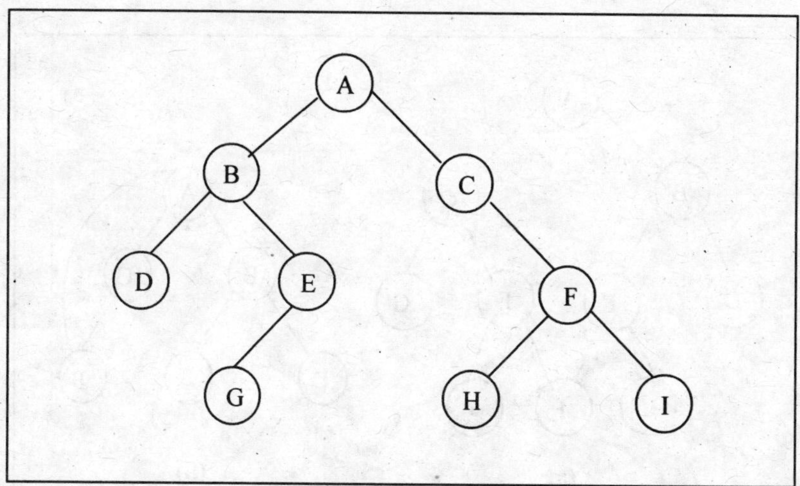

Figure 8.6

A binary tree is a finite set of elements that is either empty or is partitioned into three disjoint subsets. The first subset contains a single element called the *root* of the tree. The other two subsets are themselves binary trees, called the *left* and *right sub-trees* of the original tree. A left or right sub-tree can be empty. Each element of a binary tree is called a *node* of the tree. The binary tree shown in Figure 8.6 consists of nine nodes with *A* as its root. Its left sub-tree is rooted at *B* and its right sub-tree is rooted at *C*. This is indicated by the two branches emanating from *A* to *B* on the left and to *C* on the right. The absence of a branch indicates an empty sub-tree. For example, the left sub-tree of the binary tree rooted at *C* and the right sub-tree of the binary tree rooted at *E* are both empty. The binary trees rooted at *D*, *G*, *H* and *I* have empty right and left sub-trees. Figure 8.7 illustrates some structures that are not binary trees. Be sure that you understand why each of them is not a binary tree as just defined.

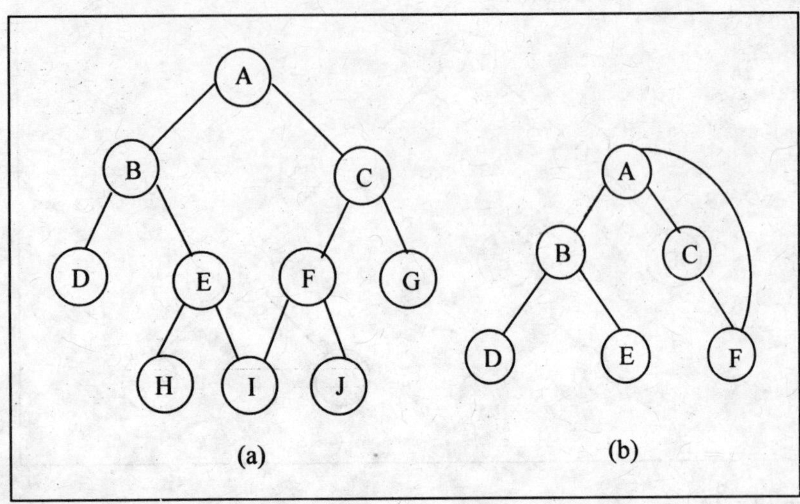

Figure 8.7

Although natural trees grow with their roots in the ground and their leaves in the air, computer scientists almost universally portray tree data structures with the root at the top and the leaves at the bottom. The direction from the root to the leaves is "down" and the opposite direction is "up". Going from the leaves to the root is called climbing the tree, and going from the root to the leaves is called descending the tree.

Traversal Of A Binary Tree

The traversal of a binary tree involves visiting each node in the tree exactly once. Binary tree traversal is useful in many applications. The order in which nodes of a linear list are visited is clearly from first to last. However, there is no such natural linear order for the nodes of a tree. The methods differ primarily in the order in which they visit the nodes. There are three popular methods of binary tree traversal. These methods are known as *inorder* traversal, *preorder* traversal and *postorder* traversal. In each of these methods nothing need be done to traverse an empty binary tree. The functions used to traverse a tree using these methods can be kept quite short if we understand the recursive nature of the binary tree. A binary tree is recursive in that each sub-tree is really a binary tree itself. Thus, traversing a binary tree involves visiting the root node and traversing its left and right sub-trees. The only difference among the methods is the order in which these three operations are performed.

To traverse a nonempty binary tree in preorder, we perform the following three operations:

(a) Visit the root.
(b) Traverse the left sub-tree in preorder.
(c) Traverse the right sub-tree in preorder.

To traverse a nonempty binary tree in inorder (or symmetric order):

(a) Traverse the left sub-tree in inorder.
(b) Visit the root.
(c) Traverse the right sub-tree in inorder.

To traverse a nonempty binary tree in postorder:

(a) Traverse the left sub-tree in postorder.
(b) Traverse the right sub-tree in postorder.
(c) Visit the root.

Many algorithms that use binary trees proceed in two phases. The first phase builds a binary tree, and the second traverses the tree. As an example of such an algorithm, consider the following sorting method. Given a list of numbers in an input file, we wish to print them in ascending order. As we read the numbers, they can be inserted into a binary tree such as the one of Figure 8.8. When a number is compared with the contents of a node in the tree, a left branch is taken if the number is smaller than the contents of the node and a right branch if it is greater or equal to the contents of the node. Thus if the input list is

20 17 6 8 10 20 7 18 13 12 5 6

the binary tree of Figure 8.8 is produced.

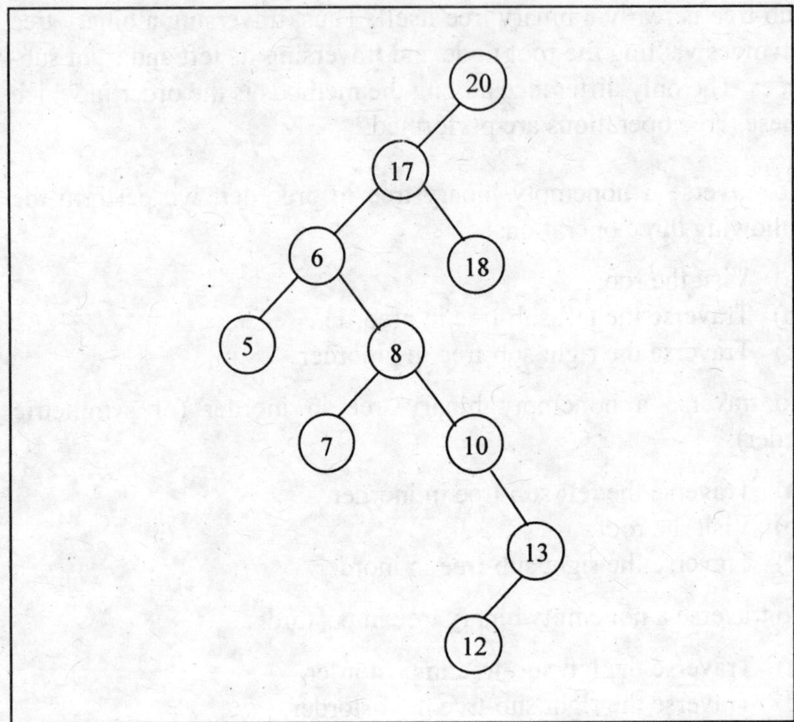

Figure 8.8

Such a binary tree has the property that all elements in the left sub-tree of a node *n* are less than the contents of *n*, and all elements in the right sub-tree of *n* are greater than or equal to the contents of *n*. A binary tree that has this property is called a *Binary Search Tree (BST)*. If a binary search tree is traversed in inorder (left, root, right) and the contents of each node are printed as the node is visited, the numbers are printed in ascending order. Convince yourself that this is the case for the binary search tree of Figure 8.8. A class that helps you to build a binary search tree and traverse it using any traversal procedure is implemented below. In addition, the class also has the capability to copy contents of one binary search tree into another and to compare the contents of the two binary search trees.

```
#include <iostream>
using namespace std ;

#define TRUE 1
#define FALSE 0

class tree
{
    private :

        struct node
        {
            node *l ;
            int data ;
            node *r ;
        } *p ;

    public :

        tree( ) ;
        void search ( int n, int &found, node * &parent ) ;
        void insert ( int n ) ;
        void traverse( ) ;
        void in ( node *q ) ;
        void pre ( node *q ) ;
        void post ( node *q ) ;
        int operator == ( tree t ) ;
        int compare ( node *pp, node *qq ) ;
        void operator = ( tree t ) ;
        node * copy ( node * q ) ;
} ;
```

```
tree::tree( )
{
    p = NULL ;
}

void tree::search ( int n, int &found, node * &parent )
{
    node *q ;
    found = FALSE ;
    parent = NULL ;

    if ( p == NULL )
        return ;

    q = p ;
    while ( q != NULL )
    {
        if ( q->data == n )
        {
            found = TRUE ;
            return ;
        }

        if ( q->data > n )
        {
            parent = q ;
            q = q->l ;
        }
        else
        {
            parent = q ;
            q = q->r ;
        }
    }
}
```

```
void tree::insert ( int n )
{
    int found ;
    node *t, *parent ;

    search ( n, found, parent ) ;

    if ( found == TRUE )
        cout << endl << "such a node already exists" ;
    else
    {
        t = new node ;
        t->data = n ;
        t->l = NULL ;
        t->r = NULL ;

        if ( parent == NULL )
            p = t ;
        else
            parent->data > n ? parent->l = t : parent->r = t ;
    }
}

void tree::traverse( )
{
    int choice ;

    cout << endl << "1. Inorder"
         << endl << "2. Preorder"
         << endl << "3. Postorder"
         << endl << "Your choice " ;
    cin >> choice ;

    switch ( choice )
    {
        case 1 :
            in ( p ) ;
```

```
            break ;

        case 2 :
            pre ( p ) ;
            break ;

        case 3 :
            post ( p ) ;
            break ;
    }
}

void tree::in ( node *q )
{
    if ( q != NULL )
    {
        in ( q->l ) ;
        cout << "\t" << q->data ;
        in ( q->r ) ;
    }
}

void tree::pre ( node *q )
{
    if ( q != NULL )
    {
        cout << "\t" << q->data ;
        pre ( q->l ) ;
        pre ( q->r ) ;
    }
}

void tree::post ( node *q )
{
    if ( q != NULL )
    {
        post ( q->l ) ;
```

```
        post ( q->r ) ;
        cout << "\t" << q->data ;
    }
}

int tree::operator == ( tree t )
{
    int flag ;

    flag = compare ( p, t.p ) ;
    return ( flag ) ;
}

int tree::compare ( node *pp, node *qq )
{
    static int flag ;

    if ( ( pp == NULL ) && ( qq == NULL ) )
        flag = TRUE ;
    else
    {
        if ( ( pp != NULL ) && ( qq != NULL ) )
        {
            if ( pp->data != qq->data )
                flag = FALSE ;
            else
            {
                compare ( pp->l, qq->l ) ;
                compare ( qq->r, qq->r ) ;
            }
        }
    }
    return ( flag ) ;
}

void tree::operator = ( tree t )
{
```

```
	p = copy ( t.p ) ;
}

tree::node * tree::copy ( node * q )
{
	node *t ;
	if ( q != NULL )
	{
		t = new node ;
		t->data = q->data ;
		t->l = copy ( q->l ) ;
		t->r = copy ( q->r ) ;
		return ( t ) ;
	}
	else
		return ( NULL ) ;
}

int main( )
{
	tree tt, ss ; int i, num ;

	for ( i = 0 ; i <= 6 ; i++ )
	{
		cout << endl << "Enter the data for the node to be inserted " ;
		cin >> num ;
		tt.insert ( num ) ;
	}

	tt.traverse( ) ;
	ss = tt ;
	ss.traverse( ) ;

	if ( ss == tt )
		cout << endl << "Trees are equal" << endl ;
	else
		cout << endl << "Trees are unequal" << endl ;
```

```
    return 0 ;
}
```

In this program the binary tree has been implemented as a linked structure in which each node has two links, one pointing to the left child of that node (this link is null if there is no left child), and another pointing to the right child (if there is one). Access to any node in the tree is possible through a pointer to the root of the tree.

In addition to the constructor there are six more member functions in the class. Their names and purposes are as under.

Function	**Purpose**
search( )	Searches the place where the node can be inserted in the binary search tree
insert( )	Inserts a new node at appropriate place in the BST
traverse( )	Displays a menu permitting the user to select the method of traversal of BST
in( )	Traverses the BST according to inorder traversal
pre( )	Traverses the BST according to preorder traversal
post( )	Traverses the BST according to postorder traversal
operator == ( )	Invokes the *compare( )* function for comparing the contents of two BSTs
compare( )	Recursive function which checks whether two BSTs are identical
operator = ( )	Invokes the *copy( )* function to copy contents of one BST into another
copy( )	Recursive function which copies the contents of one BST into another

Of all the functions listed above the one that is a bit complicated is the *search( )* function. It traverses the binary tree to find out whether the node being added already exists in the BST. If it does then it sets the flag *found* and returns. If the node is not found then it returns after having set the *parent* with the address of the node whose child the new node would become. The *insert( )* function then sets up the appropriate links between the parent and the child node. Rest of the functions are fairly straightforward.

Linked list is a very useful structure for processing dynamic lists whose maximum sizes are not known in advance and whose sizes change significantly because of repeated insertions and deletions. However, to search an item in a linked list we have to traverse the entire list. To overcome this disadvantage we can use a binary search tree, which makes the searching efficient at the same time maintaining the flexibility of a linked structure.

Deletion From A Binary Tree

In addition to techniques for inserting data in a binary tree and traversing the tree, practical situations call for deleting data from the binary tree. Assuming that we will pass the specified data item that we wish to delete to the *delete( )* function, there are four possible cases that we need to consider:

(a) No node in the tree contains the specified data.
(b) The node containing the data has no children.
(c) The node containing the data has exactly one child.
(d) The node containing the data has two children.

For case (a) we merely need to print the message that the data item is not present in the tree.

In case (b) since the node to be deleted has no children the memory occupied by this should be freed and either the left link or the right link of the parent of this node should be set to NULL. Which of these should be set to NULL depends upon whether the node being deleted is a left child or a right child of its parent.

In case (c) since the node to be deleted has one child the solution is again rather simple. We have to adjust the pointer of the parent of the node to be deleted such that after deletion it points to the child of the node being deleted.

For case (d), in which the node to be deleted has two children the solution is more complex. Consider node *C* in Figure 8.9. (Before Deletion). From the figure the inorder successor of the node *C* is node *J*. The data of this inoder successor should now be copied into the node to be deleted and a pointer should be setup to the inorder successor (node *J*). This inorder successor would have one or zero children. This node should then be deleted using the same procedure as for deleting a one child or a zero child node. Thus the whole logic of deleting a node with two children is to locate the inorder successor, copy its data and reduce the problem to a simple deletion of a node with one or zero child.

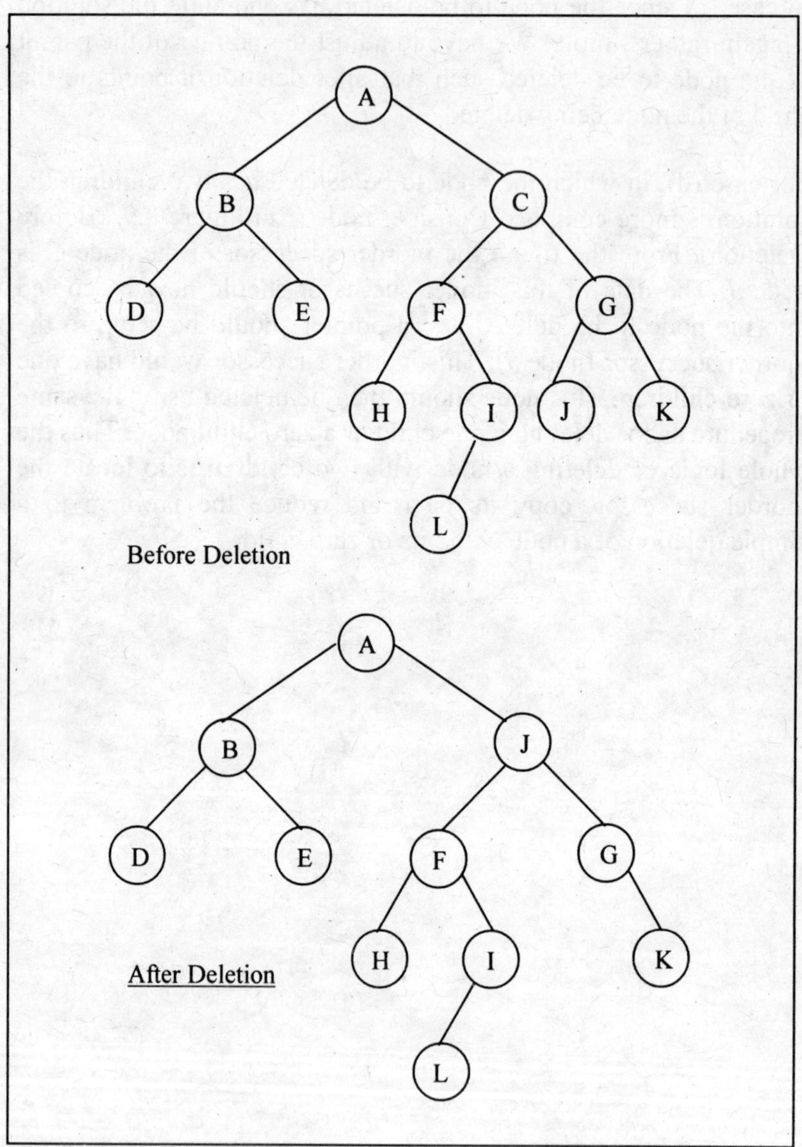
A
B
C
D
E
F
G
H
I
J
K
L
Before Deletion
A
B
J
D
E
F
G
H
I
K
L
After Deletion

Figure 8.9

The following program adds the deletion function to the binary class developed earlier. The functions that had no role to play during deletion of a node have been purposefully omitted from the class. The *search( )* function has been suitably modified. This modification is necessary for the *del( )* function to work properly. When called from *insert( )* the *search( )* function sets the variable *parent* with the address of the node whose child the new node is going to become. When called from *del( )* the *search( )* function not only sets the parent but also sets up the variable *x* with the address of the node being deleted.

```
#include <iostream>
using namespace std ;

#define TRUE 1
#define FALSE 0

class tree
{
    private :

        struct node
        {
            node *l ;
            int data ;
            node *r ;
        } *p ;

    public :

        tree( ) ;
        ~tree( ) ;
        void search ( int n, int &found, node * &parent, node * &x ) ;
        void insert ( int n ) ;
        void traverse( ) ;
        void in ( node *q ) ;
```

```
        void del ( int num ) ;
        void infordel ( node *q ) ;
} ;

tree::tree( )
{
    p = NULL ;
}

tree::~tree( )
{
    infordel ( p ) ;
}

void tree::search ( int n, int &found, node * &parent, node * &x )
{
    node *q ;
    found = FALSE ;
    parent = NULL ;

    if ( p == NULL )
        return ;

    q = p ;
    while ( q != NULL )
    {
        if ( q->data == n )
        {
            found = TRUE ;
            x = q ;
            return ;
        }

        if ( q->data > n )
        {
            parent = q ;
            q = q->l ;
```

```
        }
        else
        {
            parent = q ;
            q = q->r ;
        }
    }
}

void tree::insert ( int n )
{
    int found ;
    node *t, *parent, *x ;

    search ( n, found, parent, x ) ;

    if ( found == TRUE )
        cout << endl << "such a node already exists" ;
    else
    {
        t = new node ;
        t->data = n ;
        t->l = NULL ;
        t->r = NULL ;

        if ( parent == NULL )
            p = t ;
        else
            parent->data > n ? parent->l = t : parent->r = t ;
    }
}

void tree::traverse( )
{
    in ( p ) ;
}
```

```
void tree::in ( node *q )
{
     if ( q != NULL )
     {
          in ( q->l ) ;
          cout << endl << q->data ;
          in ( q->r ) ;
     }
}

void tree::infordel ( node *q )
{
     if ( q != NULL )
     {
          infordel ( q->l ) ;
          infordel ( q->r ) ;
          delete q ;
     }
}

void tree::del ( int num )
{
     int found ;
     node *parent, *x, *xsucc ;

     /* if tree is empty */
     if ( p == NULL )
     {
          cout << endl << "Tree is empty" ;
          return ;
     }

     parent = x = NULL ;

     /* call the search function to find the node to be deleted */
     search ( num, found, parent, x ) ;
```

```
/* if the node to deleted is not found */
if ( found == FALSE )
{
    cout << endl << "Node to be deleted not found" ;
    return ;
}

/* if the node to be deleted has two children */
if ( x->l != NULL && x->r != NULL )
{
    parent = x ;
    xsucc = x->r ;

    while ( xsucc->l != NULL )
    {
        parent = xsucc ;
        xsucc = xsucc->l ;
    }

    x->data = xsucc->data ;
    x = xsucc ;
}

/* if the node to be deleted has no child */
if ( x->l == NULL && x->r == NULL )
{
    if ( parent->r == x )
        parent->r = NULL ;
    else
        parent->l = NULL ;

    delete x ;
    return ;
}

/* ifthe node to be deleted has only right child */
if ( x->l == NULL && x->r != NULL )
```

```
    {
        if ( parent->l == x )
            parent->l = x->r ;
        else
            parent->r = x->r ;

        delete x ;
        return ;
    }

    /* if the node to be deleted has only left child */
    if ( x->l != NULL && x->r == NULL )
    {
        if ( parent->l == x )
            parent->l = x->l ;
        else
            parent->r = x->l ;

        delete x ;
        return ;
    }
}

int main( )
{
    tree tt ;
    int i, num ;

    for ( i = 0 ; i <= 6 ; i++ )
    {
        cout << endl << "Enter the data for the node to be inserted " ;
        cin >> num ;
        tt.insert ( num ) ;
    }

    tt.traverse( ) ;
    cout << endl << "Enter the value of the node to be deleted " ;
```

```
    cin >> num ;
    tt.del ( num ) ;
    cout << endl ;
    tt.traverse( ) ;
    return 0 ;
}
```

This program has plugged one loophole that the earlier program had. It has a destructor function that gets called when the tree object goes out of scope. In this function we have called the another member function *infordel( )*. This function recursively traverses the tree in inorder and calls the *del( )* function for every node that it visits, thereby destroying the entire tree.

Exercise

[A] State True or False:

(a) In a binary tree a node may have more than two children.

(b) To reach the last node in a linked list it is necessary to traverse the entire linked list.

(c) A stack can be implemented using an array or a linked list.

(d) Stacks are useful in keeping track of function calls.

(e) The keys typed from the keyboard are usually stored in a queue.

(f) Queues are FIFO lists.

(g) In a binary search tree the right child of a node always has a value greater than the value stored in the node.

(h) Binary trees can be implemented using arrays.

(i) If we traverse a BST in inorder we get the list in ascending order.

(j) A doubly linked circular linked list can exist, where each node can have a pointer to the next as well as the previous node in the list, and the last node can point to the first node and the first node to the last.

(k) To reach any node in a binary tree it is necessary to start the traversal from the root node.

[B] Answer the following:

(a) Improve the linked list class by incorporating the following functions to:

- Compare whether two linked lists' contents are same or not.
- Copy contents of one linked list into another.

(b) Change the tree class's *in( )* function to traverse a BST in inorder without using recursion.

(c) Write a program to implement a stack as a circular linked list.

(d) Write a program to implement a doubly linked list, where each node has two pointers in addition to data: one pointing to the previous node in the list and another pointing to the next node in the list.

CHAPTER NINE

Inheritance

Now that we have familiarised ourselves with classes—the building blocks of object oriented programming—let us now deal with another important C++ concept called *inheritance*. Inheritance is probably the most powerful feature of object-oriented programming after classes themselves. Inheritance is the process of creating new classes, called *derived classes*, from existing classes. These existing classes are often called *base classes*. The derived class inherits all the capabilities of the base class but can add new features and refinements of its own. By adding these refinements the base class remains unchanged.

Inheritance is one of the corner stones of object oriented programming. It has several advantages to offer. Most important amongst these is that it permits code reusability. Once a base class is written and debugged, it need not be touched again but at the same time it can be adapted to work in different situations. Reusing existing code saves time and money and increases a program's reliability. Inheritance can also help in the original conceptualization of a programming problem, and in the overall design of the program.

The code reusability is of great help in the case of distributing class libraries. A programmer can use a class created by another person or company, and, without modifying it, derive other classes from it that are suited to particular programming situations. Let us now understand the concept of inheritance using a program.

Suppose that we have designed a class called *index* that serves as a general-purpose index (counter). Assume that we have worked long and hard to make the *index* class operate just the way we want, and we're pleased with the results, except for one thing. The *index* class can only increment the counter and not decrement it. To achieve this we can insert a decrement routine directly into the source code of the *index* class. However, there are several reasons why we might not want to do this. Firstly, the *index* class works well and has been thoroughly tested and debugged. This is an exaggeration in this case, but it would be true in a larger and more complex class. Now if we start modifying the source code of the *index* class, the testing process will need to be carried out again. And then there always exists a possibility that at the end of the entire process the original class itself may not work satisfactorily.

Sometimes there might be another reason for not modifying the *index* class: We might not have access to its source code, especially if it had been distributed as part of a class library.

To avoid these problems we can use inheritance to create a new class based on *index*, without modifying *index* itself. Here's how this can be achieved.

```
#include <iostream>
using namespace std ;

class index  // base class
{
    protected :

        int count ;

    public :

        index( )  // zero argument constructor
        {
            count = 0 ;
        }

        index ( int c )  // one argument constructor
        {
            count = c ;
        }
```

```
        void display( )
        {
            cout << endl << "count = " << count ;
        }

        void operator ++ ( )
        {
            count++ ;
        }
} ;

class index1 : public index  // derived class
{
    public :

        void operator -- ( )
        {
            count-- ;
        }
} ;

int main( )
{
    index1 i ;
    ++i ;
    ++i ;
    i.display( ) ;
    --i ;
    i.display( ) ;
    return 0 ;
}
```

Here we have first declared a base class called *index* and then derived a class called *index1* from it. *index1* inherits all the features of the base class *index*. *index1* doesn't need a constructor or the *operator ++( )* functions, since they are already present in the base class.

The first line of the *index1* class,

```
class index1 : public index
```

specifies that the class *index1* has been derived from the base class *index*. We would see later on what happens if we use *private* in place of *public*. Instead of the *base - derived* terminology some authors tend to use the *parent - child* terminology. Figure 9.1 shows the relationship between the base class and the derived class. Note that the arrow in the figure means *derived from*. The direction of the arrow says that the derived class refers to the functions and data in the base class, while the base class has no access to the derived class data or functions.

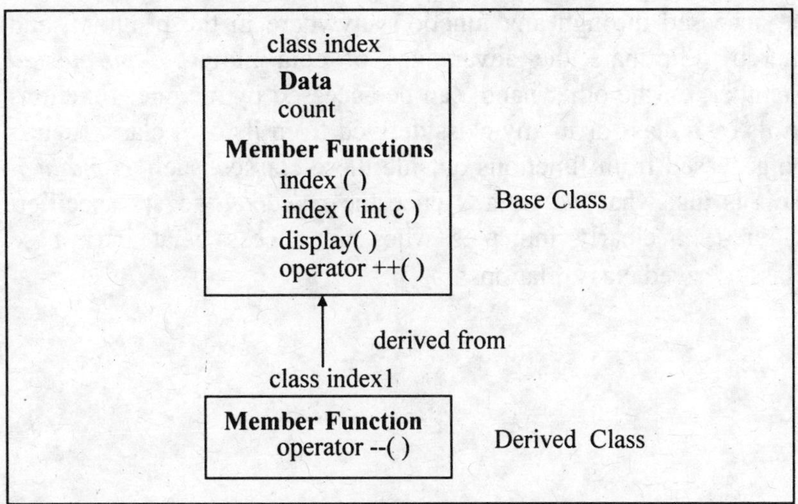

Figure 9.1

Since we have not declared any constructor in *index1*, when we create an object *i* the constructor in the base class gets called. The object *i* also uses the function *operator ++( )* from the base class to increment *count*.

The data members in the classes that we've created so far used the *private* access specifier. As against this, in the above program the data has been given a new specifier—*protected*. Let us find out why is this so.

Can member functions of the derived class access members of the base class? In other words, can *operator --( )* in *index1* access *count* in *index*? The answer is that members of a derived class can access members of the base class if the base class members are *public* or *protected*. They can't access *private* members. This rule holds good for data members as well as member functions.

We don't want to make *count public*, since that would allow it to be accessed through any function anywhere in the program, and thereby eliminate the advantages of data hiding. A *protected* member, on the other hand, can be accessed by member functions in its own class or in any class derived from its own class. It can't be accessed from functions outside these classes, such as *main( )*. This is just what we want. Hence the *protected* access specifier. Figure 9.2 clearly indicates who can access what in a base class–derived class relationship.

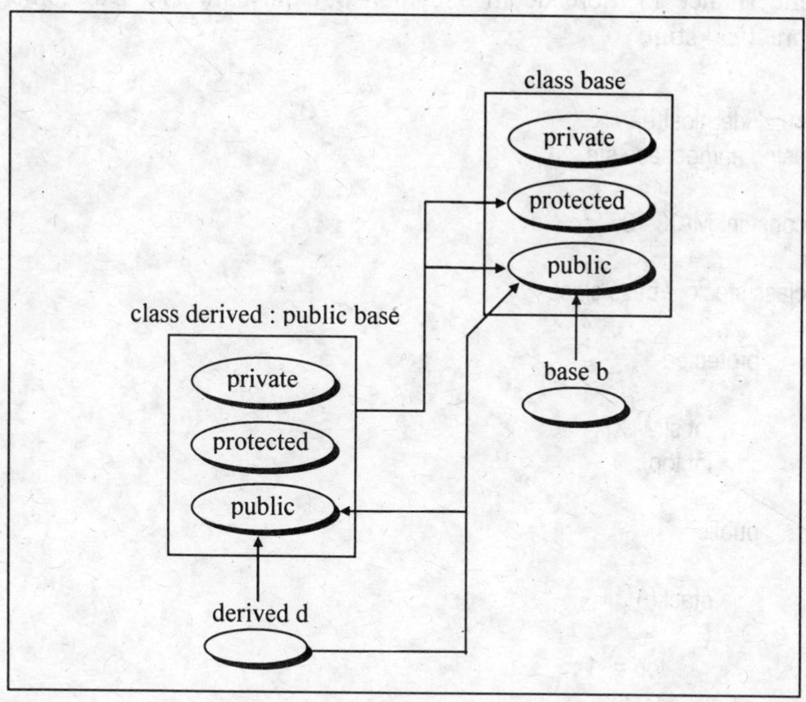

Figure 9.2

You would agree that through the derived class *index1* (and thereby through inheritance) we have increased the functionality of the *index* class without modifying it.

Note that inheritance doesn't work in reverse. That is, the base class and its objects have no knowledge about any classes derived from the base class. In our program had we built an object *j* from the class *index*, then the *operator --( )* function would have remained inaccessible to this object.

Let us now look at another example that puts inheritance to work. Go through it and understand the basic concept of inheritance. In the next few pages we'll examine a few more features of inheritance in more detail and then put the entire idea to some practical stint.

```
#include <iostream>
using namespace std ;

const int MAX = 25 ;

class stack  // base class
{
    protected :

        int s[MAX] ;
        int top ;

    public :

        stack( )
        {
            top = -1 ;
        }

        void push ( int num )
        {
            top++ ;
            s[top] = num ;
        }

        int pop( )
        {
            int num ;
            num = s[top] ;
            top-- ;
            return ( num ) ;
        }
} ;
```

```
class stack1 : public stack  // derived class
{
    public :

        void push ( int num )
        {
            if ( top == MAX - 1 )
                cout << endl << "Stack is full" ;
            else
                stack::push ( num ) ;  // calls push( ) of base class
        }

        int pop( )
        {
            int n ;
            if ( top == -1 )
            {
                cout << endl << "Stack is empty" ;
                return NULL ;
            }
            else
            {
                n = stack::pop( ) ;  // calls pop( ) of base class
                return ( n ) ;
            }
        }
} ;

int main( )
{
    int n ;
    stack1 stk ;

    stk.push ( 10 ) ;
    stk.push ( 20 ) ;
    stk.push ( 30 ) ;
```

```
    n = stk.pop( ) ;
    cout << endl << n ;

    n = stk.pop( ) ;
    cout << endl << n << endl ;
    return 0 ;
}
```

We have already learnt the *stack* data structure in Chapter 8. In this program the base class *stack* has the capability to push items on the stack and pop items off it. However, the function *stack::push( )* doesn't consider the possibility of the stack becoming full. Similarly, the *stack::pop( )* function doesn't believe that the stack would at some point in time fall empty and it cannot remove an element from an empty stack. The class *stack1* through its member functions *push( )* and *pop( )* accounts for both these possibilities. This class has been derived from the class *stack*, hence it inherits all the properties of the base class. Note that even the names of the functions in both the classes are same. This is legal. When the *push( )* function is called from *main( )* through the statement,

```
stk.push ( 10 ) ;
```

it is the *push( )* function of the *stack1* class that gets called. This is because when a base class and a derived class have *public* member functions with the same name and argument lists, the function in the derived class gets a priority when the function is called as a member of the derived class object. In *stack1::push( )* it is first verified whether the stack is full or not. If it is then a message indicating this is flashed. However, if the stack is not full then instead of implementing the logic for adding the element to the stack, it simply calls the base class *push( )* function through the statement:

```
stack::push ( num ) ;
```

Thus using inheritance we have provided additional functionality to the stack without modifying the base class.

More Inheritance

Let us reiterate a few facts that we have learnt about inheritance by now.

(a) A derived class inherits all the capabilities of the base class, but can add new features of its own. By making these additions the base class remains unchanged.

(b) *protected* members behave just like *private* members until a new class is derived from the base class that has *protected* members.

(c) If a base class has *private* members, those members are not accessible to the derived class. *protected* members are *public* to derived classes but *private* to the rest of the program.

(d) A derived class can specify that a base class is *public*, or *private* by using the following notation in the declaration of the derived classes:

```
class c : public b
class a : private b
```

The *public* access specifier means that the *protected* members of the base class are *protected* members of the derived class and the *public* members of the base class are public members of the derived class. The *private* access specifier means that the *protected* and *public* members of the base class are *private* members of the derived class. Default access specifier is *private*. Figure 9.3 depicts these accesses.

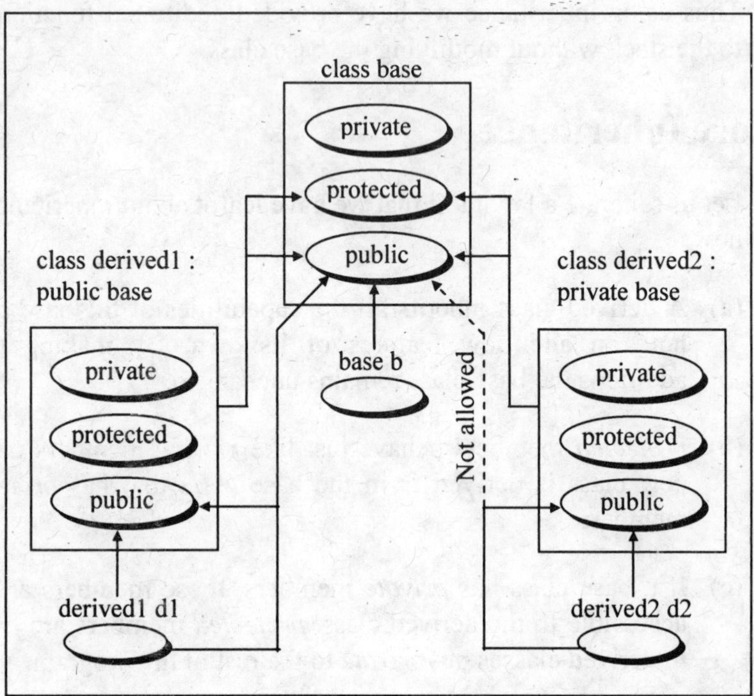

Figure 9.3

(e) When you define an object of a derived class, the compiler executes the constructor function of the base class followed by the constructor function of the derived class. The parameters list for the derived class's constructor function may be different from that of the base class's constructor function. Therefore, the constructor function for the derived class must tell the compiler what values to use as arguments to the constructor function for the base class.

(f) When a base class and a derived class have *public* member functions with the same name and parameter list types, the function in the derived class gets a priority when the function is called as a member of the derived class object.

(g) A program can declare objects of both the base and derived classes. The two objects are independent of one another.

The following program should further clarify the accessibility of data members and member functions of base class from derived class member functions or from objects of derived class.

```
class one  // base class
{
    private:

        int a ;

    protected:

        int b ;

    public :

        int c ;
} ;

class two : public one  // publicly-derived class
{
    public:

        void function1( )
        {
            int z ;

            z = a ;  // error: not accessible
            z = b ;  // works
            z = c ;  // works
        }
} ;
```

```
class three : private one  // privately-derived class
{
    public :

        void function2( )
        {
            int y ;

            y = a ;  // error: not accessible
            y = b ;  // works
            y = c ;  // works
        }
} ;

int main( )
{
    int x ;

    two second ;  // object of class two
    x = second.a ;  // error: not accessible
    x = second.b ;  // error: not accessible
    x = second.c ;  // works

    three third ;  // object of class three
    x = third.a ;  // error: not accessible
    x = third.b ;  // error: not accessible
    x = third.c ;  // error: not accessible
    return 0 ;
}
```

Some More Inheritance

Let us now put some of these concepts into action by writing a program. The following program has a base class called *linklist* and a derived class *linklist1*. The base class is capable of adding or deleting nodes from a link list. The derived class inherits these features of the base class and adds two more functions, one to display the contents of the linked list and another to count the number of nodes in it. Here is the program...

```
#include <iostream>
using namespace std ;

class linklist
{
    protected :

        struct node
        {
            int data ;
            node *link ;
        } *p ;

    public :

        linklist( ) ;
        ~linklist( ) ;
        void append ( int num ) ;
        void addatbeg ( int num ) ;
        void addafter ( int c, int num ) ;
        void del ( int num ) ;
} ;

linklist::linklist( )
{
    p = NULL ;
}

linklist::~linklist( ) // desturctor
{
    node *t ;
    while ( p != NULL )
```

```
    {
        t = p ;
        p = p->link ;
        delete t ;
    }
}

// adds nodes at the end of the linked list
void linklist::append ( int num )
{
    node *q, *t ;

    if ( p == NULL ) // if the list is empty
    {
        p = new node ;
        p->data = num ;
        p->link = NULL ;
    }
    else
    {
        q = p ;
        while ( q->link != NULL )
            q = q->link ;

        t = new node ;
        t->data = num ;
        t->link = NULL ;
        q->link = t ;
    }
}

// adds node at beginning of list
void linklist::addatbeg ( int num )
{
    node *q ;

    q = new node ;
```

```
    q->data = num ;
    q->link = p ;
    p = q ;
}

// adds a new node after the specified number of nodes
void linklist::addafter ( int c, int num )
{
    node *q, *t ;
    int i ;

    for ( i = 0, q = p ; i < c ; i++ )
    {
        q = q->link ;
        if ( q == NULL )  // if end of list is encountered
        {
            cout << endl << "There are less than " << c
                << " elements." ;
            return ;
        }
    }

    // insert new node
    t = new node ;
    t->data = num ;
    t->link = q->link ;
    q->link = t ;
}

// deletes node from the linked list
void linklist::del ( int num )
{
    node *q, *r ;

    q = p ;
    if ( q->data == num )  // if node to delete is first node
    {
```

```
        p = q->link ;
        delete q ;
        return ;
    }

    r = q ;
    while ( q != NULL )
    {
        if ( q->data == num )
        {
            r->link = q->link ;
            delete q ;
            return ;
        }
        r = q ;
        q = q->link ;
    }

    cout << endl << "Element " << num << " not found" ;
}

class linklist1 : public linklist
{
    public :
        void display( ) ;
        int count( ) ;
} ;

// displays contents of the linked list
void linklist1::display( )
{
    node *q ;

    cout << endl ;
    for ( q = p ; q != NULL ; q = q->link )
        cout << q->data << endl ;
}
```

```
// counts number of nodes in the linked list
int linklist1::count( )
{
    node *q ;
    int c = 0 ;

    for ( q = p ; q != NULL ; q = q->link )
        c++ ;

    return ( c ) ;
}

int main( )
{
    linklist1 ll ;

    cout << endl << "No. of elements in Linked List = " << ll.count( ) ;

    ll.append ( 11 ) ;
    ll.append ( 22 ) ;
    ll.append ( 33 ) ;
    ll.append ( 44 ) ;
    ll.append ( 55 ) ;
    ll.append ( 66 ) ;

    ll.addatbeg ( 100 ) ;
    ll.addatbeg ( 200 ) ;

    ll.addafter ( 3, 333 ) ;
    ll.addafter ( 6, 444 ) ;

    ll.display( ) ;

    cout << endl << "No. of elements in linked list = " << ll.count( ) ;

    ll.del ( 200 ) ;
```

```
    ll.del ( 66 ) ;
    ll.del ( 0 ) ;

    ll.display( ) ;

    cout << endl << "No. of elements in linked list = " << ll.count( ) << endl ;
    return 0 ;
}
```

So far we have seen how a class can be derived from a base class. We also know that a derived class inherits the characteristics of the base class. The derived class automatically possesses the data members and the member functions of the base class. The base class can add its own data members and member functions and it can override the member functions of the base class. Adding and overriding members is how you modify the behaviour of a base class to form a derived class. There are two reasons to derive a class. One is that you want to modify the behaviour of an existing class. The other is that you are building a well-organized object oriented class hierarchy where the user defined data types descend from one root class.

Multiple Levels Of Inheritance

You can even derive a class from a base class which itself has been derived from another base class. For example we may have a base class called *linklist* from which we derive a class *linklist1*. Then we may derive a class *linklist2* from *linklist1*. Thus, there can exist multiple levels of inheritance.

Multiple Inheritance

In the last section we saw how to derive a class from a base class which itself has been derived from another base class. We called this as multiple levels of inheritance. Let us now see another aspect of inheritance, where a class can be derived from more than one base class. This is called *Multiple Inheritance*. The syntax for multiple inheritance is similar to that for single inheritance.

Let us understand multiple inheritance, with a simple example. Imagine a company that markets both hardware and software. Suppose we create a base class *item* that stores the title of the item (a string) and its price (a *float*). Suppose we have another base class called *sales* that holds an array of three *float*s so that it can record the sale in rupees of a particular item for the last three months. Now we derive two classes *hwitem* (hardware item) and *switem* (software item) from both *item* and *sales*. The *hwitem* class holds category of the item and its original equipment manufacturer, whereas the *switem* class holds the type of the software item and the OS under which it works. Each class has its own *getdata( )* and *displaydata( )* functions to input and output data respectively. The program, which implements these classes, is given below.

```
#include <iostream>
using namespace std ;

class item
{
    private :

        char title[20] ;
        float price ;

    public :

        void getdata( )
        {
            cout << endl << "Enter title and price " ;
            cin >> title >> price ;
```

```
        }

        void displaydata( )
        {
            cout << endl << "Title and price " ;
            cout << title << "\t" << price ;
        }
} ;

class sales
{
    private :

        float salesfig[3] ;

    public :

        void getdata( )
        {
            cout << endl << "Enter sales figures for 3 months " ;
            for ( int i = 0 ; i < 3 ; i++ )
                cin >> salesfig[i] ;
        }

        void displaydata( )
        {
            cout << endl << "sales figures for 3 months " ;
            for ( int i = 0 ; i < 3 ; i++ )
                cout << salesfig[i] << "\t" ;
        }
} ;

class hwitem : private item, private sales
{
    private :

        char category[10] ;
```

```
        char oem[10] ;

    public :

        void getdata( )
        {
            item :: getdata( ) ;
            cout << endl << "Enter category and oem " ;
            cin >> category >> oem ;
            sales :: getdata( ) ;
        }

        void displaydata( )
        {
            item :: displaydata( ) ;
            cout << endl << "category and oem " ;
            cout << category << "\t" << oem ;
            sales :: displaydata( ) ;
        }
} ;

class switem : private item, private sales
{
    private :

        char category[10] ;
        char os[10] ;

    public :

        void getdata( )
        {
            item :: getdata( ) ;
            cout << endl << "Enter category and os " ;
            cin >> category >> os ;
            sales :: getdata( ) ;
        }
```

```
        void displaydata( )
        {
            item :: displaydata( ) ;
            cout << endl << "category and os " ;
            cout << category << "\t" << os ;
            sales :: displaydata( ) ;
        }
} ;
int main( )
{
    hwitem h1, h2 ;

    h1.getdata( ) ;
    h1.displaydata( ) ;
    h2.getdata( ) ;
    h2.displaydata( ) ;

    switem s1, s2 ;

    s1.getdata( ) ;
    s1.displaydata( ) ;
    s2.getdata( ) ;
    s2.displaydata( ) ;
    return 0 ;
}
```

The following figure shows the hierarchy of classes used in the program.

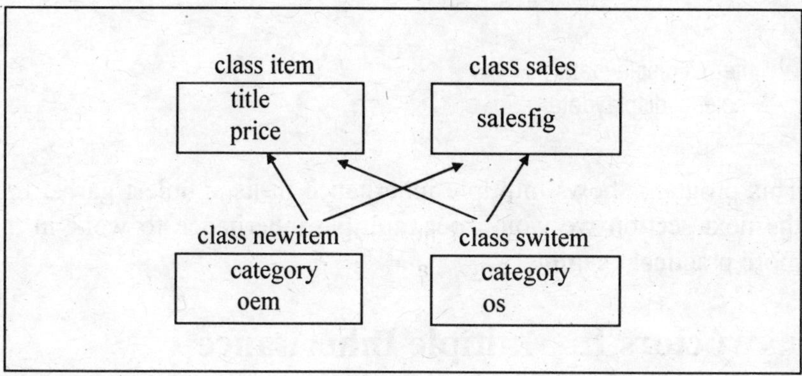

Figure 9.5

Though most of the program is simple to understand there are two points worth noting:

(a) The declaration

```
class hwitem : private item, private sales
```

indicates that the class *hwitem* has been derived from two classes *item* and *sales*. Thus it inherits the properties of both these classes. Note the comma separating *private item* and *private sales*. We could have written the same statement as

```
class hwitem : private sales, private item
```

i.e. the order in which *sales* and *item* appear in this declaration doesn't matter.

(b) When we call the *displaydata( )* function from the *displaydata( )* functions of the *hwitem* (derived class), the compiler would not know the *displaydata( )* function of which base class (*sales* or *item*) should be called. This ambiguity is easily eliminated by preceding the *displaydata( )* function with the class name and the scope resolution operator as shown below:

```
    item :: displaydata( ) ;
    sales :: displaydata( ) ;
```

This program shows multiple inheritance in its simplest garbs. In the next section we would put multiple inheritance to work in a more practical example.

Constructors In Multiple Inheritance

Let us now go one step further. Let us see how constructors are handled in multiple inheritance. For the sake of convenience we would use the same classes (except for the *switem* class) developed in the last section. The only addition that we would make is the definition of constructors in each class. The program, which implements these classes, is given below.

```
#include <iostream>
#include <string>
using namespace std ;

class item
{
    private :

        char title[20] ;
        float price ;

    public :

        item( )
        {
            strnset ( title, 0, 20 ) ;
            price = 0 ;
        }
```

```
        item ( char *t, float p )
        {
            strcpy ( title, t ) ;
            price = p ;
        }

        void getdata( )
        {
            cout << "\nEnter title and price " ;
            cin >> title >> price ;
        }

        void displaydata( )
        {
            cout << endl << "Title and price " ;
            cout << title << "\t" << price ;
        }
} ;

class sales
{
    private :

        float salesfig[3] ;

    public :

        sales( )
        {
            for ( int i = 0 ; i < 3 ; i++ )
                salesfig[i] = 0 ;
        }

        sales ( float a, float b, float c )
        {
            salesfig[0] = a ;
```

```
        salesfig[1] = b ;
        salesfig[2] = c ;
    }

    void getdata( )
    {
        cout << "\nEnter sales figures for 3 months " ;
        for ( int i = 0 ; i < 3 ; i++ )
            cin >> salesfig[i] ;
    }

    void displaydata( )
    {
        cout << endl << "sales figures for 3 months " ;
        for ( int i = 0 ; i < 3 ; i++ )
            cout << salesfig[i] << "\t" ;
    }
} ;

class hwitem : private item, private sales
{
    private :

        char category[10] ;
        char oem[10] ;

    public :

        hwitem( ) : item( ), sales( )
        {
            strnset ( category, 0, 10 ) ;
            strnset ( oem, 0, 10 ) ;
        }

        hwitem ( float a, float b, float c, char *t, float p,
                    char *cat, char *o ) :  item ( t, p ), sales ( a, b, c ),
        {
```

```
            strcpy ( category, cat ) ;
            strcpy ( oem, o ) ;
        }

        void getdata( )
        {
            item :: getdata( ) ;
            cout << endl << "Enter category and oem " ;
            cin >> category >> oem ;
            sales :: getdata( ) ;
        }

        void displaydata( )
        {
            item :: displaydata( ) ;
            cout << endl << "category and oem " ;
            cout << category << "\t" << oem ;
            sales :: displaydata( ) ;
        }
} ;

int main( )
{
    hwitem h1 ;
    hwitem h2 ( 50000.00, 125000.00, 170000.00, "IBM PC/AT", 25000,
                "FG", "IBM" ) ;
    h1.displaydata( ) ;
    h2.displaydata( ) ;
    return 0 ;
}
```

The new feature in this program is the use of constructors in the derived class *hwitem*. These constructors call the appropriate constructors in base classes *item* and *sales*.

The zero-argument constructor of the *item* class looks like this:

```
item( )
{
    strnset ( title, 0, 20 ) ;
    price = 0 ;
}
```

This constructor fills 0s for the *title*, so the user will be made aware if an attempt is made to display data for an uninitialised *item* object. You're already familiar with the zero-argument constructor in the *sales* class. The zero-argument constructor in *hwitem* calls both these constructors through the statement:

```
hwitem( ) : item( ), sales( )
```

The names of the base-class constructors follow the colon (and not ::) and are separated by commas. These base class constructors will be called in order when the *hwitem( )* constructor is invoked.

The situation in multi-argument constructors is more complex. The constructor for *hwitem* calls the multiple argument constructors of *sales* and *item*, so it must supply values for their arguments. In addition it has two arguments of its own: the category of item and the oem manufacturer. So this constructor has seven arguments. It calls the constructors of its base classes. Here's how it looks like:

```
hwitem ( float a,float b,float c,char *t, float p,
        char *cat, char *o ) : item ( t, p ), sales ( a, b, c )
{
    strcpy ( category, cat ) ;
    strcpy ( oem, o ) ;
}
```

As before, a colon signals the start of the list of constructors to be called, with the members of the list being separated by commas.

Of the first five arguments passed to *hwitem( )*, two are passed on to *item( )* and three to *sales( )*. The last two arguments are used to initialise the *category* and *oem* manufacturer of the hardware item, within the body of the constructor function.

Another small issue. If we change the order of the constructors in the list following the colon would the calling sequence also change? No. In fact the order in the list has no bearing on the order of calling. Then how is the order decided? It is decided from the order used in the declaration of the class. In our program the class declaration looked like this:

```
class hwitem : private item, private sales
{
    // code
} ;
```

Hence, even if the constructor definition is as follows

```
hwitem( ) : sales( ), item( )
{
}
```

the constructors would still get called in the order *item( )* followed by *sales( )*.

Note that the destructors in case of multiple inheritance are called in exactly the reverse order of the constructors. Why is the order of calling constructors governed by the order in the class declaration? This is because if you change the order of constructor calls while defining the constructor, you may have two different call sequences in two different constructors, but the poor destructor wouldn't know how to properly reverse the order of calls for destruction.

A Word Of Caution

Imagine a situation where a class has been derived from two base classes. The two base classes have functions with the same name, say *f( )*, while the derived class has no function with this name. Now what would happen if the derived class object tries to call the base class function *f( )*? An error would occur since the compiler can't figure out *f( )* of which base class you wish to call. This problem can be resolved using the scope resolution operator to specify the function from which base class you wish to call. This is shown below:

```
// base1 and base2 are base classes
// Both base classes contain the function f( )
// The class derived has been derived from base1 and base2
derived d ;
d.f( ) ; // Error
d.base1::f( ) ;
d.base2::f( ) ;
```

Private Inheritance

We have already seen this. When we inherit *private*ly we create a new class that has all the data and the functionality of the base class, but that functionality is hidden; i.e. the members of the base class (*private*, *protected* or *public*) can be accessed in the derived class but not outside it. You may wonder what purpose such an inheritance may serve. There may occasionally be situations where you want to hide part of the functionality of the base class. By default, when we inherit privately all *public* members of the base class become *private* for the derived class. If you want only some of them to remain *private* and the rest to be accessible from outside the class it can be done as shown in the following program.

```
#include <iostream>
using namespace std ;

class base
{
    public :

        void display( )
        {
            cout << endl << "in display" ;
        }

        void show( )
        {
            cout << "in show" ;
        }

} ;

class derived : private base
{
    public :

        base :: display ;
} ;

int main( )
{
    derived d ;
    d.display( ) ; // works
    d.show( ) ;    // error
    return 0 ;
}
```

Here we wanted *base::display( )* to be accessible in spite of *private* inheritance. We achieved this just by mentioning the name (no arguments or return values) in the *public* section of the *derived* class. As a result, *display( )* is accessible from *main( )*, whereas *show( )* is not. In other words we have been able to hide part of the functionality of the base class.

Protected Inheritance

So far we have used either *private* or *public* inheritance. We are also allowed to use *protected* inheritance. It's something that you don't use often, but it's there in the language for the sake of completeness. Before we look at protected inheritance let us reiterate two facts:

(a) If a class *derived1* is derived *public*ly from a class called *base* then the *protected* and *public* members of *base* remain *protected* and *public* members for *derived1*.

(b) If a class *derived1* is derived *private*ly from a class called *base* then the *protected* and *public* members of *base* become *private* members for *derived1*.

A similar rule for *protected* derivation would be:

If a class *derived1* is derived *protected*ly from a class called *base* then the *protected* and *public* members of base become *protected* members for *derived1*.

The following program shows *protected* inheritance at work.

```
class base
{
    protected :
```

```
        int i ;

    public :

        int j ;
} ;

class derived1 : protected base
{
    protected :

        int ii ;

    public :

        int jj ;
} ;

class derived2 : public derived1
{
    public :

        f( )
        {
            i = 10 ;  // works
            j = 10 ;  // works
            ii = 10 ; // works
            jj = 10 ; // works
        }
} ;

int main( )
{
    derived2 d1 ;

    d1.i = 10 ;  // error
    d1.j = 10 ;  // error
```

```
    d1.ii = 10 ; // error
    d1.jj = 10 ; // works
    return 0 ;
}
```

Here we have derived the class *derived2 public*ly from *derived1*. The *derived1* class in turn has been derived from the class *base* using the *protected* specifier. As a result, now *i* and *j* have become *protected* members of the class *derived1*. Since *derived2* has been *public*ly derived from *derived1* *i* and *j* remain as *protected* members of *derived2*. Hence *i* and *j* can be accessed in the function *f( )*. However, they cannot be accessed from *main( )*.

Had we derived the *derived1* class *private*ly through the following declaration, there would be a change in access rules for *i* and *j*.

```
class derived1 : private base
```

Now because of private derivation *i* and *j* would become *private* members of *derived1*. Hence they cannot be accessed in the function *f( )* of the *derived2* class. Needless to say, they cannot be accessed even from *main( )*.

Functions That Are Not Inherited

All functions do not get inherited. For example, the constructor and the destructor functions never get inherited. This would make sense if we look at a small example.

```
class base
{
    private :

        int i ;

    public :
```

```
        base( )
        {
            i = 10 ;
        }
};

class derived : public base
{
    // ...
};
```

Since *i* has been defined as *private* in the *base* class it is not available to the *derived* class. Had the constructor been inherited then in the *derived* class the initialisation of *i* would not have been possible. For the same reason the destructors are also not inherited.

In general, constructors and destructors deal with creation and destruction of an object, and they know what to do with the aspects of the object only at their particular level in the class hierarchy. Hence they are not inherited. Another function that is not inherited is the *operator = ( )* function as it performs a constructor-like activity.

If we have a zero-argument constructor, a destructor, an assignment operator function and a copy constructor in the base class, they do not get inherited in the derived class. However, if we do not provide their definitions in the derived class the compiler adds them automatically.

Incremental Development

One of the advantages of inheritance is that it supports incremental development. It allows you to introduce new code without causing bugs in existing code. By inheriting from an existing, functional class and adding data members and member functions (and redefining existing member functions) you leave the existing code—that someone else may still be using—untouched and unbugged. If a bug happens, you know it's in your new code, which is much shorter and easier to read than if you had modified the body of existing code.

It's rather amazing how cleanly the classes are separated. You don't even need the source code for the member functions to reuse the code. Just the header file describing the class and the object file or library file with the compiled member functions would do.

It's important to realize that program development is an incremental process. Nobody ever conceived the program in its entirety at the start of the project. The program should try to create and manipulate objects of various types to express a model in the terms given to you by the problem's space. Rather than constructing the program all at once it should grow out as an organic, evolutionary creature. Of course, at some point after things stabilize you need to take a fresh look at your class hierarchy with an aim to collapse it into a sensible structure. Inheritance fits this bill to perfection.

Exercise

[A] State True or False:

(a) We can derive a class from a base class even if the base class's source code is not available.

(b) Multiple inheritance is different from multiple levels of inheritance.

(c) The way a derived class member function can access base class *protected* and *public* members, the base class member functions can access *protected* and public *member* functions of derived class.

(d) It is possible to derive a derived class through *public* derivation, *private* derivation or *protected* derivation.

(e) A derived class member function has an access to *protected* and *public* members of base class, irrespective of whether the derived class has been derived *public*ly or *private*ly.

(f) If the derived class has been derived *public*ly then a derived class object, can access *public* members of base class.

(g) An object of a derived class (however derived) cannot access *private* or *protected* members of base class.

(h) *private* members of base class cannot be accessed by derived class member functions or objects of derived class.

(i) In *public* inheritance the *protected* members of the base class become *public* for the functions outside the derived class.

(j) There is no difference between *private* and *protected* inheritance.

(k) In *private* inheritance part of the base class interface can be made available to the functions outside the derived class.

(l) The size of a derived class object is equal to the sum of sizes of data members in base class and the derived class.

(m) Creating a derived class from a base class requires fundamental changes to the base class.

(n) If a base class contains a member function *func( )*, and a derived class does not contain a function with this name, an object of the derived class cannot access *func( )*

(o) If no constructors are specified for a derived class, objects of the derived class will use the constructors in the base class.

(p) If a base class and a derived class each include a member function with the same name, the member function of the derived class will be called by an object of the derived class

(q) A class *D* can be derived from a class *C*, which is derived from a class *B*, which is derived from a class *A*.

(r) It is illegal to make objects of one class members of another class.

[B] What will be the output of the following programs:

(a)
```
#include <iostream>
using namespace std ;

class base
{
    private :
```

```
        int i ;
};

class derived : public base
{
    private :
        int j ;
};

int main( )
{
    cout << endl << sizeof ( derived ) << endl << sizeof ( base ) ;
    derived o1 ;
    base o2 ;
    cout << endl << sizeof ( o1 ) << endl << sizeof ( o2 ) ;
    return 0 ;
}
```

(b)
```
#include <iostream>
using namespace std ;

class base1
{
    private :
        int b1 ;
};

class base2
{
    private :
        int b2 ;
};

class derived : public base1, public base2
{
    private :
        int d1 ;
```

```
};

int main( )
{
    cout << endl << sizeof ( base1 ) << endl << sizeof ( base2 )
        << endl << sizeof ( derived ) ;
    return 0 ;
}
```

(c)
```
#include <iostream>
using namespace std ;

class base
{
    protected :
        int i ;

    public :
        base( )
        {
            cout << endl << &i ;
        }
};

class derived: public base
{
    public :
        derived( ) : base( )
        {
            cout << endl << &i ;
        }
};

int main( )
{
    derived d1 ;
    base b1 ;
```

```
    return 0 ;
}
```

(d)
```
#include <iostream>
using namespace std ;

class base
{
    protected :
        int i ;

    public :
        void funct( )
        {
            cout << endl << &i ;
        }
} ;

class derived : public base
{
    private :
        ini i ;

    public :
        derived( )
        {
            cout << endl << &i ;
            funct( ) ;
        }
} ;

int main( )
{
    derived d1 ;
    return 0 ;
}
```

(e)
```
#include <iostream>
using namespace std ;

int top = 3 ;

class base
{
    protected :
        int top ;

    public :
        base( )
        {
            top = 2 ;
            cout << endl << top ;
        }
} ;

class derived : public base
{
    private :
        int top ;

    public :
        derived( ) : base( )
        {
            top = 1 ;
            cout << endl << top ;
            cout << endl << base::top ;
            cout << endl << ::top ;
        }
} ;

int main( )
{
    derived d1 ;
    return 0 ;
```

```
}
```

(f)
```
#include <iostream>
using namespace std ;

class index
{
    protected :
        int count ;

    public :
        index( )
        {
            count = 0 ;
        }

        void operator ++( )
        {
            count++ ;
        }

        void display( )
        {
            cout << endl << count ;
        }
} ;

int main( )
{
    index c ;
    c++ ;
    c.display( ) ;
    ++c ;
    c.display( ) ;
    return 0 ;
}
```

(g)
```
#include <iostream>
using namespace std ;

class base
{
    public :
        base( )
        {
            cout << endl << "third" ;
        }
} ;

class derived1 : public base
{
    public :
        derived1( ) : base( )
        {
            cout << endl << "second" ;
        }
} ;

class derived2 : public derived1
{
    public :
        derived2( ) : derived1( )
        {
            cout << endl << "first ;
        }
} ;

int main( )
{
    derived2 object ;
    return 0 ;
}
```

[C] Point out the errors, if any, in the following programs.

(a)
```
class base1
{
    int b1 ;
} ;

class base2
{
    int b2 ;
} ;

class derived : public base1, base2
{
} ;

int main( )
{
    return 0 ;
}
```

(b)
```
#include <iostream>
using namespace std ;

void print( ) ;

class base1
{
    protected :
        void print( )
        {
            cout << "Hello" ;
        }
} ;

class base2
{
```

```
    public :
        void print ( )
        {
            cout << "Hi" ;
            ::print( ) ;
        }
};

void print( )
{
    cout << "err" ;
}

int main( )
{
    base1 b1 ;
    base2 b2 ;
    b1.print( ) ;
    b2.print( ) ;
    return 0 ;
}
```

(c)
```
#include <iostream>
using namespace std ;

class base
{
    private :
        int i ;

    public :
        float j ;

        base( )
        {
            i = j = 99 ;
        }
```

```
};

class derived : public base
{
    public :
        derived( ) : base( )
        {
            cout << i << j ;
        }
};

int main( )
{
    derived d1 ;
    return 0 ;
}
```

(d)
```
#include <iostream>
using namespace std ;

class base
{
    protected :
        int i ;
        float j ;

    public:
        base( )
        {
            i = j = 99 ;
        }
};

class derived : public base
{
    public :
        derived( ) : base( )
```

```
        {
            cout << i << j ;
        }
};

int main( )
{
    derived d1 ;
    return 0 ;
}
```

(e)
```
#include <iostream>
using namespace std ;

class base
{
    public :
        void f1( )
        {
            cout << "cout" ;
        }
};

class derived : public base
{
    public :
        void f2( )
        {
            cout << "cin" ;
        }
};

int main( )
{
    base b1 ;
    derived d1 ;
    b1.f2( ) ;
```

```
    d1.f1( ) ;
    return 0 ;
}
```

(f)
```
#include <iostream>
using namespace std ;

class base
{
    public :
        void func1( )
        {
            cout << "Hello" ;
        }
} ;

class der1 : public base
{
    public :
        void func2( )
        {
            cout << endl << "Hi" ;
        }
} ;

class der2 : private base
{
    public :
        void func3( )
        {
            cout << endl << "Goodbye!" ;
        }
} ;

int main( )
{
    der1 o1 ;
```

```
    der2 o2 ;
    o1.func1( ) ;
    o2.func1( ) ;
    return 0 ;
}
```

(g)
```
#include <iostream>
using namespace std ;

class base
{
    public :
        base( )
        {
            cout << "base class" ;
        }
} ;

class derived : public base
{
    public :
        void a( ) : base( )
        {
            cout << "derived class" ;
        }
} ;

int main( )
{
    derived d ;
    return 0 ;
}
```

[D] Answer the following:

(a) Implement a *string* class containing the following functions:

- Overloaded + operator function to carry out the concatenation of strings.
- Overloaded = (assignment) operator function to carry out string copy.
- Overloaded += operator function.
- Function to display the length of a string.
- Function to display the size of a string.
- Function *tolower( )* to convert upper case letters to lower case.
- Function *toupper( )* to convert lower case letters to upper case.

(b) Suppose there is a base class *B* and a derived class *D* derived from *B*. *B* has two *public* member functions *b1( )* and *b2( )*, whereas *D* has two member functions *d1( )* and *d2( )*. Write these classes for the following different situations:

- *b1( )* should be accessible in *main( )*, *b2( )* should not be.
- Neither *b1( )*, nor *b2( )* should be accessible in *main( )*.
- Both *b1( )* and *b2( )* should be accessible in *main( )*.

(c) If a class *D* is derived from two base classes *B1* and *B2*, then write these classes each containing a zero-argument constructor. Ensure that while build an object of type *D* firstly the constructor of *B2* should get called followed by that of *B1*. Also provide a destructor in each class. In what order would these destructors get called?

(d) Assume a class *D* that is *private*ly derived from class *B*. Which of the following can an object of class *D* located in *main( )* access?

- *public* members of *D*
- *protected* members of *D*
- *private* members of *D*

- *public* members of *B*
- *protected* members of *B*
- *private* members of *B*

CHAPTER TEN

Virtual Functions

After classes and inheritance, polymorphism is the third essential feature of an object-oriented programming language. Programmers who switch over from C to C++ seem to do so in three steps. In the first step they start using C++ simply as "better C". During this stage they start using function prototypes, scope resolution operator, const, references, and a few more small concepts. These don't have much to do with object oriented programming.

Once comfortable with the non-object-oriented features of the language the second step is to use C++ as a "object-based" programming language. This means that you start appreciating the benefits of grouping data together with the functions that act upon it, the value of constructors and destructors, and perhaps some simple inheritance.

Many programmers carry a wrong impression that since they have started using classes, objects, function overloading, operator overloading and inheritance they have graduated to the object-oriented world. Though on the face of it everything may appear nice, neat and clean don't get fooled. If you stop here, you're missing out on the greatest part of the language, which is the jump to true object-oriented programming. You can do this only with polymorphism implemented through *virtual* functions.

Overloading of functions or operators is one kind of polymorphism (one thing with several distinct forms). We have already dealt with this type of polymorphism. The other type of polymorphism simplifies the syntax of performing the same operation with a hierarchy of classes. Thus, you can use polymorphism to keep the interface to the classes clean, because you do not have to define unique function names for similar operations on each derived class. This kind of Polymorphism is supported by the *virtual* keyword.

Foxed? Well, virtual functions are without doubt the most difficult concept for the new C++ programmer to understand. However, they're also the turning point in the understanding of object-oriented programming. If you don't use virtual functions, you don't understand OOP yet. Just read on, things would soon become clearer.

There is no analog to the virtual function in a traditional procedural language. Features in a procedural language can be understood on an algorithmic level, but virtual functions can be understood only from a design viewpoint.

Virtual means existing in appearance but not in reality. When virtual functions are used, a program that appears to be calling a function of one class may in reality be calling a function of a different class. But why on earth would we want this? Suppose we have three different classes called *line*, *circle* and *triangle*. Each class contains a *draw( )* function to draw the relevant shape on the screen. If we are to draw a picture containing numerous lines, circles and triangles we can create an array of pointers which would hold addresses of all the objects in the picture. The array definition may look like,

```
shape *arr[50] ;
```

When it is time to draw the picture we can simply run the loop,

```
for ( i = 0 ; i < 50 ; i++ )
    arr[ i ]->draw( ) ;
```

When *arr[i]* contains address of the *line* object it would call the *line::draw( )* function. Similarly, when it contains the address of the *circle* object it would call the *circle::draw( )* function. This is amazing for two reasons:

(a) Functions from different classes are executed through the same function call.

(b) The array *arr[ ]* has been defined to contain *shape* pointers and not *line* or *circle* pointers.

This concept is called polymorphism. The functions have the same appearance, the *draw( )* function, but different actual functions are used. Which *draw( )* function would get used depends on the contents of *arr[i]*. However, for this polymorphic approach to work, several conditions must be met. These are:

(a) The classes *line*, *circle* and *triangle* all must be derived from the same base class, *shape*.

(b) The *shape* base class must contain a *draw( )* function which has been declared *virtual*.

All this would be too much to digest at one shot. So let us break it into pieces and try to understand it part by part through simple programs. Here is the first one…

```
#include <iostream>
using namespace std ;

class one
{
    public :

        void display( )
        {
            cout << endl << "In base class" << endl ;
        }
} ;

class oneofone : public one
```

```
{
    public :

        void display( )
        {
            cout << endl << "In oneofone class" << endl ;
        }
};

class twoofone : public one
{
    public :

        void display( )
        {
            cout << endl << "In twoofone class" << endl ;
        }
};

int main( )
{
    one *ptr ;
    oneofone o1 ;
    twoofone o2 ;

    ptr = &o1 ;
    ptr -> display( ) ;
    ptr = &o2;
    ptr -> display( ) ;
    return 0 ;
}
```

Here *oneofone* and *twoofone* are classes derived from the base class *one*. Each of these three classes has a member function *display( )*. In *main( )* having created the objects *o1*, *o2* (from the two derived classes) and a pointer *ptr* to base class, we have assigned the address of a derived class object to the base class pointer through the statement,

```
ptr = &o1 ;
```

Should this not give us an error, since we are assigning an address of one type to a pointer of another? No, since in this case the compiler relaxes the type checking. The rule is that pointers to objects of a derived class are type-compatible with pointers to objects of the base class. Taking the address of a derived class object and treating it as the address of the base class object is called *upcasting*.

When we execute the statement,

```
ptr -> display( ) ;
```

which function gets called—*display( )* of *oneofone* or *display( )* of *one*? The function in the base class gets called. This is because the compiler ignores the contents of the pointer *ptr* and chooses the member function that matches the *type* of the pointer. Here, since *ptr*'s type matches the base class, the *display( )* of base class gets called. Same thing happens when we call *display( )* for the second time.

Sometimes this is what we want, but it doesn't provide the facility discussed at the beginning of this discussion: accessing functions of different classes using the same statement.

Let's make a small change in our program. Let's precede the declaration of the function *display( )* in the base class with the C++ keyword *virtual* as shown below.

```
class one
{
    public :

        virtual void display( ) // virtual function
```

```
    {
        cout << endl << "In Base class" ;
    }
};
```

If we execute the program now the output would be:

```
In oneofone class
In twoofone class
```

As can be seen from the output, this time instead of the base class, the member functions of the derived classes are executed. Thus the same function call,

```
ptr -> display( ) ;
```

executes different functions, depending on the contents of *ptr*. The rule here is that the compiler selects the function to be called based on the *contents* of the pointer *ptr*, and not on the *type* of the pointer. Problem is how does the compiler know which function to compile, when it doesn't know which object's address *ptr* may contain. It could be the address of an object of the *oneofone* class or of the *twoofone* class. Which version of *display( )* does the compiler call?

In fact the compiler doesn't know what to do, so it arranges for the decision to be deferred until the program is running. At run time, when it is known what object is pointed to by *ptr*, the appropriate version of *display( )* gets called. This is called *late binding* or *dynamic binding*. (Choosing functions in a normal way, i.e. during compilation, is called early or static binding.) Late binding requires some overhead but provides increased power and flexibility.

Instead of pointers had we used references the effect would have been same. The following code shows use of references instead of pointers in *main( )*.

```
int main( )
{
    oneofone o1 ;
    twoofone o2 ;
    one &ref1 = o1 ;
    one &ref2 = o2 ;
    ref1.display( );
    ref2.display( );
    return 0 ;
}
```

Pure *virtual* Functions

We can add another refinement to the virtual function declared in the base class of the last program. Since the function *display( )* in the base class never gets executed we can easily do away with the body of this virtual function and add a notation *=0* in the function declaration, as shown below:

```
class base
{
    public :

        virtual void display( ) = 0 ;
} ;
```

The *display( )* function is now known as a *pure* virtual function. Thus, a pure virtual function is a virtual function with no body and a = *0* in its declaration. The = sign here has got nothing to do with assignment; the value 0 is not assigned to anything. It is used to simply tell the compiler that a function will be pure, i.e. it will not have any body.

If we can remove the body of the virtual function can we not remove the function altogether. That would be too ambitious and moreover it doesn't work. Without a function *display( )* in the base class, statements like

```
ptr -> display( ) ;
```

would be invalid.

Since *display( )* of the base class was never getting called we made it a pure virtual function. There is another side to it. At times we may want that a user should never be able to create an object of the base class. For example, if there is base class called *shape* from which three classes *line*, *circle* and *triangle* have been derived. We would never make an object of the *shape* class; we would only make objects of the derived classes to draw specific shapes. A class from which we would never want to create objects is called an *abstract* class. Such a class exists only as a parent for the derived classes. Now how do we communicate to users who are going to use our classes that they should never create an object of the base class. One way is to document this fact and rely on the users to remember it. That's a sloppy way. Instead, a better way would be to write the base class such that any object creation from it becomes impossible. This can be achieved by placing at least one pure virtual function in the base class. Now anybody who tries to create an object from such a base class would be reported an error by the compiler. Not only will the compiler complain that you are trying to create an object of the abstract class, it will also tell you the name of the virtual function that makes the base class an abstract class.

Whenever a pure virtual function is placed in the base class, you must override it in all the derived classes from which you wish to create objects. If you don't do this in a derived class then the derived class becomes an abstract class.

virtual Functions Under The Hood

Using virtual functions is only part of the story. Knowing how compiler implements them completes the other part. We have seen the first part. Before we take up the second and the more interesting part let me reiterate a few facts that we have learnt in the last section. A clear understanding of them is utmost necessary for you to follow the subsequent discussion.

(a) The term binding refers to the connection between a function call and the actual code executed as a result of the call.

(b) If the function invoked in response to each call is known at compile-time, it is called static or early binding, because the compiler can figure out the function to be called before the program is run.

(c) Dynamic binding is so named because the actual function called at run-time depends on the contents of the pointer. It is also known as late binding, because the connection between the function call and the actual code executed by the call is determined *late* during the execution of the program and not when the program is compiled.

(d) The keyword *virtual* tells the compiler that it should not perform early binding. Instead, it should automatically install all the mechanisms necessary to perform late binding.

(e) Unlike C++, in C language there is only one kind of binding—early binding.

Consider the following simple program.

```
#include <iostream>
using namespace std ;

class sample
{
    private :

        int i ;

    public :

        virtual void display( )
        {
            cout << endl << "In sample class";
        }
};

class example
{
    private :

        int i ;

    public :

        void display( )
        {
            cout << endl << "In example class" ;
        }
};

class trial
{
    public :

        void display( )
```

```
        {
            cout << endl << "In trial class" ;
        }
};

int main( )
{
    sample s ;
    example e ;
    trial t ;

    cout << endl << sizeof ( s )
        << endl << sizeof ( e )
        << endl << sizeof ( t ) << endl ;
    return 0 ;
}
```

Here is the output that you would get if you run the program...

```
8
4
1
```

To say the least you would find the output surprising. We had only an *int* in the object *s* still the size is being reported as 8 bytes. With the same *int* in the object *e* its size is being reported only as 4 bytes. Lastly, even though we didn't have any data in the object *t* its size has turned out to be 1 byte. Let us try to find why this so happens.

With no virtual functions, the size of the object *e* is exactly what you'd expect—the size of a single *int*. With a single virtual function in *sample*, the size of the object *s* is the size of *int* plus the size of a *void* pointer. The compiler inserts this pointer (called VPTR, as we would soon see) if you have one or more virtual functions. As there are no data member in *trial* the C++ compiler forces the object *t* to be of nonzero size (in our case 1 byte) because each object must have a distinct address. If you imagine indexing into an array of zero-sized objects, you'll be able to appreciate why the size has to be nonzero. Nonzero is fine, but why *1*? Because the smallest nonzero positive integer is *1*.

Having established the fact that the compiler silently adds a void pointer to an object of a class which contains virtual functions let us see what this pointer points to and when is it set up.

To accomplish late binding, the compiler creates a table called VTABLE for each class that contains virtual functions and for the classes derived from it. The compiler places the addresses of the virtual functions for that particular class in the VTABLE. If you don't redefine a function that was declared virtual in the base class, the compiler uses the address of the base-class version in the derived class.

When objects of the base class or the derived class are created it secretly places a pointer, called the *vpointer* (abbreviated as VPTR), which points to the class's VTABLE. When you make a virtual function call through a base-class pointer the compiler quietly inserts code to fetch the VPTR and look up the function address in the VTABLE, thus calling the right function and causing late binding to take place.

The VPTR must be initialized to point to the starting address of the appropriate VTABLE. (This happens in the constructor, as we will see later in more detail.)

Once the VPTR is initialized to the proper VTABLE, the object in effect "knows" what type it is. But this self-knowledge is worthless unless it is used at the point a virtual function is called.

Suppose a pointer to the base class object contains address of the derived class object and you call a virtual function using this pointer. Now something special happens. Instead of performing a typical function call, which is simply an assembly language CALL to a particular address, the compiler generates different code to perform the function call. The compiler starts with the contents of the base-class pointer. These contents are address of the derived class object. Using this address the VPTR of the derived class object is fetched. Using VPTR the VTABLE of the derived class is accessed. From this table the address of the function being called is extracted. Lastly using this address the function of the derived class is called.

All of this—setting up the VTABLE for each class, initializing the VPTR, inserting the code for the virtual function call—happens automatically, so you don't have to worry about it.

I am sure what we said here would seem pretty abstract unless we see it working in a program. So let us write one. Figure 10.1 shows the hierarchy of classes that we propose to implement in the program.

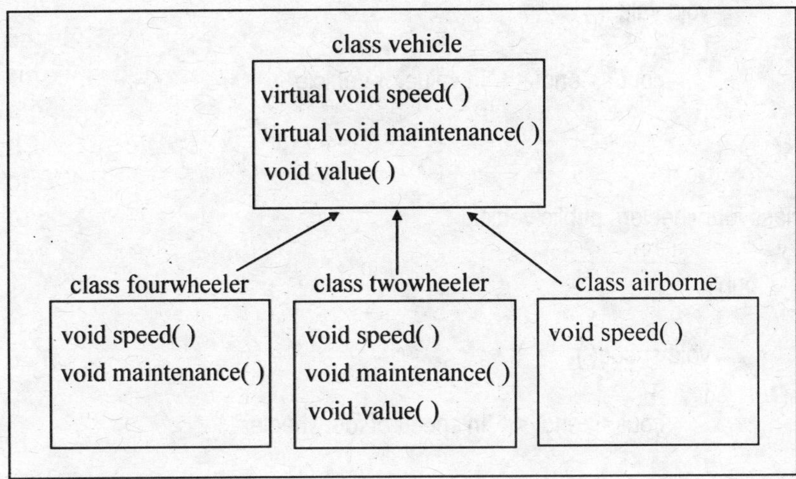

Figure 10.1

Given below is the code for the program that implements this class hierarchy.

```
#include <iostream>
using namespace std ;

class vehicle
{
    public :

        virtual void speed( )
        {
            cout << endl << "In speed of Vehicle" ;
        }

        virtual void maintenance( )
        {
            cout << endl << "In maintenance of Vehicle" << endl ;
        }
```

```
        void value( )
        {
            cout << endl << "In value of Vehicle" ;
        }
} ;

class fourwheeler : public vehicle
{
    public :

        void speed( )
        {
            cout << endl << "In speed of fourwheeler" ;
        }

        void maintenance( )
        {
            cout << endl << "In maintenance of fourwheeler" ;
        }
} ;

class twowheeler : public vehicle
{
    public :

        void speed( )
        {
            cout << endl << "In speed of twowheeler" ;
        }

        void maintenance( )
        {
            cout << endl << "In maintenance of twowheeler" ;
        }

        void value( )
        {
```

```
            cout << endl << "In value of twowheeler" ;
        }
} ;

class airborne : public vehicle
{
    public :

        void speed( )
        {
            cout << endl << "In speed of airborne" ;
        }
} ;

int main( )
{
    vehicle *ptr1 ;
    vehicle v ;

    ptr1 = &v ;
    ptr1 -> speed( ) ;
    ptr1 -> maintenance( ) ;
    ptr1 -> value( ) ;

    vehicle *ptr2, *ptr3, *ptr4 ;

    fourwheeler maruti ;
    twowheeler bajaj ;
    airborne jumbo ;

    ptr2 = &maruti ;
    ptr3 = &bajaj ;
    ptr4 = &jumbo ;

    ptr2 -> speed( ) ;
    ptr2 -> maintenance( ) ;
```

```
    ptr3 -> speed( ) ;
    ptr3 -> maintenance( ) ;

    ptr4 -> speed( ) ;
    ptr4 -> maintenance( ) ;

    ptr2 -> value( ) ;
    ptr3 -> value( ) ;

    vehicle w ;
    w.speed( ) ;

    fourwheeler f ;
    f.speed( ) ;

    airborne a ;
    a.maintenance( ) ;
    return 0 ;
}
```

Here is the output of the program…

```
In speed of vehicle
In maintenance of vehicle

In value of vehicle
In speed of fourwheeler
In maintenance of fourwheeler
In speed of twowheeler
In maintenance of twowheeler
In speed of airborne
In maintenance of vehicle

In value of vehicle
In value of vehicle
In speed of vehicle
```

```
In speed of fourwheeler
In maintenance of vehicle
```

As we saw earlier a VTABLE is created for every class that contains virtual functions and for the classes derived from it. It means in our program a VTABLE would be built for all the four classes: *vehicle*, *twowheeler*, *fourwheeler* and *airborne*. Each of these VTABLEs would contain addresses of the virtual functions. For all the objects built from these classes the compiler would automatically insert a VPTR which would point to the class's VTABLE. This is shown in the following figure.

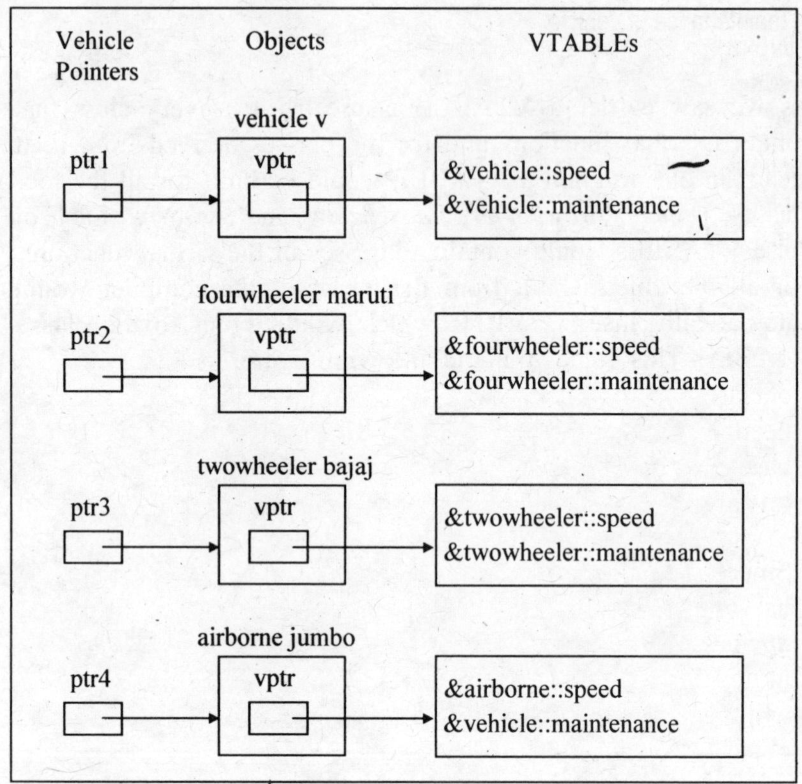

Figure 10.2

Note that the class *airborne* doesn't contain the definition of the *maintenance( )* function. Hence its VTABLE contains the address of the base class's *maintenance( )* function.

Let us now understand the working of the program a step at a time. To begin with, we have stored the address of the base class object in a pointer to the base class through the statements

```
vehicle *ptr1 ;
vehicle v ;
```

```
ptr1 = &v ;
```

Next we call the member functions of the base class through the statements

```
ptr1 -> speed( ) ;
ptr1 -> maintenance( ) ;
ptr1 -> value( ) ;
```

Though these calls appear similar, behind the screen they are built differently. This is because the first two functions have been declared as *virtual* in the base class, whereas the third has not been. Since *value( )* is not *virtual*, irrespective of the whether the base class object's or derived class object's address is stored in *ptr1* it is always the base class's *value( )* that would get called.

Since *speed( )* has been defined *virtual* in the base class, which of its implementation (of vehicle, *twowheeler*, *fourwheeler* or *airborne*) would be called depends upon whose address is stored in *ptr1*. In our case this turn's out to be *vehicle* object's address. So while calling *speed( )* firstly the *vptr* is retrieved from the vehicle object *v*. Using this pointer the VTABLE of the vehicle class is accessed. From this VTABLE the address of *speed( )* (of *vehicle*) is retrieved. Using this address *vehicle::speed( )* is ultimately called. Exactly same argument applies to calling *maintenance( )*. Because the fetching of the *vptr* and the determination of the actual function address occurs at run-time, you get the desired late binding.

The next case is more interesting. Consider the statements

```
vehicle *ptr2 ;

fourwheeler maruti ;
ptr2 = &maruti ;
```

```
ptr2 -> speed( ) ;
ptr2 -> maintenance( ) ;
```

Here we have stored the address of the derived class object in a pointer to the base class object. Now when we call *speed( )* the *vptr* of the object *maruti* would be used to access the VTABLE of the *fourwheeler* class. From this VTABLE the address of *fourwheeler::speed( )* would be retrieved. Using this address the function *fourwheeler::speed( )* would then get called.

If you think on these lines you can understand the subsequent calls made using *ptr2*, *ptr3* and *ptr4*.

Now consider the calls

```
ptr2 -> value( ) ;
ptr3 -> value( ) ;
```

Since *value( )* has not been defined as *virtual* in the base class VTABLEs are not involved in generating a call to *vehicle::value( )*. In our program we have not overridden *value( )* in the derived class. Had we done so still it is the base class implementation that would have been called.

The next three calls are interesting:

```
vehicle w ;
w.speed( ) ;

fourwheeler f ;
f.speed( ) ;

airborne a ;
a.maintenance( ) ;
```

Here the *vptr* or VTABLEs are not involved at all. While calling *f.speed( )* there is no ambiguity. As the compiler has an object (rather than its address) it knows the exact type and therefore it will not use late binding for any function calls. In general, for efficiency's sake, most compilers will perform early binding when they are making a call to a virtual function for an object because they know the exact type.

Now that we are through with the program let us look at a few more subtle issues related to virtual functions:

(a) Because of the vital role played by *vptr* while calling virtual functions it is critical that the *vptr* is always pointing to the proper VTABLE. You don't ever want to be able to make a call to a virtual function before the *vptr* is properly initialized. So the best place where this automatic initialisation can take place is the constructor. However, in our program, we didn't have a constructor in any class. That is why the compiler always adds a zero-argument constructor to our class when we don't define one—to initiate the *vptr*, if necessary.

(b) How does the compiler manage to obtain the value of *vptr* from the object. All objects have their *vptr* in the same place (often at the beginning of the object), so the compiler can pick it out of the object easily.

Why *virtual* Functions?

That's an important question. If the technique of virtual functions is so good, and if it makes the 'right' function call all the time, why is it an option? Why do we even need to know about it?

The answer is simple. The mechanism of virtual functions is not very efficient. As compared to a simple CALL to an absolute address, there are more sophisticated assembly instructions required to set up the virtual function call. This requires both code space and execution time. Some object-oriented languages like Smalltalk use late binding for all function calls. Thus it is no longer an option, and the user doesn't have to know about it. However, C++ comes from the C heritage, where efficiency is critical. C++ is supposed to make C programmers more efficient. Had all function calls in C++ been implemented through late binding the efficiency would have suffered heavily.

Hence the virtual function is an option, and by default the language uses the non-virtual virtual mechanism which is of course faster. In short, if you don't use it, you don't pay for it.

While designing your classes, however, you shouldn't worry about loss of efficiency due to use of virtual functions. If you're going to use polymorphism, use virtual functions everywhere. Because by using virtual functions there are usually much bigger gains to be had in other areas.

virtual Functions In Derived Classes

A virtual function is a complicated beast and we are not through with it as yet. We know that when we perform inheritance and redefine some of the virtual functions the compiler creates a new VTABLE for the derived class and inserts into it the new function addresses. If in the derived class we do not redefine the virtual functions, then it inserts the base-class function addresses in the derived class's VTABLE. This means there's always a full set of function addresses in the VTABLE. Thus a possibility of you calling a function and its address not existing in the VTABLE is ruled out.

Let us now consider a case when we inherit and add new virtual functions in the derived class. The following program shows this possibility.

```
#include <iostream>
using namespace std ;

class base
{
    public :

        virtual void fun1( )
        {
            cout << endl << "In base::fun1" ;
        }
} ;

class derived : public base
{
    public :

        void fun1( )
        {
            cout << endl << "In derived::fun1" ;
        }

        virtual void fun2( )
        {
            cout << endl << "In derived::fun2" ;
        }
} ;

int main( )
{
    base *ptr1, *ptr2 ;
    base b ;
    derived d ;
```

```
    ptr1 = &b ;
    ptr2 = &d ;
    ptr1->fun1( ) ;
    ptr2->fun1( ) ;
    ptr2->fun2( ) ; // error
    return 0 ;
}
```

Here the class *base* contains a single virtual function *fun1( )*. The *derived* redefines *fun1( )* and adds another virtual function called *fun2( )*. The VTABLEs created by the compiler for *base* and *derived* are shown in Figure 10.3.

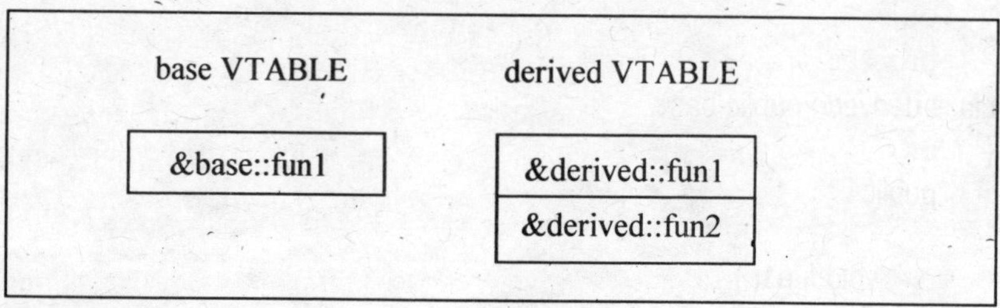

Figure 10.3

The compiler would pass the calls to *fun1( )*, but it would report an error for the call

```
ptr2->fun2( ) ;
```

In this case the compiler is working only with a pointer to a base-class object. The base class doesn't have the *fun2( )* function, so compiler cannot allow a call to *fun2( )*. The compiler doesn't know that you are working with a *derived* object, if it has only a pointer to a base-class object. Moral is that the compiler prevents you from making calls to virtual functions that exist only in derived classes. In other words, in a class hierarchy of several levels if we want a function at any level to be called through a base class pointer then the function must be declared as virtual in the base class. Defining it a s *virtual* in any intermediate class won't do.

There are some less-common cases where you may know that the address stored in the base class pointer actually points to an object of a specific derived class. In such a case you may call a function of that derived class by casting the base class pointer. For example, You can remove the error message produced by our program like this:

```
( ( derived * ) ptr2 ) -> fun2( ) ;
```

Here, you happen to know that the contents of *ptr2* point to a *derived* object, but generally you don't know that. If you come across a situation where you must know the exact types of all objects, you should probably reorganise things, because you're probably not using virtual functions properly. However, in some situations it may so happen that the design works best (or you have no choice) if you know the exact type of all objects kept in a generic container. This is done using run-time type identification.

Note that when we store a derived class object's address in a base class pointer it's completely safe. However the reverse casting—base to derived—is unsafe because there's no compile-time information about the actual types, so you must know exactly what type the object really is. If you cast it into the wrong type, you are calling for trouble.

Object Slicing

What do virtual functions achieve? They ensure that the code that manipulates objects of a base type can without change manipulate derived-type objects as well. Virtual functions should however always be called using either a pointer or a reference. If we try to do so using an object a phenomenon called *object slicing* takes place. The following program throws more light on this effect.

```
#include <iostream>
using namespace std ;

class base
{
    private :

        int i ;

    public :

        base ( int ii )
        {
            i = ii ;
        }

        virtual void fun1( )
        {
            cout << endl << i << endl ;
        }
} ;

class derived : public base
{
    private :

        int j ;

    public :

        derived ( int ii, int jj ) : base ( ii )
        {
            j = jj ;
        }

        void fun1( )
```

```
        {
            base::fun1( ) ;
            cout << endl << j << endl ;
        }
};

int main( )
{
    base b ( 10 ) ;
    derived d ( 15, 20 ) ;

    base *ptr1 = &b ;
    ptr1->fun1( ) ;

    base *ptr2 = &d ;
    ptr2->fun1( ) ;

    base &ref1 = b ;
    ref1.fun1( ) ;

    base &ref2 = d ;
    ref2.fun1( ) ;

    b = d ;  // object sliced
    b.fun1( ) ;
    return 0 ;
}
```

I am sure you would understand the calls made to *fun1( )* using pointers and references. The problem occurs during the last assignment. When we use an object instead of a pointer or reference as the recipient of the upcast, the object is *sliced* until all that remains is the subobject that corresponds to the recipient. That is, if an object of a derived class is assigned to a base class object, the compiler accepts it, but it copies only the base portion of the object. It slices off the derived portion of the object. Hence when we make the call *b.fun1( )* only the member function in the base class gets called.

Object slicing actually removes part of the object rather than simply changing the meaning of an address as when using a pointer or reference. Because of this, upcasting into an object is not often done: in fact, it's usually something to watch out for and prevent. You can explicitly prevent object slicing by putting pure virtual functions in the base class: this will cause a compile-time error when we try to create a base class object.

virtual Functions And Constructors

We would tackle three subtle issues here:

(a) Ideal place to define a constructor

(b) Order of calling constructors

(c) Calling virtual functions from within constructors

Let us begin with the first one.

Place Of Constructor Definition

Any functions which is *defined* (not *declared*) inside a class is by default treated as *inline* function. This applies to the constructor as well. Usually we define a constructor inside a class believing that by using *inlining* we would be able to avoid the overheads involved in calling a constructor. But consider what all is done inside the constructor:

- When an object containing virtual functions is created, the constructor initializes the *vptr* to point to the proper VTABLE. The compiler secretly inserts the *vptr* initialisation code into the constructor (if you have virtual functions).

- The constructor also calls the base class constructor.

- The constructor initialises the part of the object specific to the current class.

As a result, the size of the constructor grows to a limit where the savings you get from reduced function-call overheads are nullified. If you make a lot of inline constructor calls, your code size can grow without any benefits in speed. Because of the convenience of writing tiny constructors as *inline* you may still be tempted to keep them *inline*. But when you're looking for improving efficiency of your code, remember to remove *inline* constructors and define them outside the class.

Order Of Calling Constructors

Another interesting facet of constructors and virtual functions concerns the order of constructor calls. When an object is created all the base-class constructors are always called in the constructor of the derived class. The reason being a derived class has access only to its own members, and not to those of the base class; only the base-class constructor can properly initialize its own elements. If the base class constructors do not get called the object wouldn't be constructed properly. The compiler calls the default constructor if you don't explicitly call a base-class constructor in the derived class constructor. If there is no default constructor, the compiler will report an error. Having established the need for calling all the constructors in the class hierarchy what remains to be seen is the order in which they should get called.

The order of the constructor calls is important. When you inherit, you know all about the base class and can access any *public* and *protected* members of the base class. This means you must be able to assume that all the members of the base class are valid when you're in the derived class. The only way to guarantee this is for the base-class constructor to be called first. Then when you're in the derived-class constructor, all the members you can access in the base class have been initialized.

Calling *virtual* Functions From Constructors

Can we call a virtual function from a constructor? Yes. However, this time the behaviour is different than normal. If a virtual function is called from an ordinary member function the virtual call is resolved at run-time. You might think this is what should happen if the virtual function is called from a constructor. But it doesn't. Instead we find that, it is always the member function of the current class that gets called. That is, the virtual mechanism doesn't work within the constructor. The following program proves this.

```
#include <iostream>
using namespace std ;

class base
{
	private :

		int i ;

	public :

		base ( int ii )
		{
			i = ii ;
		}

		virtual void fun1( )
		{
			cout << endl << i ;
```

```
        }
};

class derived : public base
{
    private :

        int j ;

    public :

        derived ( int ii, int jj ) : base ( ii )
        {
            base *p ;
            p = this ;
            p->fun1( ) ;  // calls derived::fun1( )
            j = jj ;
        }

        void fun1( )
        {
            cout << endl << j << endl ;
        }
};

int main( )
{
    base b ( 10 ) ;
    derived d ( 15, 20 ) ;
    return 0 ;
}
```

In this program the statement

```
p = this
```

stores the address of the derived class object in the pointer to the base class object. In the constructor of the *derived* class when we call *fun1( )* it is the *derived* class's *fun1( )* that gets called.

Let us understand the reason for this. As we saw earlier the constructor's job is to bring the object into existence. Inside any constructor, the object may only be partially formed—you can only know that the base-class part of the object has been initialised. A virtual function call, however, reaches *forward* into the inheritance hierarchy. It calls a function in a derived class. If you could do this inside a constructor, you'd be calling a function that might manipulate members that hadn't been initialized yet. Disaster is likely to follow.

Also, when a constructor is called, one of the first things it does is initialize *vptr* to VTABLE of the current class and not of the base class or the class derived from the current class. If a more-derived constructor is called afterwards, that constructor sets the *vptr* to its VTABLE, and so on, until the last constructor finishes. The state of the *vptr* is determined by the constructor that is called last. This is another reason why the constructors are called in order from the base to the most derived.

As this series of constructor calls is taking place, each constructor has set the *vptr* to its own VTABLE. If it uses the virtual mechanism for function calls, it will produce only a call through its own VTABLE, not the most-derived VTABLE. Many compilers recognize that a virtual function call is being made inside a constructor, and perform early binding because they know that even by doing late binding it will produce a call only to the local function.

Destructors And *virtual* Destructors

The way the job of the constructor is to put together an object piece-by-piece, the job of the destructor is to break it part by part. While building as well as while destroying each constructor and destructor in the class hierarchy should get called. The difference is only in the order of calling. Construction starts by first calling the base constructor, then the more derived constructor and so on till the last class in the hierarchy chain. During destruction an exactly reverse order is followed. That is, the destructor starts at the most-derived class and works its way down to the base class. This is not only logical, but also safe. Let us see how.

A constructor of a derived class can access any *public* and *protected* member of the base class. Hence by the time they are accessed they must be properly set up. This can be ensured by calling the base class constructor before the derived class constructor.

Similarly while destroying an object the current destructor always knows that the base-class members are alive and active. It should not so happen that the base class members get destroyed through the base class destructor and then the derived class destructor tries to access them. This can be ensured by first calling the derived class destructor followed by the base class destructor. Thus, the destructor can perform its own cleanup, then call the base class destructor, which will perform its own cleanup. This it can do because it knows what it is derived from, but not what is derived from it.

You should keep in mind that constructors and destructors are the only place where this hierarchy of calls must happen. In all other functions, only that function will be called, whether it's virtual or not. The only way for base-class version of the same function to be called in ordinary functions (*virtual* or not) is if you explicitly call that function.

Consider a situation where a derived class object is created using *new*. The address of this object can be assigned to a pointer to a base class object. Now if we *delete* the pointer, since the pointer is a base class pointer this would result in a call to the base class destructor. Ideally, firstly the derived class destructor should be called followed by the base class destructor. This can be ensured by using a *virtual* destructor in the base class. The following program shows how this can be implemented.

```
#include <iostream>
using namespace std ;

class base
{
    public :

        base( )
        {
            cout << endl << "In base class constructor" ;
        }

        virtual ~base( )
        {
            cout << endl << "In base class destructor" ;
        }
} ;

class derived : public base
{
    public :

        derived( )
        {
```

```
        cout << endl << "In derived class constructor" ;
    }

    ~derived( )
    {
        cout << endl << "In derived class destructor" ;
    }
} ;

int main( )
{
    base *b ;
    b = new derived ;
    delete b ;
    return 0 ;
}
```

Here is the output of the program…

```
In base class constructor
In derived class constructor
In derived class destructor
In base class destructor
```

Even though the destructor, like the constructor, is an exceptional function, it is possible for the destructor to be *virtual* because the object already knows what type it is (whereas it doesn't during construction). Once an object has been constructed, its *vptr* is initialized, so virtual function calls can take place.

The way we can create a pure virtual function, we can create a pure virtual destructor as well. However, we must provide a function body to the pure virtual destructor because (unlike ordinary functions) all destructors in a class hierarchy are always called. Thus, the body for the pure virtual destructor ends up being called.

By declaring the virtual destructor as pure in the base we are in effect forcing the derived class to redefine the destructor. The base class body of the destructor is still called as part of destruction.

As a guideline, any time you have a virtual function in a class, you should immediately add a virtual destructor (even if it does nothing). This way, you can prevent any surprises later.

Calling *virtual* Functions From Destructors

When we call a virtual function from inside an ordinary member function the late-binding mechanism is used for the call. This is not true with destructors, irrespective of whether it is *virtual* or not. From inside a destructor, only the local version of the member function is called; the virtual mechanism is ignored. We had seen a similar phenomenon while calling virtual functions from a constructor. This can be confirmed from the following program.

```
#include <iostream>
using namespace std ;

class base
{
    public :

        ~base( )
        {
            cout << endl << "In virtual destructor" << endl ;
        }

        virtual void fun1( )
        {
```

```
            cout << endl << "In base::fun1( )" << endl ;
        }
};

class derived : public base
{
    public :

        ~derived( )
        {
            base *p ;
            p = this ;
            p->fun1( ) ; // calls derived::fun1( )
        }

        void fun1( )
        {
            cout << endl << "In derived::fun1( )" << endl ;
        }
};

int main( )
{
    derived d ;
    return 0 ;
}
```

Here when *fun1( )* is called from the *derived* class destructor, the derived class implementation of *fun1( )* gets called. Let us understand the reason for this.

Imagine for a moment that the virtual mechanism is used inside the destructor. Now it would be possible for the virtual call to resolve to a function that is more derived on the inheritance hierarchy than the current destructor. But destructors are called from the most-derived destructor down to the base destructor.

Hence the actual function called would rely on portions of an object that have already been destroyed. Hence the compiler resolves the calls at compile-time and calls only the local version of the function.

Note that the same is true for the constructor (as described earlier), but in the constructor's case the information wasn't available, whereas in the destructor the information (that is, the *vptr*) is there, but it isn't reliable.

virtual Base Classes

Let us look at one more subtlety of virtual functions. Consider the situation where there is one parent class called *base* and two classes derived from it, *derived1* and *derived2*. Suppose we derive a class *derived3* from *derived1* and *derived2*. Now suppose a member function of *derived3* class wants to access data or functions in the *base* class. Since *derived1* and *derived2* are derived from *base* each inherits a copy of *base*. This copy is referred to as a *subobject*. Each subobject contains its own copy of *base*'s data. This is shown in the following figure.

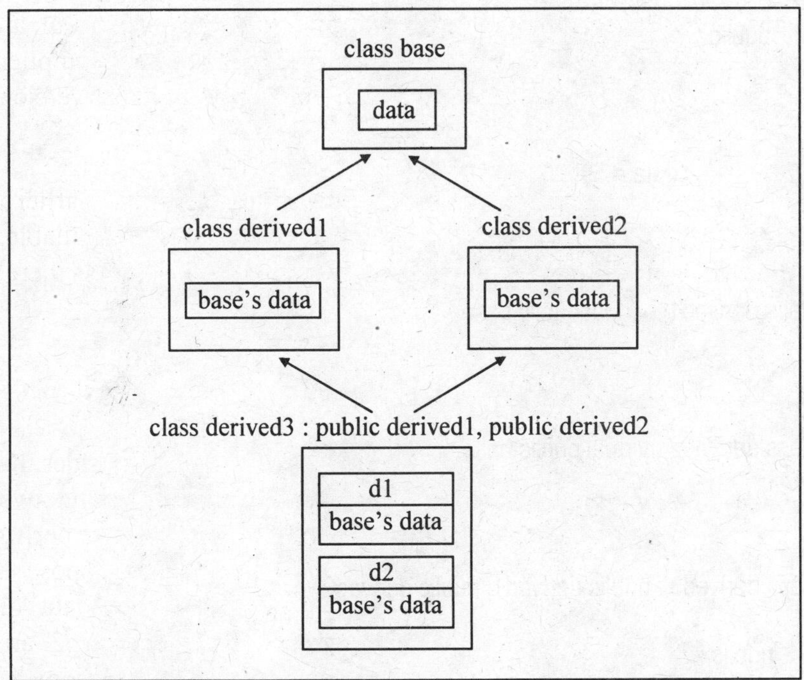

Figure 10.4

Now when *derived3* refers to the data in the *base* class, which of the two copies will it access? This is an ambiguous situation for the compiler, hence it reports an error. To get rid of this ambiguity, we should make *derived1* and *derived2* as *virtual* base classes as shown in the following program.

```
#include <iostream>
using namespace std ;

class base
{
    protected :

        int data ;
```

```
    public :

        base( )
        {
            data = 500 ;
        }
} ;

class derived1 : virtual public base
{
} ;

class derived2 : virtual public base
{
} ;

class derived3 : public derived1, public derived2
{
    public :

        int getdata( )
        {
            return data ;
        }
} ;

int main( )
{
    derived3 ch ;
    int a ;

    a = ch.getdata( ) ;
    cout << a << endl ;
    return 0 ;
}
```

Using the keyword *virtual* in the two base classes causes them to share the single subobject of the *base* class, which eliminates the ambiguity. Since there is only one subobject there is no ambiguity when it is referred in the *derived3* class. Here *derived1* and *derived2* are known as *virtual base classes.*

The ambiguity that we discussed occurs not only in the case of member data but also in case of member functions. This is shown in the following program.

```
#include <iostream>
using namespace std ;

class base
{
    public :

        void fun( )
        {
            cout << endl << "In base::fun( )" ;
        }
} ;

class derived1 : public base
{
} ;

class derived2 : public base
{
} ;

class derived3 : public derived1, public derived2
{
} ;

int main( )
```

```
{
    derived3 d ;
    d.fun( ) ;
    return 0 ;
}
```

On compilation the compiler reports an error since *derived3* inherits two copies of *fun( )*, one via *derived1* and another via *derived2*. Hence when we attempt to call *d.fun( )* the compiler would not know whether we intend to call the copy of *derived1* or that of *derived2*. Again the error can be overcome by using the *virtual* keyword in derivation of *derived1* and *derived2* as shown below:

```
class derived1 : virtual public base
{
} ;

class derived2 : virtual public base
{
} ;
```

Exercise

[A] State True or False:

(a) Virtual functions implement one form of polymorphism.

(b) Virtual functions permit calling of derived class functions using a base class pointer.

(c) Each object has its own VTABLE.

(d) There is only VTABLE per class.

(e) We can access the VTABLE using the *this* pointer.

(f) *this* pointer and *vptr* are same.

(g) There is one *vptr* per VTABLE.

(h) There is one *vptr* per object.

(i) The *vptr* always points to the VTABLE of the class.

(j) Virtual functions permit functions from different classes to be executed through the same function call.

(k) Pure virtual functions can never have a body.

(l) Pure virtual constructors can have a body.

(m) We can never build an object from a class containing a pure virtual function.

(n) A class containing a pure virtual function is called an abstract base class.

(o) Virtual function calls work faster than normal function calls.

(p) In a class hierarchy of several levels if we want a function at any level to be called through a base class pointer then the function must be declared as *virtual* in the base class.

(q) Virtual functions can be safely invoked using objects.

(r) The behaviour of virtual functions is same irrespective of whether we invoke them through pointers or references.

(s) While building an object it doesn't matter whether the base class constructor is called first or the derived class constructor is called first.

(t) While destroying an object firstly the derived class destructor should be called followed by the base class destructor.

(u) A *virtual* destructor ensures a proper calling order for the destructors in the class hierarchy.

(v) A pure *virtual* destructor can have a function body.

[B] What will be the output of the following programs:

(a)
```
#include <iostream>
using namespace std ;

class base
{
    public :

        virtual void fun1( )
        {
            cout << endl << "In base::fun1" ;
        }
};
```

```
class derived1 : public base
{
    public :

        void fun1( )
        {
            cout << endl << "In derived::fun1" ;
        }

        virtual void fun2( )
        {
            cout << endl << "In derived1::fun2" ;
        }
} ;

class derived2 : public derived1
{
    public :

        void fun1( )
        {
            cout << endl << "In derived2::fun1" ;
        }

        void fun2( )
        {
            cout << endl << "In derived2::fun2" ;
        }
} ;

int main( )
{
    base *ptr1 ;
    derived1 *ptr2 ;
    base b ;
    derived2 d ;
```

```
    ptr1 = &b ;
    ptr2 = &d ;
    ptr1->fun1( ) ;
    ptr2->fun1( ) ;
    ( ( derived1 * ) ptr2 )->fun2( ) ;
    return 0 ;
}
```

(b)
```
#include <iostream>
using namespace std ;

class base
{
    public :

        virtual void fun( )
        {
            cout << endl << "In base::fun( )" ;
        }
} ;

class derived1 : virtual public base
{
    public :

        void fun( )
        {
            cout << endl << "In derived1::fun( )" ;
        }
} ;

class derived2 : virtual public base
{
    public :

        void fun( )
        {
```

```
                cout << endl << "In derived2::fun( )" ;
            }
    } ;

    class derived3 : public derived1, public derived2
    {
        public :

            void fun( )
            {
                cout << endl << "In derived3::fun( )" ;
                derived1::fun( ) ;
            }
    } ;

    int main( )
    {
        base *b ;

        derived1 d1 ;
        b = &d1 ;
        b->fun( ) ;

        derived2 d2 ;
        b = &d2 ;
        b->fun( ) ;

        derived3 d3 ;
        b = &d3 ;
        b->fun( ) ;
        return 0 ;
    }
```

(c)
```
#include <iostream>
using namespace std ;

class base
```

```
{
    protected :
        int data ;
} ;

class derived1 : virtual public base
{
    protected :
        int data1 ;
} ;

class derived2 : virtual public base
{
    protected :
        int data2 ;
} ;

class derived3 : public derived1, public derived2
{
    private :
        int data3 ;
} ;

int main( )
{
    base b ;
    derived1 d1 ;
    derived2 d2 ;
    derived3 d3 ;
    cout << endl << sizeof ( b ) << endl << sizeof ( d1 )
         << endl << sizeof ( d2 ) << endl << sizeof ( d3 ) ;
    return 0 ;
}
```

[C] Answer the following:

(a) What are virtual base classes? When should they be used?

(b) What is the ideal place for defining a constructor and why?

(c) Improve the drawing program to include interactive drawing of line, circle and rectangle using mouse.

(d) Write a program that contains a class *derived*, derived from *base*. The *base* class should have a virtual function *fun( )* and it should be overridden in *derived*. Try to call *fun( )* from the constructor of the derived class and watch the results.

CHAPTER

ELEVEN

Input Output In C++

There are several assorted functions (easily more than 50) available in C for carrying out Input/Output (I/O). These functions put together forms what is popularly known as the standard C *stdio* library. Once you know C++ you might be tempted to convert these functions into a set of classes. It would be easier, safer and more efficient to use these classes than the assortment of functions from the *stdio* library. For example, we can design a class called *file* as shown in the following program.

```
#include <cstdio>
#include <cstdlib>
using namespace std ;
class file
{
    private :

        FILE *fp ;

    public :

        file ( const char *name, const char *mode )
        {
            fp = fopen ( name, mode ) ;
            if ( fp == NULL )
            {
                printf ( "\nCannot open file: %s\n", name ) ;
                exit ( 1 ) ;
            }
        }

        ~file( )
        {
            fclose ( fp ) ;
        }

        FILE *getfilepointer( )
```

```
        {
            return fp ;
        }
} ;

int main( )
{
    char filename[67], ch ;

    printf ( "\nEnter file name: " ) ;
    scanf ( "%s", filename ) ;
    file f ( filename, "r" ) ;

    while ( ( ch = fgetc ( f.getfilepointer( ) ) ) != EOF )
        printf ( "%c", ch ) ;

    return 0 ;
}
```

When we define the object *f* the constructor gets called. Here the file is opened using the usual *fopen( )* function. If the file opening fails a message is printed and the program is terminated. If the file is opened successfully we can now start using the normal C file I/O functions to read the contents of the file and display them on the screen. But these functions require a FILE pointer. This is defined as *private* in the *file* class and can be retrieved using the *getfilepointer( )* member function.

Let us now see what we have achieved out of the *file* class. Once the class is defined the file opening and file closing operations become very easy and safe. To open the file we just have to define a *file* object. The constructor does the rest. For closing a file we do not have to do anything. As soon as the *file* object goes out of scope the destructor gets called which promptly closes the file.

However there is a catch here. The *stdio* functions that are going to be used outside the class would need the file pointer *fp*. Wherever you need it you need to call the *getfilepointer( )* function. Does that not leave *fp* open for manipulation? Yes and no. Once the pointer is returned using it we can manipulate the contents of the FILE structure, though we cannot change the actual contents of *fp* (it being *private*). Thus *fp*'s contents can remain safe, but the contents of the FILE structure to which it points can change. In effect, this is not a perfectly safe approach. If we are to make the whole thing foolproof we need to include all file I/O functions within our *file* class. A program, which uses this class, is given below.

```
#include <cstdio>
#include <cstdlib>
#include <cstdarg>

using namespace std ;

class file
{
    private :

        FILE *fp ;

    public :

        file ( const char *name, const char *mode = "r" )
        {
            fp = fopen ( name, mode ) ;
            if ( fp == NULL )
            {
                printf ( "\nCannot open file: %s\n", name ) ;
                exit ( 1 ) ;
            }
        }
```

```
    ~file( )
    {
        fclose ( fp ) ;
    }

    int fgetc( )
    {
        int ch ;
        ch = ::fgetc ( fp ) ;
        return ch ;
    }

    void printf ( const char *fmt, ... )
    {
        va_list ptr ;
        char str[100] ;

        va_start ( ptr, fmt ) ;
        vsprintf ( str, fmt, ptr ) ;
        ::printf ( str ) ;
        va_end ( ptr ) ;
    }

    int open ( const char* path, const char* mode = "r" ) ;
    int close( ) ;

    int ungetc ( int c ) ;
    int fputc ( int c ) ;

    int puts ( const char* s ) ;
    char * gets ( char *s, int n ) ;

    int eof( ) ;
    int flush( ) ;

    int fseek ( long offset, int whence ) ;
```

```
        void rewind( ) ;
        long ftell( ) ;

        // and a few more that I may not have imagined
} ;

int main( )
{
    char filename[67], ch ;

    printf ( "\nEnter file name " ) ;
    scanf ( "%s", filename ) ;
    file f ( filename, "r" ) ;
    while ( ( ch = f.fgetc( ) ) != EOF )
        f.printf ( "%c", ch ) ;
    return 0 ;
}
```

I have defined only those member functions of *file* that are needed by *main( )*. On similar lines you can define the others. Most of them are only wrappers around the *stdio* functions. In addition to the constructor and destructor from the last class here we have also provided a zero-argument constructor. This is useful when we want to create an object but don't want to open the file. There is no *getfilepointer( )* member function any more because we don't want functions outside the class to access the *private* member *fp*. This ensures absolute safety.

Note the calls to *fgetc( )* and *printf( )* from within the class member functions. The *::* has been used to ensure that the member functions do not get called recursively. For example, *::fgetc (fp)* calls the *stdio* function and not the member function. In *file::printf( )* we have first written the output to a string by calling *vsprintf( )*. This function accepts variable-argument list as its parameter. Once the string is ready we have displayed it on the screen using *stdio*'s *printf( )*.

You can imagine making similar classes for console I/O and for reading/writing to a block of memory. With the *stdio* function turned into a few classes everything may seem neat and clean now. However, it is not so if you scratch the surface a bit. The *file* class uses *printf( )/scanf( )* and there lies the trouble. There are five major limitations of using *printf( )/scanf( )*.

(a) The specifiers used in the format string of *printf( )/scanf( )* include *%c, %d, %i, %u, %ld, %lu, %f, %lf, %Lf, %x, %X, %o, %p, %e* and *%g*. Remembering these specifiers for all types is not an easy job.

(b) *printf( )/scanf( )* do not carry out the conversions logically. So *3.5* printed using *%d* neither produces *3* nor *4*.

(c) If there is a mismatch in the specifier used and the type to be printed *printf( )/scanf( )* do not warn you. For example, if you try to print a *float* using *%d* no error/warning is reported. This is because *printf( )/scanf( )* are variable-argument list functions. The format strings used in these functions are interpreted at run-time not at compile time. Hence there cannot be any compile-time error checking for wrong type or wrong number of arguments used in these functions. C++ wants to trap errors at compile time (so that our life becomes easier) hence it has to reject the I/O library of C.

(d) The *printf( )* family of functions is not easily extensible. If we are to add a new class which does its own printing we may decide to overload *printf( )* within it. But remember that overloaded functions must have different types in their argument lists and *printf( )* hides its type information in the format string and the variable-argument list. Hence the primary goal of C++—the ability to add new data types with ease—gets defeated.

(e) An interpreter is loaded at run-time for the variable-argument list functions like *printf( )/scanf( )*. This involves unnecessary overheads. For example, even if we decide to print only a character the logic that prints out strings, *long*s and *double*s also gets loaded wasting precious space. There's no option for reducing the amount of space used.

Moral: Since we do I/O in almost every program, we need a fresh approach. An approach that is easy (no remembering of format specifiers), clean (no clutter in the program), safe (no unexpected manipulations of class elements), efficient (no overheads for doing small jobs) and adaptable (should accommodate new class's I/O). C++ offers this approach in the form of a library called *iostream* library.

The *iostream* Library

A *stream* is a general name given to the flow of data. Different streams are used to represent different kinds of data flow. For example, the standard output stream flows to the screen display, the standard input stream flows from the keyboard (these streams can be redirected, if required). In C++ a stream is represented by an object of a particular class. For example, *cin* and *cout* that we have used so far are really objects of *istream_withassign* and *ostream_withassign* classes respectively. These classes have been derived from *istream* and *ostream* classes. We don't have to define these objects because they have already been defined for us in the 'iostream.h' file. Based on the nature of data flow the *iostream* library offers several classes arranged in a complex hierarchy. Figure 11.1 shows some of the important classes from this hierarchy.

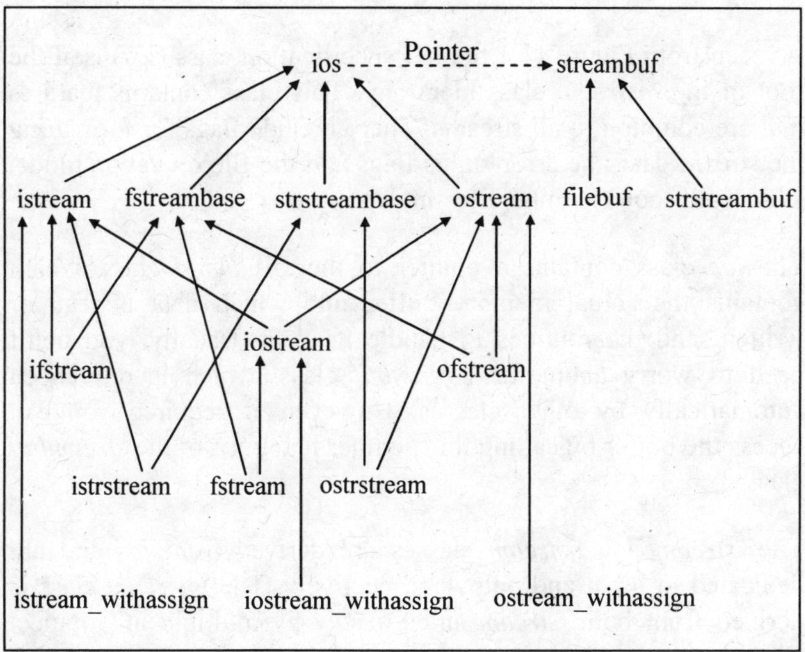

Figure 11.1

An *iostream* system consists of three parts:

(a) A buffer, which acts as an intermediary between the generalized input-output system and some particular source or sink for characters. This has been implemented in the *streambuf* class.

(b) A specification system responsible for reporting errors and controlling formats. This has been implemented in the *ios* class.

(c) A translation system that converts C++ language's typed objects to a sequence of characters or vice versa. This has been implemented in classes like *istream*, *ostream*, *iostream*, etc.

As seen from Figure 11.1 the I/O specification class (*ios*) is at the root of the *iostream* class hierarchy. This class contains features that are common to all streams. There include flags for formatting the stream data, the error-status flags and the file operation mode. We would soon examine these in detail.

The *ios* class contains a pointer to the *streambuf* class, which contains the actual memory buffer into which data is read or written, and the routines to handle its data. Usually, you don't need to worry about the *streambuf* class, which is referenced automatically by other classes. However, if required you can access the buffer by calling the member functions of the *streambuf* class.

The *istream* and *ostream* classes are derived from *ios* and are dedicated to input and output, respectively. The *iostream* class is derived from both *istream* and *ostream* by multiple inheritance. Classes derived from it can be used with devices, such as disk files, that may be opened for both input and output at the same time. Three classes—*istream_withassign*, *ostream_withassign*, and *iostream_withassign*—are inherited from *istream*, *ostream*, and *iostream*, respectively. They add assignment operators to these classes.

The classes used for input and output to the video display and keyboard are declared in the header file 'iostream.h', which we routinely included in our examples in previous chapters. The classes used specifically for disk file I/O are declared in the file 'fstream.h'. In-memory classes are declared in 'strstream.h'.

The *ios* Class

As said earlier, the *ios* class contains data members that help formatting of stream data, the error-status flags and the file operation mode. Some of the data used for formatting is stored in variables. For example, the floating-point precision, the output field width, and the character used to pad the output. The rest of the formatting is determined by flags, which are usually combined to save space. The following figure gives a complete list of the formatting flags.

Flag	Meaning
skipws	Skip (ignore) whitespace (For input; this is the default)
showbase	Use base indicator on output (0 for octal, 0x for hex)
showpoint	Show decimal point and trailing zeros for floats in output
uppercase	Use uppercase A-F for hex values and E for scientific values
showpos	Display + before positive integers
unitbuf	Unit Buffering. Flush all streams after each insertion
dec	Convert to decimal
oct	Convert to octal
hex	Convert to hexadecimal
left	Left justify output
right	Right justify output
internal	Use padding between sign or base indicator and number
scientific	Use exponential format on floating-point output
fixed	Use fixed format on floating-point output
boolalpha	Convert *bool* to "true" or "false" strings

Figure 11.2

There are two types of flags:

(a) On/Off flags

(b) Flags that work in a group

The on/off flags are simple. They can be turned on through the *setf( )* function and off through the *unsetf( )* function. For example, by default a string is displayed right justified. If we are to left-justify it we can say,

```
cout.setf ( ios::left ) ;
cout << "Open your eyes. Donate them!"
```

To remove the left justification for subsequent output we can say,

```
cout.unsetf ( ios::left ) ;
```

The flags that can be set/unset in this manner include *skipws*, *showbase*, *showpoint*, *uppercase*, *showpos*, *unitbuf* and *stdio*.

The second type of formatting flags work in a group. You can have only one of these flags on at a time. To set these flags you must use the second form of *setf( )* function. For example, there's a flag for each of the number bases: hexadecimal, decimal, and octal. Collectively, these flags are referred to as the *ios::basefield*. If the *ios::dec* flag is set and you call *setf (ios::hex)*, you'll set the *ios::hex* flag, but you won't clear the *ios::dec* bit, resulting in undefined behavior. The proper thing to do is call the another form of *setf( )* like this:

```
cout.setf ( ios::hex, ios::basefield ) ;
```

This call first clears all the bits in the *ios::basefield*, then sets *ios::hex*.

Similarly, the flags *scientific* and *fixed* are referred to as *ios::floatfield*. Also, the flags *left*, *right* and *internal* are collectively referred as *ios::adjustfield*. The following code snippet shows use of these group flags.

```
float a = 3.142800 ;
cout.setf ( ios::scientific, ios::floatfield ) ;
cout << a << endl ;
cout.setf ( ios::left, ios::adjustfield ) ;
```

```
cout << "Diamonds are for ever" ;
```

There are data members in the *ios* class that control the width of the output field, the fill character used when the data doesn't fill the output field, and the precision for printing floating-point numbers. The values of these variables can be read and written by member functions of the same name. A list of these functions is given below.

Function	**Effect**
int ios::width( )	Reads the current width. (Default is 0.)
int ios::width (int n)	Sets the width, returns the previous width.
int ios::fill( )	Reads the current fill character, (Default is space).
int ios::fill (int n)	Sects the fill character, returns the previous fill character.
int ios::precision( )	Read current floating-point precision (Default is 6)
int ios::precision (int n)	Sets floating-point precision, returns previous precision.

Figure 11.3

A small note about the field width values. When the specified width is less than the number of characters that represent the value the specified width is ignored. Thus, if you try to print 412 with a width of two, you'll still get 412. The field width specifies a minimum number of characters; there's no way to specify a maximum number.

Also, the width is reset to zero by each insertion and extraction. If we want to have a constant width, we need to call *width( )* after each insertion or extraction.

Let us now put together all that we have learnt about stream formatting in a program. Carefully go through the program and the output that follows it. I am sure it would clarify your understanding of the *iostream* formatting.

```
#include <iostream>
#include <windows.h>
using namespace std ;

int main( )
{
    int i = 52 ;
    float a = 425.0 ;
    float b = 123.500328 ;
    char str[ ] = "Dream. Then make it happen!" ;

    system ( "cls" ) ;
    cout.setf ( ios::unitbuf ) ;

    cout.setf ( ios::showpos ) ;
    cout << i << endl ;

    cout.setf ( ios::showbase ) ;
    cout.setf ( ios::uppercase ) ;
    cout.setf ( ios::hex, ios::basefield ) ;
    cout << i << endl ;

    cout.setf ( ios::oct, ios::basefield ) ;
    cout << i << endl ;

    cout.fill ( '0' ) ;
    cout << "Fill character: " << cout.fill( ) << endl ;

    cout.setf ( ios::dec, ios::basefield ) ;
    cout.width ( 10 ) ;
    cout << i << endl ;
```

```
cout.setf ( ios::left, ios::adjustfield ) ;
cout.width ( 10 ) ;
cout << i << endl ;

cout.setf ( ios::internal, ios::adjustfield ) ;
cout.width ( 10 ) ;
cout << i << endl ;
cout << i << endl ; // without width ( 10 )

cout.width ( 10 ) ;
cout << str << endl ;
cout.width ( 40 ) ;
cout << str << endl ;
cout.setf ( ios::left, ios::adjustfield ) ;
cout.width ( 40 ) ;
cout << str << endl ;

cout.precision ( 6 ) ;
cout << "Precision: " << cout.precision( ) ;
cout.setf ( ios::showpoint ) ;
cout.unsetf ( ios::showpos ) ;
cout << endl << a ;
cout.unsetf ( ios::showpoint ) ;
cout << endl << a ;

cout.setf ( ios::fixed, ios::floatfield ) ;
cout << endl << b ;
cout.setf ( ios::scientific, ios::floatfield ) ;
cout << endl << b ;

b = 5.375 ;
cout.precision ( 14 ) ;
cout.setf ( ios::fixed, ios::floatfield ) ;
cout << endl << b ;
cout.setf ( ios::scientific, ios::floatfield ) ;
cout << endl << b << endl ;
```

```
    cout.unsetf ( ios::showpoint ) ;
    cout.unsetf ( ios::unitbuf ) ;
    return 0 ;
}
```

Here is the output of the program…

```
+52
0X34
064
Fill character: 0
0000000+52
+520000000
+000000052
+52
Dream. Then make it happen!
0000000000000Dream. Then make it happen!
Dream. Then make it happen!0000000000000
Precision: +6
425.000
425
123.500328
1.235003E+02
5.37500000000000
5.37500000000000E+000
```

Most of the output is self-explanatory. The *unitbuf* and *stdio* flag deserve some explanation. The unit buffering should be turned on when we want to ensure that each character is output as soon as it is inserted into an output stream. You can also use unbuffered output, but unit buffering provides better performance.

The value of any format flag can be enquired using *ios::flags( )* member function. This function takes no arguments and returns a *long* (*typedef*ed to *fmtflags*) that contains the current format flags.

Manipulators

Calling the member functions of the *ios* class to set the formatting data of the stream is a little tedious. The actions of these functions can be more easily (and cleanly) duplicated using *manipulators*. When we use manipulators the formatting instructions are inserted directly into a stream. Out of the several manipulators available, we have been using one quite often: *endl*. As we know, this manipulator sends a newline to the stream and flushes it.

Manipulators come in two flavors: those that take an argument and those that don't. Manipulators with no arguments are provided in 'iostream.h', whereas those that take arguments are provided in 'iomanip.h'. The following figure gives a list of all manipulators along with their function.

Manipulator	**Purpose**
skipws	Skip whitespace on input
noskipws	Do not skip whitespace on input
dec	Convert to decimal
oct	Convert to octal
hex	Convert to hexadecimal
left	Left align, pad on right
right	Right align, pad on left
internal	Use padding between sign or base indicator and value
endl	Insert newline and flush the output stream
showpos	Shows plus sign for positive values

Continued...

...Continued

Manipulator	**Purpose**
noshowpos	Do not show plus sign for positive values
uppercase	Display uppercase A-F for hex values, and E for scientific values
nouppercase	Do not display hex values in uppercase
showpoint	Show decimal point and trailing zeros for *float* values
noshowpoint	Do not show decimal point & trailing zeros for *float* values
scientific	Use scientific notation for printing *float* values
fixed	Use fixed notation for printing *float* values
ends	Insert null character to terminate an output string
flush	Flush the output stream
lock	Lock file handle
unlock	Unlock file handle
setw (int n)	Changes the field width for output to *n*
setfill (char n)	Changes the fill character to *n* (default is a space)
setprecision (int n)	Changes the precision to *n* places after decimal point
setbase (base n)	Changes base to *n*, where *n* is 8, 10 or 16. If *n* is zero, output is base 10, but input uses the C convention: 10 is 10, 010 is 8, and 0xC is 12
setiosflags (fmtflags n)	Sets format flags specified by *n.* Setting remains in effect until next change
resetiosflags (fmtflags n)	Clears only the format flags specified by *n*. Setting remains in effect until next change

Figure 11.4

The following program shows how to use these manipulators. It produces the same output as the previous program. However, you would find this program more compact and clean.

```
#include <iostream>
#include <windows.h>
#include <iomanip>
using namespace std ;

int main( )
{
    int i = 52 ;
    float a = 425.0 ;
    float b = 123.500328f ;
    char str[ ] = "Dream. Then make it happen!" ;

    system ( "cls" ) ;
    cout << setiosflags ( ios::unitbuf | ios::showpos ) ;
    cout << i << endl ;

    cout << setiosflags ( ios::showbase | ios::uppercase ) ;
    cout << hex << i << endl ;

    cout << oct << i << endl ;

    cout << setfill ( '0' ) ;
    cout << "Fill character:" << cout.fill( ) << endl ;

    cout << dec << setw ( 10 ) << i << endl ;
    cout << setiosflags ( ios::left )
         << dec << setw ( 10 ) << i << endl ;

    cout << setiosflags ( ios::internal )
         << dec << setw ( 10 ) << i << endl ;
    cout << i << endl ;
```

```
    cout << setw ( 10 ) << str << endl ;
    cout << setw ( 40 ) << str << endl ;
    cout << setiosflags ( ios::left ) << setw ( 40 ) << str << endl ;

    cout.precision ( 6 ) ;
    cout << "Precision: " << cout.precision( ) ;
    cout << setiosflags ( ios::showpoint ) << resetiosflags ( ios::showpos )
         << endl << a ;
    cout << resetiosflags ( ios::showpoint )
         << endl << a ;

    cout << setiosflags ( ios::fixed ) << endl << b ;
    cout << setiosflags ( ios::scientific ) << endl << b ;

    b = 5.375 ;
    cout.precision ( 14 ) ;
    cout << setiosflags ( ios::fixed ) << endl << b ;
    cout << setiosflags ( ios::scientific ) << endl << b ;

    cout << resetiosflags ( ios::showpoint | ios::unitbuf ) << endl ;
    return 0 ;
}
```

The aim of the above program was to generate the same output as the previous one. As a result, all the manipulators in Figure 11.4 couldn't be used here.

Creating Our Own Manipulators

Though the list of manipulators provided by the *iostream* library is quite impressive, at times you may want to create your own manipulators. Here I would demonstrate how to create both types of manipulators: those that do not take arguments and those that do. Let us begin with the first one.

To understand how to develop a zero-argument manipulator we need to understand the internal working of some existing manipulator, say *endl*. *endl* is simply a function that take as its argument an *ostream* reference. The declaration for *endl( )* in 'iostream.h' looks like this.

```
ostream& endl ( ostream& ) ;
```

Consider the statement

```
cout << endl ;
```

Since << is an overloaded operator, internally this statement becomes,

```
cout.operator << ( endl ) ;
```

endl( ) being a function what is being passed to the overloaded operator is a pointer to a function. The << operator has been defined in 'iostream.h' as follows:

```
ostream & ostream::operator << ( ostream & ( *_f ) (ostream & ) )
{
    return ( *_f )( *this ) ;
}
```

This indicates that when we pass the address of *endl( )* to this function it collects it in a pointer to a function that receives an *ostream* reference and returns an *ostream* reference. If you observe carefully this matches the prototype of the *endl( )* function. Since this operator function is called through the *cout* object the *this* pointer contains the address of *cout*. Hence **this* yields the object. This object is then passed to the *endl( )* function through the statement.

```
( *_f )( *this ) ;
```

On getting called all that the *endl( )* function does is emit a '\n' to the output stream.

Simple enough! Now we can proceed to develop our own manipulator called *tab*. Here it is.

```
#include <iostream>
using namespace std ;

ostream & tab ( ostream &o )
{
    return o << '\t' ;
}

int main( )
{
    cout << "Don't" ;
    cout << tab << tab ;
    cout << "panic" << endl ;
    return 0 ;
}
```

This program works exactly on the similar lines as the previous one. The only difference is instead of calling the function *endl( )*, here the *tab( )* function gets called. Trace the flow of control in the program. This would help you understand its working better.

User-defined Manipulators With Arguments

As we saw in the previous section it is easy to create zero-argument manipulators. However, the way to create manipulators with arguments is pretty convoluted. Hence, let us try to understand it with an example. Here we would try to create a manipulator called *roman* which would receive an *unsigned long* as an argument and output its roman equivalent. To implement this *roman( )* manipulator we need to define a class called *roman*. This class consists of a constructor and an overloaded << operator function. This function has been implemented as a *friend* function.

Here we would not discuss why the function has to be a *friend* function. If you can't wait and want to know friend functions this very moment you can jump to Chapter 12. Others can take a look at the listing of the program that defines and uses the *roman* class.

```
#include <iostream>
using namespace std ;

class roman
{
    private :

        unsigned long num ;

    public :

        roman ( unsigned long n ) ;
        friend ostream & operator << ( ostream& o, roman& r) ;
} ;

roman::roman ( unsigned long n )
{
    num = n ;
}

ostream & operator << ( ostream& o, roman& r)
{
    struct key
    {
        char ch ;
        int val ;
    } ;
    key z[ ] = {
                    'm', 1000,
                    'd', 500,
                    'c', 100,
```

```
                'l', 50,
                'x', 10,
                'v', 5,
                'i', 1
            } ;
    int sz ;
    int k ;

    sz = sizeof ( z ) / sizeof ( z[0] ) ;

    for ( int i = 0 ; i < sz ; i++ )
    {
        k = r.num / z[i].val ;
        for ( int j = 1 ; j <= k ; j++ )
            o << z[i].ch ;

        r.num = r.num % z[i].val ;
    }
    return o ;
}

int main( )
{
    long yr = 1999 ;
    cout << roman ( yr ) ;
    cout << endl << roman ( 1752 ) << endl ;
    return 0 ;
}
```

Observe the following statement carefully

```
cout << roman ( yr ) ;
```

Here *roman (yr)* creates a temporary object of the type *roman*. Naturally, while creating this temporary object the constructor gets called and the value passed to it gets set in the *private* variable *num*. This temporary object and the *cout* object are then passed to the overloaded *operator <<( )* function. Note that in case of a *friend* the call to the operator function *doesn't* get converted into the form

```
cout.operator << ( roman ( yr ) ) ;
```

Within the operator function we have converted the value in *num* into its roman equivalent and outputted it using the reference of the *cout* object. At the end we have returned the reference. This returning of reference is necessary if we are to use the manipulator in a cascaded *cout* like

```
cout << endl << roman ( 1752 ) << endl ;
```

Thus we can implement any other manipulator with an argument—by developing a class for it. Does this mean that for every one-argument manipulator provided by the *iostream* library there is a separate class? Yes. However, instead of writing a separate class for each manipulator, the writers of the *iostream* library have put together a generic class hidden behind a complicated set of *#define*s in the file 'iomanip.h'. You can examine this file and try to understand this generic class.

Come GUI And...

All along we have been using *cin* and *cout* which work well with text based interfaces. But with GUIs like Windows 95 *cin* and *cout* are simply not going to work (unless you are running your C++ program as a console application). Does that mean all that we have learnt in this chapter has come to a big zero? Not at all! For GUIs, instead of sending the output to console we should send it to a file (which is identical to sending it to *cout*) or use the data display facilities of the GUI. Similarly, instead of reading input from the keyboard we can read it from a file. Note that even while sending the output to a file, or reading it from a file, all the stream formatting functions and manipulators that we have learnt in this chapter would work without any change.

So much about the formatting capabilities of the *ios* class. We would discuss its error status flags and file opening modes later. Right now let us turn our attention to other stream classes like *istream*, *ostream*, *iostream* etc. The capabilities of these classes are summarised below in brief. Should you so desire, you can skip their discussion for now and return to it later when a need arises to know how to perform a specific activity related with a stream.

The *istream* Class

The *istream* class is derived from the *ios* class. It performs activities specific to input. One of the most commonly used member function of this class is the overloaded >> operator. It has been overloaded to extract values of all basic types. We can extract even a string using this operator:

```
char str[10] ;
cin >> str ;
```

However, in this case we have no control over the number of characters that would get extracted into the string. If the array overflows, it might be dangerous. Instead of this we can use the *get( )* member function. This function comes in several forms. These are as under:

Function	**Purpose**
get (ch)	Extracts one character into *ch*
get (str, MAX)	Extracts up to MAX characters into *str*
get (str, DELIM)	Extracts characters into array *str* until specified delimiter (typically '\n'). Leaves delimiting character in stream
get (str, MAX, DELIM)	Extracts characters into array *str* until MAX characters or the DELIM character. Leaves delimiting character in stream
getline (str, MAX, DELIM)	Extract characters into array *str*, until MAX characters or the DELIM character. Extracts delimiting character.

Figure 11.5

In addition to these, the *istream* class supports a few miscellaneous functions. These are given below.

Function	**Purpose**
putback (ch)	Inserts last character read, back into input stream
peek (ch)	Reads one character, leaves it in stream
num = gcount( )	Returns number of character read by a (immediately preceding) call to *get( )*, *getline( )*, or *read( )*
ignore (MAX, DELIM)	Extracts and discards up to MAX characters until (and including) the specified delimiter (typically '\n')

Figure 11.6

The following program puts these functions to work.

```
#include <iostream>
using namespace std ;

int main( )
{
    char ch ;

    cout << endl << "Enter a character: " ;
    cin.get ( ch ) ;
    cout << ch ;
    cin.putback ( ch ) ;
    cin.get ( ch ) ;
    cout << endl << ch ;
    int count = cin.gcount( ) ;
    cout << endl << "Characters extracted in last get( ) = " << count ;

    // stuff stream with a Z
    cin.putback ( 'Z' ) ;
    ch = cin.peek( ) ;
    cout << endl << ch ;

    // Z is still in stream
    cin.get ( ch ) ;
    cout << endl << ch << endl ;
    return 0 ;
}
```

Lastly, *istream* class consists of functions that work specifically with disk files. These would be discussed when we do disk I/O.

The *ostream* Class

The *ostream* class handles output or insertion activities. Once again the most commonly used member function of this class is the overloaded << operator function. Two other useful member functions of this class are *put( )* and *flush( )*. The first one puts a character into the stream, whereas, the second flushes the buffer contents and inserts a newline.

Like *istream* class this class too contains some functions that deal specifically with disk files. These would be taken up later.

The *iostream* Class

The *iostream* class is derived from both *istream* and *ostream* by multiple inheritance. It acts only as a base class from which other classes can be derived. Other than the constructors and destructors, it doesn't contain any other member functions. As you can guess, classes derived from *iostream* can perform both input and output.

The *_withassign* Classes

There are three *_withassign* classes. They are *istream_withassign*, *ostream_withassign*, and *iostream_withassign*. These classes are derived from *istream*, *ostream*, and *iostream* respectively.

The *_withassign* classes are much like their base classes except that they include overloaded assignment operators. Using these operators the objects of the *_withassign* classes can be copied. The *istream*, *ostream*, and *iostream* classes are made uncopyable by making their overloaded copy constructors and assignment operators *private*.

Predefined Stream Objects

So far we have used two predefined stream objects: *cin* and *cout*. They are objects of *istream_withassign* and *ostream_withassign* classes respectively. As we know, these objects are used for keyboard input and screen display respectively. There are two other predefined objects that are used frequently: *cerr* and *clog*. *cerr* is an object of *ostream_withassign* class and is used for displaying error messages. As the name suggests, the *cerr* object is used to display error messages on the screen. Output of *cout, cerr*, and *clog* can be redirected to devices and files. The output sent to *cout* is buffered, whereas the one sent to *cerr* is displayed immediately.

clog is an object of the class *ostream_withassign* and is used for logging messages. It is a fully buffered version of cerr. The C equivalents of *cin*, *cout*, and *cerr* are *stdin*, *stdout* and *stderr* respectively. There is no C equivalent for *clog*.

Outputting Strings

Really speaking outputting strings should not deserve a section devoted to it. After all, outputting them should be as straight as outputting other standard types.

Consider the following statements:

```
char str[ ] = "Only thing that we should fear is fear itself."
cout << str ;
```

On execution would *cout* output the string or its address? If it prints the string then how do we get the address and vice versa. Examine the following program and its output to get the answer.

```
#include <strstream>
#include <iostream>
using namespace std ;

int main( )
{
    char str1[ ] = "Be silent. Let performance speak!" ;
    char *p1 = "Be eloquent. Express yourself!" ;
    char *p2 ;

    p2 = str1 ;

    cout << endl << str1 << endl << p1 ;
    cout << endl << p2 ;
    cout << endl << ( void * ) str1 ;
    cout << endl << ( void * ) p1 ;
    cout << endl << ( void * ) p2 << endl ;
    return 0 ;
}
```

This program produces the following output:

```
Be silent. Let performance speak!
Be eloquent. Express yourself!
Be silent. Let performance speak!
0x1f7cffd4
0x1f7c00cc
0x1f7cffd4
```

Note that to get the address of the string we need to cast the *char* * into a *void* *.

A Brief Review

We are about to begin our discussion of stream classes that perform file I/O. Before we do that, let us reiterate what we have learnt about stream classes so far. Figure 11.7 shows it in brief.

Class	**What It Does**
streambuf	Provides methods for memory buffers
ios	Handles stream state variables and errors
istream	Handles formatted and unformatted character conversions *from* a *streambuf*
ostream	Handles formatted and unformatted character conversions *to* a *streambuf*
iostream	Combines *istream* and *ostream* to handle bi-directional operations on a single stream
istream_withassign	Provides copy constructor and assignment operators for the *cin* stream
ostream_withassign	Provides copy constructor and assignment operators for *cout*, *cerr* and *clog*

Figure 11.7

File I/O With Streams

Almost all programs need to carry out disk file I/O. To carry out reading/writing from/to files we need to use another set of classes. These are as under.

Class	Derived From	Purpose
ifstream	istream, fstreambase	Input from file
ofstream	ostream, fstreambase	Output to file
fstream	iostream, fstreambase	Both input and output

Figure 11.8

The *ifstream*, *ofstream* and *fstream* classes are declared in the file 'fstream.h'.

Let us now look at a simple program that writes standard data types to a disk file and then reads them back and displays them on the screen.

```
#include <fstream>
#include <iostream>
using namespace std ;

int main( )
{
    // create file for output
    ofstream outfile ( "SAMPLE.TXT" ) ;

    char ch = 'Z' ;
    int i = 25 ;
    float a = 473.14f ;
    char str[ ] = "Hyperbole!" ;

    // send data to file
    outfile << ch << endl << i << endl << a << endl << str ;

    outfile.close( ) ;

    ifstream infile ( "SAMPLE.TXT" ) ;
```

```
    // read data from file
    infile >> ch >> i >> a >> str ;

    // send data to screen
    cout << ch << endl << i << endl << a << endl << str << endl ;
    return 0 ;
}
```

Opening File

To begin with, we have defined an object called *outfile* of type *ofstream* class through the statement

```
ofstream outfile ( "SAMPLE.TXT" ) ;
```

This invokes the one argument constructor of the *ofstream* class. This constructor allocates resources and opens the file SAMPLE.TXT. But we didn't mention whether the file is to be opened for reading or writing. This is not necessary since the constructor uses the defaults. The prototype of the constructor looks like this.

```
ofstream ( const char*, int = ios::out, int = filebuf::openprot ) ;
```

When we do not pass the second parameter to this constructor it uses the *ios::out* as the default file opening mode. Hence the file gets opened for writing.

The third parameter corresponds to the access permission under DOS, and it is used unless *ios::nocreate* is specified in the file opening mode. The default value is set to read and write permission.

Sometimes, we may not know the name of the file when the *ofstream* object is created. In such a case we may first create the object and then call *ofstream::open( )* function to open the file. This procedure is shown below.

```
ofstream outfile ;
outfile.open ( "SAMPLE.TXT" ) ;
```

Once again we have not mentioned the file opening mode. The reason is same–*ios::out* has been binarily included (ORed) into the mode (second parameter).

Later when the file is opened for reading once again a one-argument constructor of *ifstream* class is invoked. This constructor uses the *ios::in* by default to open the file for input.

Writing Data

The insertion operator << has been appropriately overloaded in the *ostream* class (from which *ofstream* is derived) to write different data types to the relevant stream. We can use the same operator functions to output data to the file. This we have done through the statement

```
outfile << ch << endl << i << endl << a << endl << str ;
```

Note that while writing this data we have separated each data item from the other using a newline. This is necessary because when we attempt to write numbers like 25 and 473.14 they are written as numeric strings. That is, 473.14 is written as '4', '7', '3', '.', '1', '4'. This results into two disadvantages:

(a) 473.14 which occupied only four bytes in memory ends up occupying 6 bytes in the file. This means more the number of digits in the number more space would it demand in the file.

(b) Every data item needs to be separated from the other using a delimiter (usually '\n'). This is necessary otherwise while reading the file it would not be possible for the extraction operator to figure out where one number is ending and the other beginning. Also, using this method if we write a multiword string, during extraction only the first word of the string would be read back.

Reading Data

For reading the data back we have built an object of the *istream* class. Constructor of this object opens the 'SAMPLE.TXT' file for reading. Once opened we have used the overloaded extraction operator of the class *istream* to read the data from the file. The '\n' written at the end of every data item helps the overloaded operator to distinguish the various items. When the numeric strings are read back from the file they are converted back to their binary representation for storage in program variables.

Closing File

We have specifically closed the file once writing is over by calling the function *ostream::close( )*. This is necessary since we wanted to open the same file for reading. Ideally, we should have opened the file for reading as well as writing. This file opening mode we would see later.

Note that we didn't close the file once reading from the file was over. This is because on termination of the program the *infile* object goes out of scope. As a result, the destructor gets called which closes the file.

The *ifstream*, *ofstream*, and *fstream* classes are declared in the header file 'fstream.h'. This file also includes the 'iostream.h' header file, so there is no need to include it explicitly.

A Better Way

Not being able to read multi-word strings is a serious limitation. We can overcome it by using the *getline( )* function in place of the extraction operator as shown below.

```
#include <fstream>
#include <iostream>
using namespace std ;

int main( )
{
    // create file for output
    ofstream outfile ( "SAMPLE.TXT" ) ;

    // send text to file
    outfile << "You should be enthusiastic about your future\n" ;
    outfile << "That is where you are going to spend the rest of your life\n" ;

    outfile.close( ) ;

    const int MAX = 100 ;
    char str[MAX] ;

    // create file for input
    ifstream infile ( "SAMPLE.TXT" ) ;

    // so long as end of file is not encountered
    while ( !infile.eof( ) )
    {
        // read a line of text
        infile.getline ( str, MAX ) ;

        // display the text read from the file
        cout << endl << str ;
    }
```

```
    return 0 ;
}
```

Here we have read the text from the file one line at a time using the *getline( )* function. This function is a member of *istream* (from which *ifstream* is derived). It reads characters until it encounters the end of line character, '\n', and places the resulting string in the buffer *str* supplied as an argument. The maximum size of the buffer is given as the second argument. The contents of the buffer are displayed after each line is read. This goes on till all the lines have been read.

Detecting End Of File

Within the *while* loop we keep checking whether we are through with reading the entire contents of the file. For this we have called the function *ifstream::eof( )*. This function returns a value zero if the end of file is reached, non-zero otherwise.

At times the same effect can be obtained through a statement like

```
while ( infile )
```

It seems truly magical that in this case a zero or non-zero value is correctly returned. Let us try to understand what is happening behind the screen. When the statement *while (infile)* gets executed the following function gets called

```
ios::operator void * ( )
{
    return fail( ) ? 0 : this ;
}
```

This is a conversion function that tries to convert an *ifstream* object into a *void* pointer. Within it, it calls a *ios::fail( )* function which looks like this:

```
int fail( )
{
    return state & ( failbit | badbit | hardfail ) ;
}
```

Here *state* is an *ios* class variable and what is being tested is the status of various error flags (these are discussed towards the end of this chapter). If this function returns a non-zero value (meaning end of file is not reached) then the conversion function simply returns the address of the object (*this*), otherwise it returns a zero. It is this address or zero that is checked in the *while* loop. If zero is returned the control jumps out of the *while* loop.

Note that the address returned has no significance except to be tested for a zero or non-zero value.

A Filecopy Program

Let us now try to write a program that copies the contents of one file into another. To perform file copying we would read the source file character by character and keep writing every character read to the target file. The process would continue till the end of file is not reached. Here is the program.

```
#include <fstream>
#include <iostream>
using namespace std ;

int main( )
{
```

```
    char source[67], target[67] ; // max allowable path length usually 66
    char ch ;

    cout << endl << "Enter source filename" ;
    cin >> source ;

    cout << endl << "Enter target filename" ;
    cin >> target ;

    // create file for input
    ifstream infile ( source ) ;

    // create file for output
    ofstream outfile ( target ) ;

    // continue reading file until EOF is reached
    while ( infile )
    {
        infile.get ( ch ) ;
        outfile.put ( ch ) ;
    }
    return 0 ;
}
```

Here the characters are read using the *istream::get( )* function and they are written to the target file using *ostream::put( )*.

File Opening Modes

So far we have opened a stream object either for reading or for writing. There are several other modes in which a stream object can be opened. Each mode is defined by a bit in the *ios* class. We can combine these bits using the logical OR operator. Each combination of mode bits specifies various aspects of how a stream object will be opened. Figure 11.9 shows the various possibilities.

Mode Bit	**Result**
in	Open for reading (default for *ifstream*)
out	Open for writing (default for *ofstream*)
ate	Start reading or writing at end of file (AT End)
app	Start writing at end of file (APPend)
trunc	Truncate file to zero length if it exists (TRUNCate)
norcreate	Error when opening if file does not already exist
noreplace	Error when opening for output if file already exists, unless *ate* or *app* is set
binary	Open file in binary (not text) mode

Figure 11.9

If we want to preserve whatever was in the file we should use *ios::app*. In this case whatever we write to the file will be added at the end of the existing contents.

If we want to perform both input and output on the file in binary mode we can use the following open command.

```
fstream file ;
file.open ( filename, ios::in | ios::out | ios::binary ) ;
```

The vertical bars between the flags cause the bits representing these flags to be logically combined into a single integer, so that several flags can be applied simultaneously.

Quick now! Can you suggest the bit flag combination for opening a file for reading as well as writing. If the file does not exist a new one should get created, whereas if it is already existing then it should not get overwritten. The answer is

```
fstream file ;
file.open ( filename, ios::in | ios::out | ios::noreplace ) ;
```

Binary I/O

Imagine that we wish to read/write records from/to file. Assume that each record contains employee information like name, age, basic salary and gross salary. If we use the overloaded operator << to write such records we would end up consuming more space for a record on the disk as compared to the space occupied by the same record in memory. This is because normally each number (integer or float) is written as a character string rather than as binary bits of the number. If the records were huge in number this would lead to a lot of wastage of precious disk space. If we are to avoid this we need to open the file in binary mode and then carry out the record input/output. The following program shows how this can be achieved.

```
#include <fstream>
#include <iostream>
using namespace std ;

int main( )
{
    struct employee
    {
        char name[20] ;
        int age ;
        float basic ;
        float gross ;
    } ;
```

```
    employee e ;
    char ch = 'Y' ;

    // create file for output
    ofstream outfile ;
    outfile.open ( "EMPLOYEE.DAT", ios::out | ios::binary ) ;

    while ( ch == 'Y' || ch == 'y' )
    {
        cout << endl << "Enter a record" ;
        cin >> e.name >> e.age >> e.basic >> e.gross ;
        outfile.write ( ( char * ) &e, sizeof ( e ) ) ;
        cout << endl << "Add another Y/N" << endl ;
        cin >> ch ;
    }

    outfile.close( ) ;

    // create file for input
    ifstream infile ;
    infile.open ( "EMPLOYEE.DAT", ios::in | ios::binary ) ;

    while ( infile.read ( ( char * ) &e, sizeof ( e ) ) )
    {
        cout << endl << e.name << '\t' << e.age << '\t'
               << e.basic << '\t' << e.gross << endl ;
    }
    return 0 ;
}
```

On execution the program asks the user to enter employee records. Each record entered is written to disk using the *ofstream::write( )* function. Once all the records are written the file is closed. The same file is then opened for reading in binary mode and it is read record by record. Every record read is displayed on the screen.

We have used two new functions here: *write( )*, a member of *ofstream*; and *read( )*, a member of *ifstream*. These functions think about data in terms of bytes. They don't care how the data is formatted, they simply transfer a buffer full of bytes from and to a disk file. Consider the call to *write( )*.

```
outfile.write ( ( char * ) &e, sizeof ( e ) ) ;
```

Here we are trying to tell *write( )* to write everything from the address given by *&e* upto the next *sizeof (e)* bytes. Note that it is necessary to cast the address passed to *write( )* into a *char* *, since *write( )* doesn't know about an *employee* *.

The parameters passed to *read( )* are identical to the ones passed to *write( )*—the address of the data buffer and its length in bytes.

Elementary Database Management

Having spent enough time reading/writing from/to a file let us now write a program which carries out elementary operations on a database. These include adding records, listing them out, modifying them, deleting them, undeleting them, etc. Naturally these operations should be implemented using a menu system. Hence I have built a simple menu through which the appropriate member functions of the class *group* get called.

If we are to delete a record permanently from a file we have to open another file, write all records into it except the one that we want to delete, delete the original file and rename the new one back to original. Though apparently crude this is the way we can get rid of a record permanently. But this would be a pretty slow operation if the database already contains lot of records. To improve the efficiency we have two menu items: 'Delete' and 'Pack'. Selecting 'Delete' would only mark the record for deletion. The record would not be physically removed from the file. This marking is done by placing a '*' besides the record to be deleted. When we select 'Pack' all starred records would be eliminated from the file permanently. Since on deleting the record it is only marked for deletion, we can provide a facility to even undelete the record. This is achieved through the menu item 'Recall'.

To be able to recall the records that have been deleted, an additional field called *flag* has been used in the structure *person*. Any time a record is deleted a '*' is placed in this field of the record. During recalling of a record the '*' is replaced by a space. All other member functions of the class have been written taking into account the presence of this *flag* field in the structure. The program that implements all these operations is given below.

```
#include <fstream>
#include <cstdlib>
#include <cstdio>
#include <string>
#include <iomanip>
#include <iostream>
#include <windows.h>

using namespace std ;

void gotoxy ( short, short ) ;

class group
{
    private:
        struct person
        {
            char flag ;
            char empcode[5] ;
            char name[40] ;
            int age ;
            float sal ;
```

```
        } p ;

        fstream file ;

    public:

        group( ) ;
        void addrec( );
        void listrec( ) ;
        void modirec( ) ;
        void delrec( );
        void recallrec( ) ;
        void packrec( ) ;
        void exit( ) ;
} ;

int main( )
{
    char choice ;
    group g ;

    do
    {
        system ( "cls" ) ;
        gotoxy ( 30, 10 ) ;
        cout << "1. Add records" ;
        gotoxy ( 30, 11 ) ;
        cout << "2. List records" ;
        gotoxy ( 30, 12 ) ;
        cout << "3. Modify record" ;
        gotoxy ( 30, 13 ) ;
        cout << "4. Delete record" ;
        gotoxy ( 30, 14 ) ;
        cout << "5. Recall record" ;
        gotoxy ( 30, 15 ) ;
        cout << "6. Pack records" ;
        gotoxy ( 30, 16 ) ;
```

```
cout << "0. Exit" ;
gotoxy ( 30, 18 ) ;
cout << "Your choice? " ;
cin >> choice ;
system ( "cls" ) ;

switch ( choice )
{
    case '1' :

        g.addrec( ) ;
        break ;

    case '2' :

        g.listrec( ) ;
        break ;

    case '3' :

        g.modirec( ) ;
        break ;

    case '4' :

        g.delrec( ) ;
        break ;

    case '5' :

        g.recallrec( ) ;
        break ;

    case '6' :

        g.packrec( ) ;
        break ;
```

```
            case '0' :

                g.exit( ) ;
                exit ( 1 ) ;
        }
    } while ( choice != 0 ) ;
    return 0 ;
}

group::group( )  // zero-argument constructor
{
    file.open ( "EMP.DAT", ios::binary | ios::in | ios::out ) ;
    if ( !file )
    {
        cout << endl << "Unable to open file" ;
        exit( ) ;
    }
}

// adds records to the file at end
void group::addrec( )
{
    char ch ;

    file.seekp ( 0L, ios::end ) ;

    do
    {
        cout << endl << "Enter emp code, name, age & salary" << endl ;
        cin >> p.empcode >> p.name >> p.age >> p.sal ;

        p.flag = ' ' ;
        file.write ( ( char * ) &p, sizeof ( p ) ) ;
        cout << "Add another record? (Y/N) " ;
        cin >> ch ;
```

```
    } while ( ch == 'y' || ch == 'Y' ) ;
}

// lists all records in the file
void group::listrec( )
{
    int j = 0 ;

    // position get pointer at the beginning of file
    file.seekg ( 0L, ios::beg ) ;

    // so long as end of file is not reached,
    // read each record and display it
    while ( file.read ( ( char * ) &p, sizeof ( p ) ) )
    {
        if ( p.flag != '*' )
            cout << endl << "Record# " << j++
                << setw ( 6 ) << p.empcode
                << setw ( 20 ) << p.name
                << setw ( 4 ) << p.age
                << setw ( 9 ) << p.sal ;
    }

    file.clear( ) ;
    cout << endl << "Press any key..." ;
    fflush ( stdin ) ;
    getchar( ) ;
}

// modifies a given record from the file
void group::modirec( )
{
    char code[5] ;
    int count = 0 ;
    long int pos ;

    cout << "Enter employee code: " ;
```

```
    cin >> code ;

    // position get pointer at beginning of file
    file.seekg ( 0L, ios::beg ) ;

    // search for the employee code
    while ( file.read ( ( char * ) &p, sizeof ( p ) ) )
    {
        // if record is found
        if ( strcmp ( p.empcode, code ) == 0 )
        {
            // receive new record
            cout << endl << "Enter new record" << endl ;
            cin >> p.empcode >> p.name >> p.age >> p.sal ;
            p.flag = ' ' ;

            // position put pointer such that the existing record is
            // overwritten
            pos = count * sizeof ( p ) ;
            file.seekp ( pos, ios::beg ) ;
            file.write ( ( char * ) &p, sizeof ( p ) ) ;
            return ;
        }
        count++ ;
    }

    cout << endl << "No employee in file with code = " << code ;
    cout << endl << "Press any key..." ;
    getchar( ) ;

    file.clear( ) ;
}

// marks a record for deletion
void group::delrec( )
{
    char code[5] ;
```

```
    long int pos ;
    int count = 0 ;
    cout << "Enter employee code: " ;
    cin >> code ;

    // position get pointer at the beginning of file
    file.seekg ( 0L, ios::beg ) ;

    // search for the employee code
    while ( file.read ( ( char * ) &p, sizeof ( p ) ) )
    {
        // if employee code is found
        if ( strcmp ( p.empcode, code ) == 0 )
        {
            p.flag = '*' ;

            // position put pointer
            pos = count * sizeof ( p ) ;
            file.seekp ( pos, ios::beg ) ;
            file.write ( ( char * ) &p, sizeof ( p ) ) ;
            return ;
        }
        count++ ;
    }

    cout << endl << "No employee in file with code = " << code ;
    cout << endl << "Press any key..." ;
    getchar( ) ;

    file.clear( ) ;
}

// recalls the record which was earlier marked for deletion
void group::recallrec( )
{
    char code[5] ;
    long int pos ;
```

```
    int count = 0 ;

    cout << "Enter employee code: " ;
    cin >> code ;

    // position get pointer at the beginning of file
    file.seekg ( 0L, ios::beg ) ;

    // search for the employee code
    while ( file.read ( ( char * ) &p, sizeof ( p ) ) )
    {
        if ( strcmp ( p.empcode, code ) == 0 )
        {
            p.flag = ' ' ;

            // position put pointer
            pos = count * sizeof ( p ) ;
            file.seekp ( pos, ios::beg ) ;
            file.write ( ( char * ) &p, sizeof ( p ) ) ;
            return ;
        }
        count++ ;
    }

    cout << endl << "No employee in file with code = " << code ;
    cout << endl << "Press any key..." ;
    getchar( ) ;

    file.clear( ) ;
}

// removes all records which have been marked for deletion
void group::packrec( )
{
    // create a temporary file of stream outfile ;
    ofstream outfile ;
    outfile.open ( "TEMP", ios::out ) ;
```

```
    // position get pointer at the beginning of file
    file.seekg ( 0, ios::beg ) ;

    // search for records which have been marked for deletion

    while ( file.read ( ( char * ) &p, sizeof ( p ) ) )
    {
        if ( p.flag != '*' )
            outfile.write ( ( char * ) &p, sizeof ( p ) ) ;
    }

    outfile.close( ) ;
    file.close( ) ;

    remove ( "EMP.DAT" ) ;
    rename ( "TEMP", "EMP.DAT" ) ;

    file.open ( "EMP.DAT", ios::binary | ios::in | ios::out ) ;
}

void group::exit( )
{
    file.close( ) ;
}

void gotoxy ( short col, short row )
{
    HANDLE h = GetStdHandle ( STD_OUTPUT_HANDLE ) ;
    COORD position = { col, row } ;
    SetConsoleCursorPosition ( h, position ) ;
}
```

File Opening

To ensure that the file operations are carried out efficiently we propose to open the file only once, perform all possible operations on it and finally close it. To this effect we have opened the file in the constructor. The file is closed finally when the user selects 'Exit' from the menu. While performing all other operations the file is considered to be open (and it indeed would be).

To open the file we have called the *open( )* function through the statement

```
file.open ( "EMP.DAT", ios::binary | ios::in | ios::out ) ;
```

We have used the mode bits *in*, *out*, and *binary* because we want to perform both input and output on the file in binary mode. The vertical bars between the flags cause the bits representing these flags to be logically ORed together.

Seeking In iostreams

Each stream has two long integers associated with it—a *get* pointer and a *put* pointer. The value present in the *get* pointer indicates the byte number in the file from where the next character would be read. Similarly, the value in the *put* pointer specifies where in the file would the next write take place. The term *pointer* in this context should not be confused with the normal C/C++ pointers. We can change the values of these pointers (using member functions) if we want to exercise control over where the next read/write should take place.

In our program while adding records we would like to carry out the addition at the end of existing records in the file. While listing records we would like to start reading records from the first record onwards. Similarly, while modifying records we would like to modify a record present at any place in the file. This means to carry out these operations we would be required to move the *get* and the *put* pointers.

The *istream::seekg( )* and *ostream::seekp( )* functions allow us to set the *get* and the *put* pointer respectively. To enquire their current positions we can use the functions *istream::tellg( )* and *ostream::tellp( )*.

The seek functions come in two forms. The first form needs the absolute position within the file. For example,

```
file.seekg ( 1000L ) ;
```

would position the *get* pointer at 1000th byte in the *file* stream.

The other form requires two arguments. The first argument specifies an offset from a location in the file, whereas the second specifies the location from which the offset is measured. The first argument can take positive or negative values. The second argument would be one of these: *beg*, *cur* and *end*. For example,

```
file.seekg ( -25L, ios::cur ) ;
```

would position the *get* pointer *25* bytes before its *current* position.

In our program we have used the *seekg( )/seekp( )* functions to suitably locate the *get* and *put* pointers in the file.

The Catch In Reading Files

Do you find anything odd in the following code:

```
file.seekg ( 0L, ios::beg ) ;
while ( file.read ( ( char * ) &p, sizeof ( p ) ) )
{
    if ( p.flag != '*' )
        cout << endl << "Record# " << j++
            << setw ( 6 ) << p.empcode
```

```
        << setw ( 20 ) << p.name
        << setw ( 4 ) << p.age
        << setw ( 9 ) << p.sal ;
}
```

Here, to begin with, we have positioned the *get* pointer at the beginning of the file stream. Next through the loop we have read each record and then displayed it on the screen. When we execute this code for the first time it displays all the records in the file. But this seemingly innocuous code creates a problem if executed the second time. It doesn't display any records at all, even though we are repositioning the pointer using *seekg( )*. Let us understand why this happens.

When we reach the end of the input file the end of file bit in the *state* variable of the *ios* class gets set. This would remain set even if we reposition the *get* pointer to the beginning of the file. Hence when we try to read the records second time the end of file condition is still satisfied. Hence no reading takes place. To rectify this situation, whenever we reach end of file and still want to use the file we should call the *ios::clear( )* function as shown below:

```
file.clear( ) ;
```

Classes That Read/Write themselves

Let us now see how we can create classes that can perform I/O for themselves. Given below is a menu-driven program that lets you choose the shape that you intend to draw. When a shape is selected from the menu it won't be efficient to have a member function for that object open the file, write one object to it, and then close it. It would be much faster to work on the following lines. We would consider two possibilities here:

(a) A filename is supplied as command-line argument

(b) No command-line argument is supplied.

If no filename is supplied at command line we should perform the following steps:

(a) As objects are created put them in a linked list.

(b) When the application is terminated ask for the name of the file and open that file for writing.

(c) Write all the objects in the linked list to the open file and then close it.

If filename is supplied at command line we should perform the following steps:

(a) Open the specified file for reading and writing.

(b) Read objects from the file and put them in a linked list.

(c) If more objects are created add them to the linked list.

(d) When the application is terminated write all the objects in the linked list to the open file and then close it.

The linked list is maintained by the *objarray* class. As each object is created a pointer to it is stored in the linked list. The *objarray* class can also report how many objects are present in the linked list. The following figure would help you imagine how the linked list is constructed.

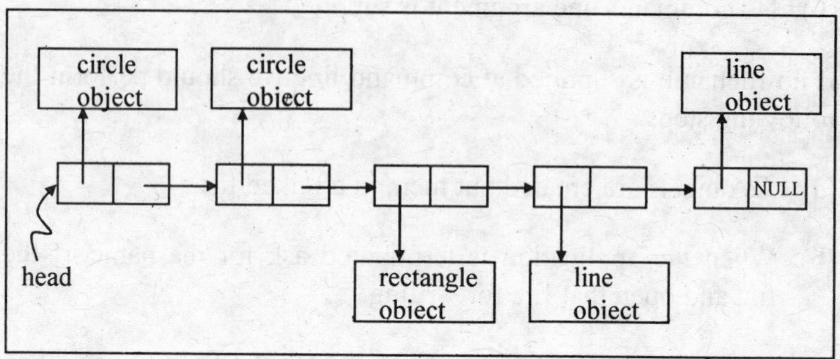

Figure 11.10

When it's time to write the objects to the disk the linked list is traversed writing each object in turn. What complicates the matter is the fact that the size of each object (line, circle and rectangle) is different since they contain different amounts of data. If such objects were written to the disk then reading them back would be a problem because we would not know how many bytes to read for a particular object. Hence while writing the objects to the disk we have also written a character 'L', 'C' or 'R' to indicate whether the bytes that follow it represent the data for line, circle or rectangle. An alternative strategy could be to write the size of the object, followed by the object data.

Note that we are not going to actually draw the shapes on the screen as that would involve creating window, selecting pen and brush and then calling Windows API functions to carry out the drawing. Instead of complicating the program with these calls, we would simply display a relevant message on the screen when it is time to draw these shapes.

Here is the program…

```
#include <iostream>
#include <fstream>
#include <string>
#include <cstdio>
#include <cstdlib>
#include <ctime>

using namespace std ;

class shapes
{
    public :

        virtual void draw( ) = 0 ;
        virtual void save ( fstream &out ) = 0 ;
        virtual void open ( fstream &in ) = 0 ;
} ;

class myline : public shapes
{
    private :

        int sx, sy, ex, ey, color ;

    public :

        myline( )
        {
        }

        myline ( int x1, int y1, int x2, int y2, int clr )
        {
            sx = x1 ;
            sy = y1 ;
            ex = x2 ;
            ey = y2 ;
            color = clr ;
```

```
        }

        void draw( )
        {
            cout << "Line - draw( )" << endl ;
        }

        void save ( fstream &out )
        {
            out << "L" << "\n" ;
            out << sx << " " << sy << " " << ex << " " << ey << " "
                << color << "\n" ;
        }

        void open ( fstream &in )
        {
            in >> sx >> sy >> ex >> ey >> color ;
        }
} ;

class myrectangle : public shapes
{
    private :

        int sx, sy, ex, ey, color ;

    public :

        myrectangle( )
        {
        }

        myrectangle ( int x1, int y1, int x2, int y2, int clr )
        {
            sx = x1 ;
            sy = y1 ;
            ex = x2 ;
```

```
            ey = y2 ;
            color = clr ;
        }

        void draw( )
        {
            cout << "Rectangle - draw( )" << endl ;
        }

        void save ( fstream &out )
        {
            out << "R" << "\n" ;
            out << sx << " " << sy << " " << ex << " " << ey << " "
                << color << "\n" ;
        }

        void open ( fstream &in )
        {
            in >> sx >> sy >> ex >> ey >> color ;
        }
} ;

class mycircle : public shapes
{
    private :

        int sx, sy, radius, color ;

    public :

        mycircle( )
        {
        }

        mycircle ( int x1, int y1, int r, int clr )
        {
            sx = x1 ;
```

```
        sy = y1 ;
        radius = r ;
        color = clr ;
    }

    void draw( )
    {
        cout << "Circle - draw( )" << endl ;
    }

    void save ( fstream &out )
    {
        out << "C" << "\n";
        out << sx << " " << sy << " " << radius << " " << color
            << "\n" ;
    }

    void open ( fstream &in )
    {
        in >> sx >> sy >> radius >> color ;
    }
} ;

struct node
{
    void *obj ;
    node *link ;
} ;

class objarray
{
    private :

        node *head ;

    public :
```

```
objarray( )
{
    head = NULL ;
}

void add ( void *o )
{
    node *temp = new node ;
    temp -> obj = o ;
    temp -> link = NULL ;

    if ( head == NULL )
        head = temp ;
    else
    {
        node *q ;

        q = head ;
        while ( q -> link != NULL )
            q = q -> link ;

        q -> link = temp ;
    }
}

void* getobj ( int i )
{
    node *q ;
    q = head ;

    int n ;
    for ( n = 1 ; n < i ; n++ )
    {
        q = q -> link ;
    }

    return ( q -> obj ) ;
```

```
        }

        int getcount( )
        {
            int n = 0 ;

            node *q ;
            q = head ;

            while ( q != NULL )
            {
                q = q -> link ;
                n++ ;
            }

            return n ;
        }

        ~objarray( )
        {
            node *q ;
            q = head ;

            while ( q != NULL )
            {
                head = head -> link ;
                delete q ;
                q = head ;
            }
        }
} ;

int main ( int argc, char *argv[ ] )
{
    fstream file ;
    char choice ;
    int clrnum, sx, sy, ex, ey, rad ;
```

```
shapes *ptr ;
objarray arr ;

char a[2] ;
int i ;

if ( argc == 2 )
    file.open ( argv[1], ios::in | ios::out ) ;

while ( file )
{
    file >> a ;

    // determine the type of the object read
    if ( strcmp ( a, "L" ) == 0 )
    {
        myline *l = new myline( ) ;
        l -> open ( file ) ;
        arr.add ( l ) ;
    }

    if ( strcmp ( a, "R" ) == 0 )
    {
        myrectangle *r = new myrectangle( ) ;
        r -> open ( file ) ;
        arr.add ( r ) ;
    }

    if ( strcmp ( a, "C" ) == 0 )
    {
        mycircle *c = new mycircle( ) ;
        c -> open ( file ) ;
        arr.add ( c ) ;
    }
}
```

```
int count = arr.getcount( ) ;
for ( i = 1 ; i <= count ; i++ )
{
    ptr = ( shapes * ) arr.getobj ( i ) ;
    ptr -> draw( ) ;
}


srand ( ( unsigned ) time ( NULL ) ) ;

while ( 1 )
{
    cout << endl << "1. Line  2. Rectangle  3. Circle  4. Exit " << endl ;

    cout << "Your choice: " ;
    fflush ( stdin ) ;
    cin.get ( choice ) ; ;

    clrnum = rand() % 16 ;
    sx = rand() % 638 ;
    sy = rand() % 478 ;
    ex = rand() % 638 ;
    ey = rand() % 478 ;
    rad = rand() % 200 ;

    myline *l ;
    myrectangle *r ;
    mycircle *c ;

    switch ( choice )
    {
        case '1' :

            l = new myline ( sx, sy, ex, ey, clrnum ) ;
            if ( l == NULL )
                exit ( 1 ) ;
```

```
        arr.add ( l ) ;
        cout << "Following Line added to array" << endl ;
        cout << "sx = " << sx << " sy = " << sy << " ex = " << ex
            << " ey = " << ey << " color = " << clrnum << endl ;
        break ;

    case '2' :

        r = new myrectangle ( sx, sy, ex, ey, clrnum ) ;
        if ( r == NULL )
            exit ( 1 ) ;

        arr.add ( r ) ;
        cout << "Following Rectangle added to array" << endl ;
        cout << "sx = " << sx << " sy = " << sy << " ex = " << ex
            << " ey = " << ey << " color = " << clrnum << endl ;
        break ;

    case '3' :

        c = new mycircle ( sx, sy, rad, clrnum ) ;
        if ( c == NULL )
            exit ( 1 ) ;

        arr.add ( c ) ;
        cout << "Following Circle added to array" << endl ;
        cout << "sx = " << sx << " sy = " << sy << " rad = " << rad
            << " color = " << clrnum << endl ;
        break ;

    case '4' :

        if ( argc == 1 )
        {
            cout << "Enter file name: " ;
            char name[67] ;
            cin >> name ;
```

```
                file.open ( name, ios::out ) ;
            }

            count = arr.getcount( ) ;
            file.seekp ( 0L, ios::beg ) ;
            file.clear( ) ;
            for ( i = 1 ; i <= count ; i++ )
            {
                ptr = ( shapes * ) arr.getobj ( i ) ;
                    ptr -> save ( file ) ;
            }

            file.close( ) ;
            cout << "Array saved to file... exiting" << endl ;
            exit ( 1 ) ;
        }
    }
    return 0 ;
}
```

Go through the program carefully. This concept of objects reading/writing themselves is very commonly used in Visual C++ applications.

Errors During I/O

The I/O programs that we wrote so far were not sand-papered with error checks. Error checking, if any, was restricted only to reaching end-of-file condition. However, no professional program can stand the test of time unless exhaustive error checking is done in it. This involves error checking which opening a file and while reading/writing a file. The following program shows how these checks can be performed.

```
#include <fstream>
#include <stdlib>
#include <iostream>
using namespace std ;

int main( )
{
    void report ( ofstream& ) ;

    ofstream file ;
    file.open ( "SAMPLE.TXT", ios::noreplace ) ;

    if ( ! file )
    {
        report ( file ) ;
        exit ( 1 ) ;
    }
    else
    {
        file << "Had cars been built like the OS," << endl
            << "we would have had more hospitals than homes" ;
        if ( ! file )
        {
            report ( file ) ;
            exit ( 2 ) ;
        }
    }
    file.close( ) ;
    return 0 ;
}

void report ( ofstream &file )
{
    cout << endl << "Unable to open SAMPLE.TXT" ;
    cout << endl << "Error state = " << file.rdstate( ) ;
    cout << endl << "good( ) = " << file.good( ) ;
    cout << endl << "eof( ) = " << file.eof( ) ;
```

```
    cout << endl << "fail( ) = " << file.fail( ) ;
    cout << endl << "bad( ) = " << file.bad( ) ;
}
```

So far when we opened a file for reading we assumed that it was already existing. Similarly, when we opened it for writing we assumed that it could get created. It is not safe to rely on such assumptions if we want to make the program foolproof. Hence whenever we open a file we must check whether the file opening was successful or not. Also, when we write to the disk the possibilities like the disk getting full, or the disk being write-protected cannot be ruled out. While reading from a file if you don't consider the possibility of a hardware error you are away from reality.

In the above program we have opened the file for writing. If this fails then we report an error. You may recall that in the statement

```
file.open ( "SAMPLE.TXT", ios::noreplace ) ;
```

file becomes zero if we are enable to open the file. So we can check the status of *file* for success/failure in file opening:

```
if ( ! file )
```

If this condition is satisfied we have called the *report( )* function where details of various error flags are printed. The *ios* class maintains a state variable whose bits signify the various error states. The position of these bits and their meaning is given in the following figure.

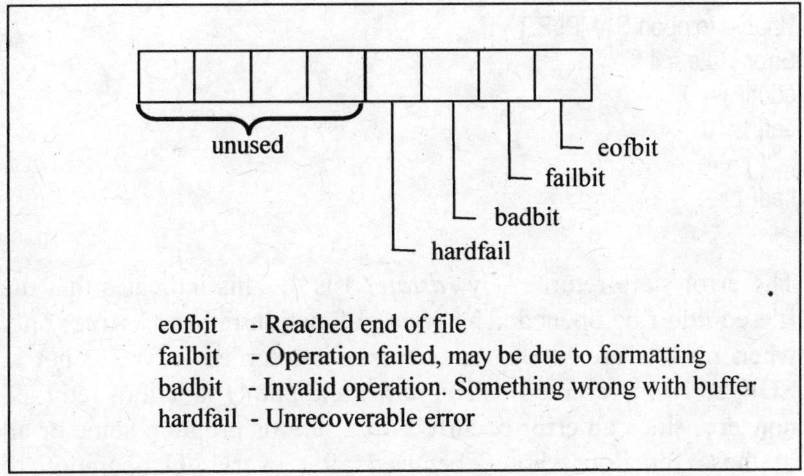

Figure 11.11

The value of the state variable can be obtained through the function *ios::rdstate( )*. Other functions like *eof( )*, *good( )*, *fail( )*, *hard( )*, and *bad( )* return the status of other bits. The meanings of these functions are as under.

Function	**Purpose**
eof( )	Returns true if EOF flag is set
fail( )	Returns true if *failbit* or *badbit* or *hardfail* flag is set
bad( )	Returns true if *badbit* or *hardfail* flag is set
good( )	Returns true if everything OK; no flags set
clear (int = 0)	With no argument, clears all error bits; otherwise sets specified flags, as in *clear (ios::failbit)*

Figure 11.12

Here's the output of the program when SAMPLE.TXT was existing and *noreplace* didn't permit replacement of it with a new file...

```
Unable to open SAMPLE.TXT"
Error state = 4
good( ) = 0
eof( ) = 0
fail( ) = 4
bad( ) = 4
```

The error state returned by *rdstate( )* is 4. This indicates that the file couldn't be opened. The *good( )* function returns 1 (true) only when no bits are set, so in our case it returned 0. We're not at EOF, so *eof( )* returned 0. The *fail( )* and *bad( )* functions returned nonzero, since an error occurred. In a serious program some or all of these functions should be used after every I/O operation to ensure that things went as expected.

Filecopy Program Revisited

In an earlier section we wrote a filecopy program which read the source file character by character using the *ifstream::get( )* function and wrote these characters into the target file using *ofstream::put( )* function. There exists one more way to do so. This involves a concept called stream buffering. Let us understand this concept first and then we would return to file copying.

As we know, the *istream* and *ostream* classes are derived by multiple inheritance from the *ios* and *streambuf* classes. The *streambuf* class manages a buffer. Normally while dealing with the stream classes you don't directly deal with this buffer. To hide the underlying implementation of this buffer and still provide an access to it through functions it has been abstracted into a *streambuf* class. Each stream object contains a pointer to a *streambuf* object. This pointer can be accessed through a member function called *rdbuf( )*. Every stream object has this function. It returns a pointer to the *streambuf* object.

One of the most interesting things that you can do with this pointer is to connect it to another stream object using the << operator. This would move all the bytes from the buffer of one object into that of another. We can use this facility for file copying. The program to achieve this is given below:

```
#include <fstream>
#include <iostream>
using namespace std ;

int main( )
{
    char source[67], target[67] ;

    cout << endl << "Enter source filename" ;
    cin >> source ;

    cout << endl << "Enter target filename" ;
    cin >> target ;

    // create file for input
    ifstream infile ( source ) ;

    // create file for output
    ofstream outfile ( target ) ;

    outfile << infile.rdbuf( ) ;
    return 0 ;
}
```

All the copying is done through a single statement

```
outfile << infile.rdbuf( ) ;
```

This causes the entire contents of the source file to be sent to *outfile*. You would agree that this method avoids the reading and writing of file a byte at a time and hence is more efficient. Moreover, what can be more elegant than a one line copying process.

Overloading << and >>

One of the major objectives of OOP is to make sure that user-defined objects work similar to the standard objects. This can be extended even to I/O. We can output standard objects like *char*, *int*, *float*, *double* etc. using statements like:

```
cout << ch << i << a << d ;
```

We should be allowed to use the same format for user-defined objects like, say, *complex*. However, *complex* being user-defined the compiler would not know how to output it. Hence we got to teach the same to the compiler. This means that we got to overload << operator in the *complex* class. This overloading involves usage of *friend* keyword, which is a topic of the next chapter. Hence we will have to postpone this issue till then.

Strstreams

So far we have handled two types of iostreams: standard and file. The third type of iostream works with memory and is called *strstream*. The beauty of iostreams is that even with this stream we can use the same reading and formatting functions. The class names for strstreams are similar to those for file streams. If we are to extract characters from a strstream, we create an *istrstream*. If we are to insert characters into a strstream, we create an *ostrstream*.

Readers familiar with Windows programming must have come across several functions (*MessageBox( )* for example) which needs a string as one of the parameters. If we are to display a char, a float an integer and a string through *MessageBox( )* we are first required to convert them into strings, concatenate these strings and then pass the resultant string to *MessageBox( )*. We may think of using *itoa( )*, *gcvt( )* and *strcat( )* to do the job. Or we may employ a *sprintf( )* which can do the same job in one shot. Alternately, in C++ we can use strstreams. This is shown below. We have formatted the data as it goes to the strstream.

```
#include <strstream>
#include <iomanip>
#include <iostream>
using namespace std ;

int main( )
{
    const int MAX = 100 ;

    char ch = 'Z' ;
    int i = 350 ;
    float a = 3.14152869f ;
    char str[ ] = "strstreams at work" ;
    char buffer[MAX] ;

    ostrstream s ( buffer, MAX ) ;

    s << endl
      << setw ( 8 ) << "ch = "  << ch << endl
      << setw ( 8 ) << "i = "  << hex << i << endl
      << setw ( 8 ) << "a = "  << setiosflags ( ios::fixed ) << a << endl
      << setw ( 8 ) << "str = " << str
      << ends ;

    cout << s.rdbuf( ) << endl ;
    return 0 ;
}
```

Here when we build an object *s* the constructor of *ostrstream* gets called. Its prototype looks like this:

```
ostrstream:: ostrstream ( char*, int, int = ios::out ) ;
```

The first argument is a pre-allocated buffer where the characters will end up, the second is the size of the buffer, and the third is the mode. The default mode is *ios::out*. If default mode is used, characters are written into the buffer from the starting address onwards. Instead if we use either *ios::ate* or *ios::app* (same effect), the buffer is assumed to already contain a zero-terminated string, and any new characters are added starting at the zero terminator.

The second constructor argument is the size of the array and is used by the object to ensure it doesn't overwrite the end of the array. If you fill the array up and try to add more bytes, they won't get added.

Once we have created an *ostrstream* we can insert into it anything that we want, using the normal formatting ways that we used with *cout*.

An important thing to remember about *ostrstreams* is that the zero terminator we normally need at the end of a character array is not inserted for us. We need to specifically insert it using the manipulator *ends*.

In our program once the information is formatted in *buffer* we have sent it out through the statement

```
cout << s.rdbuf( ) ;
```

The output would look like this:

```
ch = Z
  i = 15E
  a = 3.141529
```

```
str = strstreams at work
```

When we *rdbuf* the contents of the buffer the *get* pointer inside the *streambuf* is moved forward as the characters are output. For this reason, if we say *cout << s.rdbuf( )* a second time, nothing happens because the *get* pointer is already at the end.

Using *istrstreams*

Instead of writing formatted data into memory we can do the reverse too. We can extract bytes from memory using *istrstreams*. Here is a simple program that shows how this can be achieved.

```
#include <strstream>
#include <iostream>
using namespace std ;

int main( )
{
    int age ;
    float salary ;
    char name[50] ;
    char str[ ] = "35 12004.50 Sammer Shekhar Deshpande" ;

    istrstream s ( str ) ;

    s >> age >> salary >> name ;

    cout << age << endl
         << salary << endl
         << name ;

    cout << endl << s.rdbuf( ) << endl ;
    return 0 ;
}
```

When we build the object *s* the constructor of *istrstream* gets called. It takes a pointer to a zero-terminated character array. Instead of an array we can also pass it a pointer to a zero-terminated string allocated on the heap.

Once the *istrstream* object is built we can now extract bytes from it until the '\0' present at the end of the string is encountered.

There is one more form of *istrstream* constructor available. In addition to the pointer to array it also requires the size of the array. In this case the array doesn't have to be zero-terminated. If an *istrstream* object is created using this constructor you can extract bytes all the way to *buf[size]*, whether or not you encounter a zero along the way.

The statement

```
s >> age >> salary >> name ;
```

extracts the *age*, *salary* and the *name* from the *istrstream*.

You would agree that this is a more flexible and general approach to transforming character strings to typed values than using the C library functions like *atof( )*, *atoi( )*, etc.

However there is a minor hiccup here. While extracting the name only the first name could be extracted. The balance is extracted using *rdbuf( )*.

Note that while extracting an integer or a float it wasn't the first whitespace-delimited set of characters that were being extracted. How many characters got extracted was dependent on the data type they are being extracted into. As against this, while extracting the name it is only the next whitespace-delimited word that got extracted.

In general we can conclude that the best place to use the extractor in *iostreams* is when you know the exact sequence of data in the input stream and you're converting to some type other than a character string.

Automatic Storage Allocation

While using output *strstreams* (but not *istrstreams*) we have an option of allowing the *ostrstream* to do its own memory allocation. For this we need to create an *ostrstream* object with no constructor arguments:

```
ostrstream s ;
```

Now *s* takes care of all its own storage allocation on the heap. We can stuff as many bytes into it as we want. If it falls short of memory, it will allocate more memory. If it cannot, it may even move the block of memory. When the object goes out of scope, the heap storage is automatically released. This is a more flexible approach if we do not know how much space we are going to need.

If we want the physical address of the memory used by *s* we can obtain it by calling the *str( )* member function:

```
char* p = s.str( ) ;
```

There's a catch here. Once *str( )* has been called then the block of memory allocated by *ostrstream* cannot be moved. This is logical. It can't move the block since we are now expecting it to be at a particular location. In such a case we say that *ostrstream* has freezed itself. Once frozen we can't add any more characters to it. Adding characters to a frozen *ostrstream* results in undefined behavior. In addition, the *ostrstream* is no longer responsible for cleaning up the storage. You took over that responsibility when you asked for the *char ** with *str( )*.

We can clean the storage in two ways:

(a) Using the *delete* operator as shown below:

```
ostrstream s ;
char *p ;
p = s.str( ) ;
delete p ;
```

(b) By unfreezing the *ostrstream*. You do this by calling *freeze( )*, with an argument *1*. During freezing it is called with the default argument of 0.

The following program puts both these methods into action.

```
#include <strstream>
#include <iostream>
using namespace std ;

int main( )
{
    ostrstream s1, s2 ;

    s1 << "If you can't digest this..." << ends ;
    char *p = s1.str( ) ;
    delete p ;

    s2 << endl << "You must always know," << ends ;
    p = s2.str( ) ;
    s2.rdbuf( )->freeze ( 0 ) ;

    s2.seekp ( -1, ios::cur ) ;
    s2 << endl << "What is it that you do not know." << ends ;
    cout << s2.rdbuf( ) ;
    return 0 ;
```

```
}
```

The first method is straightforward. In the second method the *ostrstream* gets frozen on calling *str( )*. Now the storage cannot be deallocated when *s2* goes out of scope. Also, we can't add more characters to it. To be able to add more characters to it we got to defreeze it. This we have done through the call

```
s2.rdbuf( )->freeze ( 0 ) ;
```

Here *rdbuf( )* fetches the underlying *streambuf* pointer.

Before adding more characters we have moved the *put* pointer to position it on '\0' so that it gets overwritten. Next we have added some more characters. When *s2* goes out of scope the cleanup will now occur automatically, through the destructor.

Note that the pointer obtained when *s2* was frozen should not be used now. Adding more characters must have caused the memory block to move, so the pointer is no longer reliable.

Sending Output To Printer

Most operating systems define special filenames for standard hardware devices. Some of these predefined filenames are shown in Figure 11.13. Using these filenames we can treat the devices as if they were files. Thus doing I/O with the devices is as straight as doing I/O with the files associated with them.

Name	Device
con	Console (keyboard and screen)
aux or com1	First serial port
com2	Second serial port
prn or lpt1	First parallel printer
lpt2	Second parallel printer
lpt3	Third parallel printer
nul	Dummy (nonexistent) device

Figure 11.13

In most systems the printer is connected to the first parallel port, so the filename for the printer should be *prn* or *lpt1*. (You can substitute the appropriate name if your system has a different configuration).

The following program prints the contents of a disk file on the printer. It is a simple matter of reading a character from one file and sending it to another. After printing the entire file contents a The '\x0C' is sent to the printer. This causes the page to eject from the printer. This program can be used to print any text file.

```
#include <fstream>
#include <iostream>
#include <cstdlib>
using namespace std ;

int main( )
{
    char filename[67] ;

    cout << endl << "Enter filename" ;
    cin >> filename ;

    ifstream infile ( filename ) ;
```

```
    if ( ! infile )
    {
        cerr << endl << "Unable to open file" << endl ;
        exit ( 1 ) ;
    }

    ofstream outfile ( "PRN" ) ;
    if ( ! outfile )
    {
        cerr << endl << "Unable to open file" << endl ;
        exit ( 2 ) ;
    }

    char ch ;
    while ( infile.get ( ch ) != 0 )
        outfile.put ( ch ) ;

    outfile.put ( '\x0C' ) ;
    return 0 ;
}
```

Exercise

[A] State True or False:

(a) In the *iostream* library the *ios* class is at the root.

(b) Some of the *ios* flags can be set either through the *setf( )* function or through the manipulators.

(c) Only for those manipulators which need an argument we need to include the file 'iomanip.h'.

(d) When we are using a manipulator we are in fact calling a member function.

(e) It is possible to create your own manipulators.

(f) The *istream_withassign* class has been derived from the *istream* class and overloaded assignment operator has been added to it.

(g) *cout*, *cin* and *cprn* are predefined stream objects.

(h) Objects can read and write themselves.

(i) *strstreams* serve the same purpose as *sprintf( )* and *sscanf( )*.

(j) The *istream::getline( )* function cannot tackle multi-words strings.

[B] Answer the following:

(a) What are the disadvantages of using *scanf( )/printf( )* functions?

(b) Draw a chart showing hierarchy of various classes in the *iostream* library.

(c) What are the three parts of an *iostream* system?

(d) Why is *ios::* necessary in the following statement:

```
cout << setiosflags ( ios::showbase ) ;
```

(e) How can the following statement work for testing the end of file, if *infile* is an *ifstream* object:

```
while ( infile ) ;
```

(f) What do the *nocreate* and *noreplace* flag ensure when they are used for opening a file?

(g) What problem do you think would we face if the following code is executed twice:

```
file.seekg ( 0L, ios::beg ) ;
while ( file.read ( char * ) &p, sizeof ( p ) )
    cout << t.name << endl << p.age ;
```

How would you solve the problem ?

(h) How would you obtain the value of a *state* variable?

[C] What would be the output:

(a)
```
#include <iostream>
using namespace std ;

int main( )
{
    char str[ ] = "The boring stuff" ;
    char *p = "That's interesting" ;
    cout << endl << str ;
    cout << endl << p ;
```

```
    cout << endl << ( void * ) str ;
    cout << endl << ( void * ) p ;
    return 0 ;
}
```

(b)
```
#include <iostream>
using namespace std ;

int main( )
{
    int i = 650 ;
    float a = 425.123 ;
    cout << setiosflags ( ios::showbase | ios::uppercase ) ;
    cout << hex << i << endl ;
    cout.precision ( 4 ) ;
    cout << setiosflags ( ios::showpoint ) << a ;
    return 0 ;
}
```

(c)
```
#include <iostream>
using namespace std ;

int main( )
{
    char str[ ] = "Just listing" ;
    cout.width ( 40 ) ;
    cout << str << endl ;
    cout.setf ( ios::left, ios::adjustfield ) ;
    cout.width ( 40 ) ;
    cout << str ;
    return 0 ;
}
```

[D] Attempt the Following:

(a) Write a program that will create a manipulator with arguments. If row number and column number are passed as arguments to this manipulator it should position the cursor at that row and column.

(b) There are 100 records present in a file with each record containing a 6-character item code, a 20-character item name and an integer quantity. Write a program to read these records, arrange them in the ascending order and write them in the same file overwriting the earlier records.

CHAPTER TWELVE

Advanced Features

This chapter covers a collection of topics that a beginner would usually not be faced with. But as you spend more time in C++ programming you would start appreciating the utility of these concepts. I plan to cover here topics like containership, friend functions, overloading insertion/extraction operators, smart pointers, pointers to members, *explicit* and *mutable* keywords, namespaces, RTTI and the new casting syntax. Let's begin with containership.

Classes Within Classes

If two classes are related with one another there can be two types of relationships between them: a *kind of* relationship or a *has a* relationship. The *kind of* relationship is supported by inheritance, whereas, the *has a* relationship is supported by *composition* or *containership*.

In inheritance if a class *Y* is derived from class *X*, we can say that the new class *Y* is like that old class *X*. Or in other words "*Y* is a kind of *X*". This is because the class *Y* has all the characteristics of *X*, and in addition some of its own. It is like saying a car is a kind of automobile: a car has the characteristics shared by all automobiles (has wheels and engine, runs on fuel etc.) but has some distinctive characteristics of its own (such as a four stroke engine and a steering wheel). For this reason inheritance is often called a *kind of* relationship.

In a *has a* relationship you simply create objects of your existing class inside the new class. For example, if there is a class called *carburettor* we can create an object of this class in the new class *car* as shown below.

```
class carburettor
{
};
```

```
class car
{
    carburettor c ;
} ;
```

Actually, we have been using composition in almost every class designed so far. We were composing classes using built-in types. Using composition with user-defined types is equally straightforward, as you would realise in the following program.

```
#include <iostream>
#include <string>
using namespace std ;

class carburettor
{
    private :

        char type ;
        float cost ;
        char mfr[30] ;

    public :

        void setdata ( char t, float c, char *m )
        {
            type = t ;
            cost = c ;
            strcpy ( mfr, m ) ;
        }

        void displaydata( )
        {
            cout << endl << type << endl << cost << endl << mfr << endl ;
        }
} ;
```

```
class car
{
    private :

        char model[25] ;
        char drivetype[20] ;

    public :

        void setdata ( char *m, char *d )
        {
            strcpy ( model, m ) ;
            strcpy ( drivetype, d ) ;
        }

        void displaydata( )
        {
            cout << endl << model << endl << drivetype << endl ;
        }

        carburettor c ;  // embedded object
} ;

int main( )
{
    car mycar ;
    mycar.c.setdata ( 'A', 8500.00, "Mico" ) ;
    mycar.setdata ( "sports", "4-wheel" ) ;

    mycar.c.displaydata( ) ;
    mycar.displaydata( ) ;
    return 0 ;
}
```

Since the data members of the *carburettor* class are *private* it is completely safe to embed an object of type *carburettor* as a *public* object in the new class *car*. To access the member functions of the *carburettor* class we simple have to use the '.' operator twice.

In composition it is more common to make the embedded objects *private*. This permits us to make a change in the implementation of the embedded object, if required. For example, in the following program the function *carburettor::displaydata( )* is retained as it is in the *car* class's interface, but the functions *setcarbudata( )* and *getcost( )* have been used within member functions of *car*, thereby changing the interface.

```
#include <iostream>
#include <string>
using namespace std ;

class carburettor
{
    private :

        char type ;
        float cost ;
        char mfr[30] ;

    public :

        void setcarbudata ( char t, float c, char *m )
        {
            type = t ;
            cost = c ;
            strcpy ( mfr, m ) ;
        }

        void displaydata( )
        {
```

```
        cout << endl << type << endl << cost << endl << mfr << endl ;
    }

    float getcost( )
    {
        return cost ;
    }
} ;

class car
{
    private :

        char model[25] ;
        char drivetype[20] ;
        carburettor cc ;  // embedded object

    public :

        void setdata ( char t, float c, char *mf, char *m, char *d )
        {
            strcpy ( model, m ) ;
            strcpy ( drivetype, d ) ;
            cc.setcarbudata( t, c, mf ) ;
        }

        void displaydata( )
        {
            cout << endl << model << endl << drivetype << endl ;
        }

        float getcost( )
        {
            return 2 * cc.getcost( ) ;
        }

} ;
```

```
int main( )
{
    car mycar ;
    mycar.setdata ( 'A', 8500.00, "Mico", "sports", "4-wheel" ) ;

    mycar.displaydata( ) ;
    cout << endl << mycar.getcost( ) << endl ;
    return 0 ;
}
```

Which One To Use

If we are to do code reuse in C we have two ways:

(a) Copy code and change it
(b) Use good libraries

Both the approaches haven't worked very well. C++ has much more sophisticated mechanisms for code reuse in the form of composition and inheritance. Both permit reuse of existing classes without changing their existing code. Composition is useful when classes act like a data type. Then an object of that type can be used in a class in almost the same way as a basic type like *int* would be. Other situations would demand a more close examination of the problem. Often inheritance is simpler to implement and doesn't blur the clear-cut class boundaries.

friend Functions

So far we have learnt that that only member functions can access *private* data of a class. This is the essence of data encapsulation. However, sometimes we have to make an exception to this rule to avoid programming inconvenience. At such times we have to allow functions outside a class to access and manipulate the class's data members. To achieve this C++ provides a keyword called *friend*. It permits a function or all the functions of another class to read and write the original class's *private* data members.

Suppose we want a function to operate on objects of two different classes. If the two classes are inherited from the same base class, then we may be able to put the function in the base class. But what if the classes are unrelated? This is an ideal situation where a *friend* function can be used as a bridge between two classes. The following program will help you in understanding how this concept is put to work.

```
#include <iostream>
using namespace std ;

class two ;

class one
{
    private :

        int data1 ;

    public :

        one( )
        {
            data1 = 100 ;
        }

        friend int accessboth ( one, two ) ;
} ;

class two
{
    private:
```

```
        int data2 ;
    public:
        two( )
        {
            data2 = 200 ;
        }
        friend int accessboth ( one, two ) ;
};

int accessboth ( one a, two b )
{
    return ( a.data1 + b.data2 ) ;
}

int main( )
{
    one a ;
    two b ;
    cout << accessboth ( a, b ) << endl ;
    return 0 ;
}
```

Here, we have declared two classes *one* and *two*. The constructors in these classes initialize their *private* data items to a fixed value (*100* in *one* and *200* in *two*). We want the function *accessboth( )* to have access to both these *private* data members. Hence we have made it a *friend* function. It has been declared with the *friend* keyword in both the classes as,

```
friend int frifunc ( alpha, beta ) ;
```

This declaration can be placed either in the *private* section or the *public* section of the class.

An object of each class has been passed as an argument to the function *accessboth( )*. Being a *friend* function it can access the *private* data member of both classes through these arguments. Though the function doesn't do much, I think the program serves to illustrate the concept.

A function like *accessboth( )* is often called a global friend function. It doesn't belong to either of the two classes (otherwise in its definition we would have been required to use *one::accessboth* or *two::accessboth*) but can access *private* data of both of them. Note that the *friend* declaration is necessary in both the classes. Try commenting it out from class *one*. Immediately the compiler would flash an error that it can't access *data1*, which belongs to class *one*.

Note that the function *accessboth( )* has not been declared as global. This is because when we mention *friend* in the class it declares the function and also gives it a *friend* status.

Observe the declaration at the beginning of the program:

```
class two ;
```

This declaration is necessary since a class can't be referred to until it has been declared. Class *two* is being referred to in the declaration of the function *accessboth( )* in class one. So *two* must be declared before one. This declaration tells the compiler that the class *two* is defined later.

Overloading << And >>

In the last chapter we said that we can overload >> and << to perform I/O for user-defined types. For example, if we have an object *c1* of class *complex*, then we can display it through the statement

```
cout << c1 ;
```

Or we can read it by saying,

```
cin >> c1 ;
```

This makes the user-defined types' handling similar to that of basic data types. The following program shows how this overloading can be achieved.

```
#include <iostream>
using namespace std ;

class complex
{
    private :

        double real, imag ;

    public :

        complex( )
        {
        }

        complex ( double r, double i )
        {
            real = r ;
            imag = i ;
        }

        friend ostream& operator << ( ostream& s, complex& c ) ;
        friend istream& operator >> ( istream& s, complex& c ) ;
} ;

ostream& operator << ( ostream& s, complex& c )
{
    s << "( " << c.real << ", " << c.imag << " )" ;
    return s ;
```

```
}

istream& operator >> ( istream& s, complex& c )
{
	s >> c.real >> c.imag ;
	return s ;
}

int main( )
{
	complex c1 ( 1.5, 2.5 ), c2 ( 3.5, 4.5 ), c3 ;
	cout << endl << "c1 = " << c1 << endl << "c2 = " << c2 ;
	cout << endl << "Enter a complex number: " ;
	cin >> c3 ;
	cout << "c3 = " << c3 << endl ;
	return 0 ;
}
```

You may note that the statements

```
cout << endl << "c1 = " << c1 << endl << "c2 = " << c2 ;
cout << endl << "Enter a complex number: " ;
cin >> c3 ;
cout << "c3 = " << c3 ;
```

are much more expressive and are similar to the way we would perform I/O with standard data types.

Here we have defined two *friend* functions *operator << ( )* and *operator >> ( )*. Since the *friend* declaration of these functions occurs only in the *complex* class and not in *istream* or *ostream* classes these functions can access only the private data of the *complex* class.

The operator functions are not members of the class *complex*. Hence the statement *cin >> c3 doesn't* get converted into the form

```
cin.operator >> ( c3 )
```

The object on either side of >> gets passed to the operator function. Both are collected as references. This prevents creation of copies of these objects. The *complex* object accesses the *private* data of the *complex* class. The function returns the *istream* object by reference to permit cascading, as in

```
cin >> c4 >> c5 ;
```

Exactly same argument applies to the *operator << ( )* function.

One More Use Of *friend* Function

Friend functions are useful in two situations:

(a) To access *private* data of a class from a non-member function.

(b) To increase the versatility of overloaded operators.

In the last section we saw the usage of the friend functions in the first situation mentioned above. Let us now try to understand the second situation. Consider the following program.

```
#include <iostream>
using namespace std ;

class example
{
    private :

        int i ;
        float j ;
```

```
    public :

        example( )
        {
            i = 0 ;
            j = 0.0 ;
        }

        example ( int ii )
        {
            i = ii ;
            j = 0.0 ;
        }

        example ( int ii, float jj )
        {
            i = ii ;
            j = jj ;
        }

        void showdata( )
        {
            cout << i << "  " << j << endl ;
        }
        example operator * ( example ) ;
} ;

example example :: operator * ( example e )
{
    example temp ;
    temp.i = i * e.i ;
    temp.j = j * e.j ;
    return ( temp ) ;
}

int main( )
```

```
{
    example e1 ( 10, 3.14f ), e2 ( 2, 1.5f ), e3, e4, e5 ;
    e3 = e1 * e2 ;
    e4 = e1 * 2 ;
    e3.showdata( ) ;
    e4.showdata( ) ;
    // e5 = 2 * e1 ; // int * example causes an error
    return 0 ;
}
```

In this program we have defined a class *example* having an *int* and a *float* as its *private* data members. There are three constructors: zero-argument, one-argument and two-argument. There also exists an overloaded * operator to multiply two objects of type *example*.

When we use a statement like

```
e4 = e1 * 2 ;
```

internally it becomes

```
e4 = e1.operator * ( 2 )
```

The *2* being passed to the operator function needs to be converted to an object of the type *example*. The compiler will use the one-argument constructor to convert this *int* to a *example* value, and then carry out the multiplication.

Would the following statement work?

```
e5 = 2 * e1 ;
```

No, because internally this would become

```
e5 = 2.operator ( e1 ) ;
```

which would not make any sense since *2* is not an object to begin with. The compiler can't handle this situation hence it flashes an error. A *friend* can help you out in this situation. The following program shows how this can be achieved.

```
#include <iostream>
using namespace std ;

class example
{
    private :

        int i ;
        float j ;

    public :

        example( )
        {
            i = 0 ;
            j = 0.0 ;
        }

        example ( int ii )
        {
            i = ii ;
            j = 0.0 ;
        }

        example ( int ii, float jj )
        {
            i = ii ;
            j = jj ;
        }

        void showdata( )
        {
            cout << endl << i << endl  << j << endl ;
        }

        friend example operator * ( example, example ) ;
```

```
};

example operator * ( example k, example l )
{
    example temp ;

    temp.i = k.i * l.i ;
    temp.j = k.j * l.j ;
    return ( temp ) ;
}

int main( )
{
    example e1 ( 10, 3.14f ), e2 ( 1, 1.5f ), e3, e4, e5 ;

    e3 = e1 * 2 ;
    e4 = 2 * e2 ;
    e5 = e1 * e2 * 2 ;

    e1.showdata( ) ;
    e2.showdata( ) ;
    e3.showdata( ) ;
    e4.showdata( ) ;
    e5.showdata( ) ;
    return 0 ;
}
```

Note that, in the previous program the *operator *( )* function took only one argument, whereas in this program it takes two. This is because the operator function is no longer a member function of the class. It is a *friend* of the class *example*. Thus the statement

```
e3 = e1 * 2 ;
```

doesn't take the form *e3.operator * (2)*.

This program shows that using *friend* permits the overloaded operators to be more versatile.

friend Classes

If we make the entire class as a *friend* then automatically all the member functions of the class become *friend*s. This is shown in the following program.

```
#include <iostream>
using namespace std ;

class two ;

class one
{
    private :

        int i ;

    public :

        one( )
        {
            i = 10 ;
        }

        friend two ;
} ;

class two
{
    public :

        void fun1 ( one o )
        {
```

```
        cout << endl << o.i << endl ;
    }

    void fun2 ( one o )
    {
        cout << endl << o.i << endl ;
    }
} ;

int main( )
{
    one a ;
    two b ;

    b.fun1 ( a ) ;
    b.fun2 ( a ) ;
    return 0 ;
}
```

In class *one* we have declared the entire class *two* as a *friend*. As a result, all the member functions of *two* can access the *private* data of *one*.

A Word Of Caution

Usage of *friend* functions is controversial. Though it adds flexibility to the language and makes programming convenient in certain situations, it goes against the philosophy that only member functions can access a class's *private* data. Unless you have the source code of the class you cannot make the declaration of the *friend* functions inside that class. Thus the integrity of the class is not violated to a great extent.

C++ is not a pure OO language. Facility to access *private* data from outside the class through *friend*s is one of the reasons for it.

But then C++ was designed to solve practical programming problems, not to win prizes for purity. If *friends* violate a few lofty ideals but serves programming convenience, so be it.

On the flip side, if you find yourself using many *friends*, then maybe there is a basic flaw in the design of your program and you would be better off redesigning it.

Smart Pointers

A *container* is a way to organize data in memory. Hence stacks, linked lists, arrays are all containers. An *iterator* is an object that moves through a container accessing various elements of the container. The process of moving from element to element is called *iteration*. Hence the object that permits you to do this is called an *iterator*.

We can iterate through an ordinary C++ array by using a pointer as shown below.

```
#include <iostream>
using namespace std ;

int main( )
{
    const int MAX = 5 ;
    int arr[ MAX] = { 10, 20, 30, 40, 50 } ;
    int *p ;

    p = arr ;
    for ( int i = 0 ; i < MAX ; i++ )
    {
        cout << *p << endl ;
        p++ ;
    }
```

```
    return 0 ;
}
```

However, with more sophisticated containers plain C++ pointers won't work. If the items stored in a container are not placed in adjacent memory locations, incrementing the pointer becomes complicated. For example, moving to the next node in the linked list doesn't merely involve incrementing a pointer. We have to follow the link to the next node. The solution to this is to create a class of *smart* pointers.

An object of a smart pointer class wraps its member functions around an ordinary pointer. The + and the * operator are overloaded in this class. So it knows how to tackle situations when the container elements are not in adjacent memory locations. Iterators are thus nothing but objects of the smart pointer class. The typical skeleton of the smart pointer class is shown below.

```
class smartpointer
{
    private :

        int *p ;  // ordinary pointer

    public :

        int operator ++ ( int n )
        {
        }

        int operator * ( )
        {
        }
} ;
```

The following program illustrates the use so smart pointers in accessing various nodes of a linked list.

```
#include <iostream>
using namespace std ;

class container
{
    private :

        struct node
        {
            int data ;
            node *link ;
        } *head, *current ;

        int count ;

    public :

        container( )
        {
            head = current = NULL ;
            count = 0 ;
        }

        void add ( int n )
        {
            node *temp = new node ;
            temp -> data = n ;
            temp -> link = NULL ;

            if ( head == NULL )
                head = current = temp ;
            else
            {
```

```
                node *q ;
                q = head ;

                while ( q -> link != NULL )
                    q = q -> link ;

                q -> link = temp ;
            }

            count++ ;
        }

        int getcount( )
        {
            return count ;
        }

        friend class smartpointer ;
} ;

class smartpointer
{
    private :

        container *cptr ;

    public :

        smartpointer ( container *t )
        {
            cptr = t ;
        }

        int operator *( )
        {
            if ( cptr->current == NULL )
                return NULL ;
```

```
            else
            {
                int i = cptr->current->data ;
                return i ;
            }
        }

        void operator ++ ( int n )
        {
            if ( cptr->current != NULL )
                cptr->current = cptr->current->link ;
        }

} ;

int main( )
{
    container c ;

    c.add ( 10 ) ;
    c.add ( 20 ) ;
    c.add ( 0 ) ;
    c.add ( -40 ) ;
    c.add ( 50 ) ;

    smartpointer sptr ( &c ) ;

    for ( int i = 0 ; i < c.getcount( ) ; i++ )
    {
        cout << *sptr << endl ;
        sptr++ ;
    }
    return 0 ;
}
```

Here the *container* class implements the linked list. It has three data members: *head*, *current* and *count*. Of these, *head* and *current* are pointers to nodes, whereas *count* is an integer. The *head* pointer always points to the first node in the linked list. If the linked list is empty *head* contains NULL. As the name suggests *current* always points to the current node in the list. The 'current node' means the one which would be returned if we say **current*. *count* keeps track of the number of nodes in the linked list. Every time a new node is added, the value of *count* is incremented by *1*.

The *smartpointer* class has been declared as a *friend* of the *container* class. This in effect means that all the member functions of the *smartpointer* class would have an access to the *private* data members of the *container* class.

In the *smartpointer* class we have two overloaded operator functions. The *operator * ( )* function returns the integer in the current node. The *operator ++ ( )* function advances the *current* pointer to point to the next node in the linked list.

In *main( )* we have added nodes to the linked list. Then we have built an object of *smartpointer* class through the statement

```
smartpointer sptr ( &c ) ;
```

The constructor sets up the *container c*'s address being passed to it in a *container* pointer. Using this pointer the member functions can access the *private* data members of the *container*.

The crux of the program is the *for* loop.

```
for ( int i = 0 ; i < c.getcount( ) ; i++ )
{
    cout << endl << *sptr ;
    sptr++ ;
}
```

Here *getcount( )* returns the number of nodes currently in the linked list. *cout << *sptr* invokes the overloaded *operator * ( )* function. This returns the integer contained in the node at which *current* is currently pointing. Through *sptr++* the *operator ++ ( )* function gets called. It moves *current* to make it point to the next node in the linked list.

More Smart Pointers

Another use of smart pointer is to make an object appear like a pointer. This offers programming convenience. To understand its usage firstly we would write a program without using smart pointers and then we would improve it by incorporating smart pointers. Here is the program without smart pointers.

```
#include <iostream>
using namespace std ;

class sample
{
    private :

        int i ;
        float a ;

    public :

        sample( )
        {
        }

        sample ( int ii, float aa )
        {
            i = ii ;
            a = aa ;
```

```
        }

        void fun1( )
        {
            cout << endl << i << endl << a << endl ;
        }

        void fun2( )
        {
            cout << endl << i * a << endl ;
        }
} ;

class container
{
    private :

        enum { size  = 100 } ;
        sample *arr[size] ;
        int count ;

    public :

        container( )
        {
            count = 0 ;
            memset ( arr, 0, size * sizeof ( sample * ) ) ;
        }

        void add ( int ii, float aa )
        {
            if ( count >= size )
                return ;

            arr[count] = new sample ( ii, aa ) ;
            count++ ;
        }
```

```
        int getcount( )
        {
            return count ;
        }

        friend class smartpointer ;
} ;

class smartpointer
{
    private :

        container *c ;

    public :

        smartpointer ( container *pctr )
        {
            c = pctr ;
        }

        sample * getaddress ( int i )
        {
            return c->arr[i] ;
        }
} ;

int main( )
{
    container c ;

    c.add ( 10, 3.14f ) ;
    c.add ( 20, 6.28f) ;
    c.add ( 30, 9.45f ) ;
    c.add ( 40, 8.66f ) ;
```

```
    smartpointer sp ( &c ) ;

    for ( int i = 0 ; i < c.getcount( ) ; i++ )
    {
        sp.getaddress ( i ) -> fun1( ) ;
        sp.getaddress ( i ) -> fun2( ) ;
    }
    return 0 ;
}
```

Here we have a class called *sample* whose objects are stored in an array of pointers in the *container* class. The storage is done through the *container::add( )* function. To access the functions *sample::fun1( )* and *sample::fun2( )* we have to use a clumsy syntax:

```
c.getaddress ( i ) -> fun1( ) ;
c.getaddress ( i ) -> fun2( ) ;
```

Instead, if we overload the -> operator then we can use a more clean syntax like:

```
sp->fun1( ) ;
sp->fun2( ) ;
```

The beauty of the whole thing lies in the fact that even though *sp* is an object we can make it work like a pointer. Moreover, even though *fun1( )* and *fun2( )* are not member functions of the *smartpointer* class we can still call them in a direct way. The overloaded *operator ->* is often called a smart pointer operator. The full-fledged program is given below:

```
#include <iostream>
using namespace std ;

class sample
{
    private :

        int i ;
        float a ;

    public :

        sample( )
        {
        }

        sample ( int ii, float aa )
        {
            i = ii ;
            a = aa ;
        }

        void fun1( )
        {
            cout << endl << i << endl << a << endl ;
        }

        void fun2( )
        {
            cout << endl << i * a << endl ;
        }
} ;

class container
{
    private :
```

```
        enum { size  = 100 } ;
        sample *arr[size] ;
        int index ;

    public :

        container( )
        {
            index = 0 ;
            memset ( arr, 0, size * sizeof ( sample * ) ) ;
        }

        void add ( int ii, float aa )
        {
            if ( index >= size )
                return ;

            arr[index] = new sample ( ii, aa ) ;
            index++ ;
        }

        friend class smartpointer ;
} ;

class smartpointer
{
    private :

        container *c ;
        int index ;

    public :

        smartpointer ( container *pctr )
        {
            c = pctr ;
            index = 0 ;
```

```
        }

        int operator ++ ( int n )
        {
            if ( index >= c->size )
                return 0 ;

            index++ ;
            if ( c -> arr[index] == 0 )
                return 0 ;

            return 1 ;
        }

        sample * operator -> ( )
        {
            if ( c -> arr[index] )
                return c->arr[index] ;

            static sample dummy ;
            return &dummy ;
        }
};

int main( )
{
    container c ;
    c.add ( 10, 3.14f ) ;
    c.add ( 20, 6.28f ) ;
    c.add ( 30, 9.45f ) ;
    c.add ( 40, 8.66f ) ;

    smartpointer sptr ( &c ) ;

    do
    {
        sptr->fun1( ) ;
```

```
        sptr->fun2( ) ;
    } while ( sptr++ ) ;
    return 0 ;
}
```

The crux of the program lies in the fact that even though *fun1( )* and *fun2( )* are not members of the *smartpointer* class, the smart pointer mechanism calls those functions for *sample* * that is returned by the *operator -> ( )* function. The compiler performs all the checking to ensure that the function call works properly. Note that the overloaded smart pointer operator must be a member function. Also it must return either an object or its address.

Although the underlying working of the smart pointer is complex, it provides a convenient syntax, which perhaps outweighs the complexity.

Pointers To Members

We know that to access a structure member we use a '.' or a '->' operator. Also, to dereference a pointer we use the * operator. Following example shows this at work.

```
int i ;
int *ptr ;
struct emp
{
    char name ;
    int age ;
} ;
emp e, *empptr ;
ptr = &i ;

cout << *ptr ; // dereferencing
cout << e.name ; // access
```

```
cout << empptr -> name ; // access
```

If we want we can set up pointers to particular members of a structure. Since the elements of a structure are laid out in contiguous memory locations, the address of any structure element is really an offset from the starting address of the structure. Now to access the structure element through this pointer we need '.' or '->' to reach the element and '*' to dereference the pointer. To carry out the access and the dereferencing simultaneously, C++ provides two new operators: '.*' and '->*'. These are known as *pointer to member* operators. The following program shows their usage.

```
#include <iostream>
using namespace std ;

struct sample
{
	int a ;
	float b ;
} ;

int main( )
{
	int sample::*p1 = &sample::a ;
	float sample::*p2 = &sample::b ;

	sample so = { 10, 3.14f } ;
	cout << endl << so.*p1 << endl << so.*p2 ;

	sample *sp ;
	sp = &so ;
	cout << endl << sp->*p1 << endl << sp->*p2 ;

	// we can even assign new values
	so.*p1 = 20 ;
```

```
    sp->*p2 = 6.28f ;
    cout << endl << so.*p1 << endl << so.*p2 ;
    cout << endl << sp->*p1 << endl << sp->*p2 ;

    sample soarr[ ] = {
                        { 30, 9.22f },
                        { 40, 7.33f },
                        { 60, 8.88f }
                      };

    for ( int i =0 ; i <= 2 ; i++ )
        cout << soarr[i].*p1 << endl << soarr[i].*p2 << endl ;
    return 0 ;
}
```

Note the definition of the pointers *p1* and *p2*:

```
int sample::*p1 = &sample::a ;
float sample::*p2 = &sample::b
```

Consider the part before the assignment operator. The stars indicate that *p1* and *p2* are pointers. *sample::* indicates they are pointers to an *int* and a *float* within *sample*. We have also initialised these pointers while declaring them, with addresses of *a* and *b* respectively.

Really speaking there is no "address of" *sample::a* because we are referring to a class and not to an object of that class. *&sample::a* merely produces an offset into the class. The actual address would be produced when we combine that offset with the starting address of a particular object.

Hence *&sample::a* is nothing more than the syntax of pointer to member. If we use *p1* and *p2* with one object we would get one set of values, if we use it with another we would get another set of values. This is what is shown towards the end of the program, where we have built an array of objects and accessed all objects' elements using *p1* and *p2*. Moral is that the pointers to members are not tied with any specific object.

On the left hand side of '.*' there would always be a structure variable (object) or a reference and on the left hand side of '->*' there would always be a pointer to a structure (object).

Go through the following program carefully. I think it would help you fix your ideas about pointers to members.

```
#include <iostream>
#include <windows.h>
using namespace std ;

struct sample
{
    int a ;
    float b ;
    int *c ;
    float *d ;
    int **e ;
    float **f ;
};

int main( )
{
    int sample::*p1 = &sample::a ;
    float sample::*p2 = &sample::b ;

    int * sample::*p3 = &sample::c ;
    float * sample::*p4 = &sample::d ;

    int ** sample::*p5 = &sample::e ;
    float ** sample::*p6 = &sample::f ;
```

```
    sample so = { 10, 3.14f, &so.a, &so.b, &so.c, &so.d } ;
    sample *sp ;

    sp = &so ;

    sytem ( "cls" ) ;

    cout << endl << so.*p1 << endl << so.*p2 ;
    cout << endl << * ( so.*p3 ) << endl << *(so.*p4) ;
    cout << endl << ** ( so.*p5 ) << endl << ** ( so.*p6 ) ;

    cout << endl << sp->*p1 << endl << sp->*p2 ;
    cout << endl << * ( sp->*p3 ) << endl << * ( sp->*p4 ) ;
    cout << endl << ** ( sp->*p5 ) << endl << ** ( sp->*p6 ) ;

    // store new values
    * ( so.*p3 ) = 20 ;
    ** ( sp->*p6 ) = 6.28f ;

    // output changed values through p1 and p2
    cout << endl << so.*p1 << endl << so.*p2 << endl ;
    return 0 ;
}
```

You may have understood the concept of pointers to members, but two questions still remain unanswered:

(a) Why should we use them?

(b) If we use them with classes then won't we be required to make our data *public*?

Let me answer the second one first. We would certainly be required to make the data *public*. And this would violate the rules of encapsulation. Hence pointer to members are more often used with member functions (which are usually *public*) rather than the data members of a class.

Now the answer to the first one. By using pointers to members we can have the flexibility of choosing a member function to be called, at run time. This permits us to select or change the behaviour at run time. Sounds abstract? Well, you would soon understand it. For that firstly we will have to understand a pointer to a function. The following program shows how it works.

```
#include <iostream>
using namespace std ;

int main( )
{
    void fun ( int, float ) ;
    void ( *p ) ( int, float ) ;
    p = fun ;
    ( *p ) ( 10, 3.14f ) ;
    return 0 ;
}

void fun ( int a, float b )
{
    cout << endl << a << endl << b << endl ;
}
```

Here *p* is a pointer to a function that receives an *int* and a *float* and returns a *void*. Note that the parentheses around **p* are necessary. In their absence *p* would become a function that receives an *int* and a *float* and return a *void* *.

We have initialised *p* to address of the function *fun( )*. Mentioning the function name without a pair of parentheses gives its address in memory. If we want, we can still use the & operator to take the address:

```
p = &fun ;
```

The syntax for calling *fun( )* using *p* is as follows:

```
( *p )( 10, 3.14 ) ;
```

If we want we can have even an array of pointers to functions and then call each function in turn using this array. The following code snippet shows this.

```
void ( *p[3] ) ( int, float ) = { fun1, fun2, fun3 } ;
for ( int i = 0 ; i <= 2 ; i++ )
    ( *p[ i ] ) ( 14 + i, 5.54 + i ) ;
```

One basic condition for this code to work is that the prototypes of functions *fun1( )*, *fun2( )* and *fun3( )* must be same, otherwise we cannot gather their addresses in the array *p[ ]*.

Let's now go a step further. Let's make *fun1( )*, *fun2( )* and *fun3( )* *public* members of class *sample* and then try to call them in a manner similar to the one shown above.

```
#include <iostream>
using namespace std ;

class sample
{
    public :

        void fun1( )
        {
            cout << endl << "  In Fun1" ;
        }
```

```
        void fun2( )
        {
            cout << endl << "  In Fun2" ;
        }

        void fun3( )
        {
            cout << endl << "  In Fun3" ;
        }
} ;

int main( )
{
    sample so ;
    void ( *p[3] )( ) = { fun1, fun2, fun3 } ;

    for ( int i = 0 ; i <= 2 ;i++ )
        ( so.*p[ i ] )( ) ;
    }
    return 0 ;
}
```

This program would not clear even the compilation hurdle. An error would be reported in the declaration of *p[ ]*. This is to be expected since we cannot refer to the member functions directly. The following two declarations would also be wrong.

```
void ( *p[3] )( ) = { fun1, fun2, fun3 } ;
void ( *p[3] )( ) = { so.fun1, so.fun2, so.fun3 } ;
```

The only way we can make the declaration work is:

```
void ( sample::*p[3] )( ) = { &sample::fun1, &sample::fun2, &sample::fun3 } ;
```

Now if we are to call the member functions using *p[ ]* the only way to do so is by using the *pointer to member* syntax. The following program shows how this can be done.

```
#include <iostream>
using namespace std ;

class sample
{
    public :

        void fun1( )
        {
            cout << endl << this << "  In fun1"  ;
        }

        void fun2( )
        {
            cout << endl << this << "  In fun2" ;
        }

        void fun3( )
        {
            cout << endl << this << "  In fun3" ;
        }
} ;

int main( )
{
    sample so[4] ;
    void (sample::*p[3] )( )={&sample::fun1, &sample::fun2, &sample::fun3} ;

    for ( int j = 0 ; j <= 3 ;j++ )
    {
        for ( int i = 0 ; i <= 2 ; i++ )
            ( so[ j ].*p[ i ] )( ) ;
```

```
    }
    return 0 ;
}
```

Using the '.*' syntax now we can call different member functions using different objects. While doing so we have also printed the address of each object with reference to whom the member function is being called. The output looks like this…

```
0x1feffff2 In fun1
0x1feffff2 In fun2
0x1feffff2 In fun3
0x1feffff3 In fun1
0x1feffff3 In fun2
0x1feffff3 In fun3
0x1feffff4 In fun1
0x1feffff4 In fun2
0x1feffff4 In fun3
0x1feffff5 In fun1
0x1feffff5 In fun2
0x1feffff5 In fun3
```

The *explicit* Keyword

In Chapter 7 we saw that data conversion from standard type to user-defined type is possible through conversion operator and the class's constructor. However, there may be some conversion which you want should *not* take place. It's easy to prevent conversion performed by the conversion operator: just don't define the operator. However, the same doesn't apply to the constructor. We may want it for building the object. At the same time you may want that it should not get used for carrying out conversions. Through the *explicit* keyword we can prevent such unwanted conversions. This keyword is available in Standard C++ and as on date may not be supported by some compilers. The following program shows the use of this keyword.

```
#include <iostream>
using namespace std ;

class complex
{
	private :

		float real, imag ;

	public :

		complex( )
		{
			real = imag = 0.0 ;
		}

		explicit complex ( float r, float i = 0.0 )
		{
			real = r ;
			imag = i ;
		}

		complex operator + ( complex c )
		{
			complex t ;
			t.real = real + c.real ;
			t.imag = imag + c.imag ;
			return t ;
		}

		void display( )
		{
			cout << endl << real << "  " << imag ;
```

```
    }
};

int main( )
{
    complex c1 ( 1.5, 3.5 ), c2 ;
    c2 = c1 + 1.25 ;
    c2.display( ) ;
    return 0 ;
}
```

In the statement

```
c2 = c1 + 1.25 ;
```

the compiler would find that here the overloaded *operator + ( )* functions should get called. When it finds that there is a wrong type on the right hand side of + it would look for a conversion function which can convert a *float* to *complex*. The two-argument constructor can meet this requirement. Hence the compiler would decide to call it. This is an implicit conversion, one that you may not have intended to make possible. We can prevent such implicit conversions by declaring the constructor as *explicit*. With this keyword in place now the compiler would report that it cannot do the conversion.

There is one small disadvantage, however. We can no longer create objects by saying,

```
complex c3 = 2.25 ;
```

Note that the *explicit* keyword works only with the constructors.

The *mutable* Keyword

When we create a *const* object none of its data members can change. In a rare situation, however, you may want some data member should be allowed to change despite the object being *const*. This can be achieved by the *mutable* keyword as shown in the following program.

```
#include <iostream>
#include <string>
using namespace std ;

class car
{
    private :

        char model[20] ;
        mutable char owner[30] ;
        int yrofmfg ;
        char regno[10] ;

    public :

        car ( char *m, char *o, int y, char *r )
        {
            strcpy ( model, m ) ;
            strcpy ( owner, o ) ;
            yrofmfg = y ;
            strcpy ( regno, r ) ;
        }

        void changeowner ( char *o ) const
        {
            strcpy ( owner, o ) ;
        }

        void changemodel ( char *m )
        {
            strcpy ( model, m ) ;
        }
```

```
        void display( ) const
        {
            cout << endl << model << endl
                << owner << endl
                << yrofmfg << endl
                << regno << endl ;
        }
} ;

int main( )
{
    const car c1 ( "VX", "Fundu", 2000, "MH31-G6175" ) ;
    c1.display( ) ;

    c1.changeowner ( "mahafundu" ) ;
    c1.display( ) ;

    // c1.changemodel ( "AX" ) ;
    c1.display( ) ;
    return 0 ;
}
```

When the car is sold its owner would change, rest of its attributes would remain same. Since the object *c1* is declared as *const* none of its data members can change. An exception is however made in case of *owner* since its declaration is preceded by the keyword *mutable*. The change is brought about through the function *changeowner( )*. Try removing the comment in *main( )*. This would result in an error as the *model* data member has not been declared as *mutable* and hence cannot be changed. Had *c1* been a non-*const* object we would have been allowed to change the *owner* as well as the *model*.

Namespaces

Trivial it may seem, but creating names is one of the most basic activities in programming. Variable names, function names, structure names, class names, union names, enumeration names, all fall under one general category: *names*. While writing big programs involving several programmers things are likely to go out of hand if proper control is not exercised over visibility of these names. For example, consider the following two header files.

```
// mylib.h
char fun1( ) ;
void display( ) ;
class bignumbers { ... } ;
```

```
// somelib.h
class bignumbers { ... } ;
void display( ) ;
```

If both these header files are included in a program; there would be a clash between the two *bignmuber* classes and the two *display( )* functions. One solution to this could be to create long names such that there is a less likelihood of a clash. But then you are required to type these long names. Moreover, it is a compromise solution invented by programmers and not a language supported solution. C++ offers a better solution to such problems through a keyword called *namespace*.

C++ provides a single global name space. We can subdivide the global name space into more manageable pieces using the *namespace* feature of C++. The following code shows how.

```
// mylib.h
namespace myheader
```

```
{
    char fun1( ) ;
    void display( ) ;
    class bignumbers { ... } ;
}
```

```
// somelib.h
namespace someLib
{
    class bignumbers { ... } ;
    void display( ) ;
}
```

Now the class names will not clash because they become *mylib::bignumbers* and *somelib::bignumbers*, respectively. Same thing would happen to the function names. They would become *mylib::display( )* and *somelib::display( )*, thereby avoiding a clash.

Thus it is now possible to use the same name in separate namespaces without conflict. As long as they appear in separate namespaces, each name will be unique because of the addition of the namespace identifier.

Now a few points worth noting about the namespaces:

(a) The syntax for creation of a *namespace* is similar to that of a class except for the semicolon beyond the closing brace.

(b) Declarations that fall outside all namespaces are still members of the global namespace.

(c) A namespace definition can be continued over multiple header files as shown below:

```
// mylib.h
namespace mylib
{
    char fun1( ) ;
    void display( ) ;
}


// mylib1.h
namespace mylib
{
    extern int var1 ;
    void display( ) ;
}
```

When a namespace is continued in this manner, after its initial definition, the continuation is called an *extension-namespace-definition*.

(d) We can give an alternative name for a namespace. This is often called a namespace-alias. This prevents typing of unwieldy names as shown below:

```
namespace hard_and_soft_library
{
    class hwitem
    {
    };

    class switem
    {
    };
}

namespace hwsw = hard_and_soft_library ;
```

(e) A global namespace-name cannot be the same as any other global entity name in a given program.

(f) Members of a namespace may be defined within that namespace. For example:

```
namespace a
{
    void f( )
    {
        // some code here
    }
}
```

(g) Members of a named namespace can be defined outside the namespace in which they are declared. In this case it is necessary to explicitly qualify the name being defined as shown below:

```
namespace mine
{
    void fun1( ) ;
}

void mine::fun1( )
{
}
```

(h) If a name in a namespace is being defined outside it, then the definition must appear after the point of declaration. For example:

```
void mine::fun2( )  // error, fun2( ) is not yet a member of mine
{
```

```
}

namespace mine
{
    void fun2( ) ;
}
```

(i) A namespace definition can only appear at the global scope. Thus the following code would cause an error.

```
int main( )
{
    namespace local         // error: not at global scope
    {
    }
    return 0 ;
}
```

(j) A namespace definition can be nested within another namespace definition. For example:

```
namespace outer
{
    int n = 6;
    int fun2( ) ;

    namespace Inner
    {
        float a = 3.14 ;
    }
}
```

Using A Namespace

There are two ways to refer to a name within a namespace:

(a) Using the scope resolution operator
(b) Through the *using* keyword

Let us understand these methods one by one.

Using Scope Resolution

We can specify any name in a namespace using the scope resolution operator, as shown below.

```
#include <iostream>
#include <string>
using namespace std ;

namespace mine
{
    class myclass
    {
        private :

            int yr ;

        public :

            void changeyear( ) ;
    } ;

    class yourclass ;
    void fun1( ) ;
}

void mine::myclass::changeyear( )
```

```
{
    yr = 2000 ;
    cout << "years don't change" ;
}

class mine::yourclass
{
    public :

        yourclass( ) ;
        void show( ) ;
} ;

mine::yourclass::yourclass( )
{
        cout << endl << "Reached yourclass's zero-argument constructor"
    << endl ;
}

void mine::yourclass::show( )
{
    cout << endl << "Do it. Then don't think about it" << endl ;
}

void mine::fun1( )
{
    cout << endl << "Be impulsive. Exercise Caution" << endl ;
}

int main( )
{
    mine::myclass m ;
    m.changeyear( ) ;

    mine::fun1( ) ;

    mine::yourclass y ;
```

```
    y.show( ) ;
    return 0 ;
}
```

To reach a name in a namespace using the scope resolution operator can get tedious soon. Better solution comes in the form of the *using* keyword.

The *using* Keyword

Instead of being required to use the scope resolution operator before every name, the *using* keyword allows you to import an entire namespace at once. Let us write the previous program on these lines and appreciate the convenience of this method.

```
#include <iostream>
#include <string>
using namespace std ;

namespace mine
{
    class myclass
    {
        private :

            int yr ;

        public :

            void changeyear( ) ;
    };

    class yourclass ;
    void fun1( ) ;
}
```

```
void mine::myclass::changeyear( )
{
    yr = 2000 ;
    cout << "years don't change" ;
}

class mine::yourclass
{
    public :

        yourclass( ) ;
        void show( ) ;
} ;

mine::yourclass::yourclass( )
{
        cout << endl << "Reached yourclass's zero-argument constructor"
    << endl ;
}

void mine::yourclass::show( )
{
    cout << endl << "Do it. Then don't think about it" << endl ;
}

void mine::fun1( )
{
    cout << endl << "Be impulsive. Exercise Caution" << endl ;
}

int main( )
{
    using namespace mine ;

    myclass m ;
    m.changeyear( ) ;
```

```
    fun1( ) ;
    yourclass y ;
    y.show( ) ;
    return 0 ;
}
```

The *using* keyword declares all the names in the namespace to be in the current scope. So we can use the names without any qualifiers.

RTTI

RTTI stands for *Run Time Type Identification*. In an inheritance hierarchy, using RTTI we can find the exact type of the object using a pointer or reference to the base class. The idea behind virtual functions is to upcast the derived class object's address into a pointer to a base class object and then let the virtual function mechanism implement the correct behaviour for that type. Does this mean that an attempt to know the type of the derived class object from the base class pointer (RTTI) a step backward? No. At times it is useful to know the exact type of the object from the base class pointer. You may require this information to perform some specific operation more efficiently.

There is also a practical reason for providing RTTI as a language feature. Most class libraries were using RTTI of some form internally. So if RTTI is made a language feature you would have a consistent syntax for each library and would not be required to worry whether it is built into a new library that you intend to use.

Knowing Types At Runtime

Let us take that classical example of virtual functions where we have a base class called *shape* and two classes—*circle* and *rectangle*—derived from it. Suppose that in an array of pointers to *shapes* we store the addresses of some *circle* and *rectangle* objects. Now using this array at runtime we want to determine whether the pointers in the array point to *circle* or *rectangle* objects. It means we want to identify the type at runtime. The following program shows an elementary way to do so.

```
#include <iostream>
#include <cstdlib>
#include <ctime>

using namespace std ;

class shape
{
    public :
        virtual char typeof( ) = 0 ;
};
class circle : public shape
{
    private :

        int xc, yc, radius ;

    public :

        circle ( int x, int y, int r )
        {
            xc = x ;
            yc = y ;
            radius = r ;
        }

        char typeof( )
        {
            return 'C' ;
        }
```

```
};

class rectangle : public shape
{
    private :

        int x1, y1, x2, y2 ;

    public :

        rectangle ( int xx1, int yy1, int xx2, int yy2 )
        {
            x1 = xx1 ;
            y1 = yy1 ;
            x2 = xx2 ;
            y2 = yy2 ;
        }

        char typeof( )
        {
            return 'R' ;
        }
};

int main( )
{
    shape *s[5] ;
    int i, num ;

    srand ( ( unsigned ) time( NULL ) ) ;

    for ( i = 0 ; i <= 4 ; i++ )
    {
        num = rand( ) % 2 ;
        if ( num == 0 )
            s[i] = new circle ( 10, 20, 15 ) ;
        else
```

```
            s[i] = new rectangle ( 11, 12, 15, 70 ) ;
    }

    for ( i = 0 ; i <= 4 ; i++ )
        cout << s[i]->typeof( ) << endl ;
    return 0 ;
}
```

To determine the type of object at runtime we have declared a pure virtual function called *typeof( )* in the *shape* class and provided its implementation in the derived classes. Depending upon which *typeof( )* gets called either a 'C' or a 'R' is returned.

Now let us understand when would we like to know the type at runtime. In context of our program we may want to change the colors of all circles, then through a loop we can ask 'if you are a circle, tell me so, I would then change your color'.

In different class libraries different function names may be present instead of *typeof( )*. Instead, if we use the C++ RTTI feature the syntax of our program would remain consistent irrespective of the class library that we use. Let us understand the C++ RTTI support now.

C++ RTTI Support

C++ provides two ways to obtain information about the object' class at runtime. These are:

(a) Using *typeid( )* operator
(b) Using the *dynamic_cast* operator

Let us explore them one by one.

typeid( )

This operator takes an object, a reference or a pointer and returns a reference to a global *const* object of the type *typeinfo*. The following program shows how to use it.

```
#include <typeinfo>
#include <iostream>
using namespace std ;

class base
{
    public :

        virtual void fun1( )
        {
        }
} ;

class myclass : public base
{
} ;

class yourclass : public base
{
} ;

int main( )
{
    base *b1 ;
    cout << endl << typeid ( b1 ).name( ) ;

    myclass m ;
    b1 = &m ;
    cout << endl << typeid ( *b1 ).name( ) ;
```

```
    base *b2 ;
    yourclass y ;
    b2 = &y ;
    cout << endl << typeid ( *b2 ).name( ) ;

    if ( typeid ( *b1 ) == typeid ( *b2 ) )
        cout << endl << "Equal" ;
    else
        cout << endl << "Unequal" ;

    cout << endl << typeid ( 45 ).name( ) ;
    cout << endl << typeid ( '4' ).name( ) ;
    cout << endl << typeid ( 4.5 ).name( ) << endl ;
    return 0 ;
}
```

Here is the output of the program…

```
Class base *
Class myclass
Class yourclass
Unequal
int
char
double
```

Here we have a base class called *base*. We have derived two classes from it: *myclass* and *yourclass*. Then we have created two pointers to the base class objects: *b1* and *b2*. We can ask for the name of the type using the function *name( )*. It returns a string indicating the typename. When we pass it on a *base* * it returns the name "base". If we want the exact type it is pointing to we must dereference the pointer as in,

```
cout << endl << typeid ( *b1 ).name( ) ;
```

The return value of *typeid( )* can also be compared using == and != operators as show below:

```
if ( typeid ( *b1 ) == typeid ( *b2 ) )
    cout << endl << "Equal" ;
else
    cout << endl << "Unequal" ;
```

For the sake of consistency, we can use *typeid( )* with built-in types as well. Hence towards the end of the program we could write statements like:

```
cout << endl << typeid ( 45 ).name( ) ;
```

RTTI should be used only with polymorphic classes i.e. those, which have a *virtual* function in the base class. In absence of polymorphism the static type information is used.

Also runtime type identification doesn't work with *void* pointers, because a *void* * truly means no type information at all.

I ran the program given above in VC++ compiler version 5.0. It gave strange and misleading errors. That's because I had not enabled the RTTI option. To do so perform the following steps.

(a) Select 'Settings' from the 'Project' menu and click the 'C/C++' tab.
(b) From the category listbox, select 'C++ language'.
(c) Click the checkbox named 'Enable Run-time Type Information'.

Type Checking With *dynamic_cast*

Another way to obtain type information at runtime is by using the *dynamic_cast* operator. Its usage is shown in the following program.

```
#include <typeinfo>
#include <iostream>
using namespace std ;

class base
{
    public :

        virtual void fun1( )
        {
        }
} ;

class myclass : public base
{
} ;

class yourclass : public base
{
} ;

int main( )
{
    base *b ;
    myclass m, *mp ;
    b = &m ;

    if ( mp = dynamic_cast <myclass *> ( b ) )
        cout << endl << "Of type myclass" ;
    else
        cout << endl << "Not of type myclass" ;

    yourclass y ;
    b = &y ;

    if ( mp = dynamic_cast <myclass *> ( b ) )
```

```
        cout << endl << "Of type myclass" << endl ;
    else
        cout << endl << "Not of type myclass" << endl ;
    return 0 ;
}
```

The *dynamic_cast* operator attempts to convert the pointer *b* (which can contain either the address of a *myclass* object or the address of *yourclass* object) into a pointer to *myclass*. If the result is non-zero then *b* was indeed pointing at *myclass*. If the result is zero it means it pointed to something else.

Although here we have used the *dynamic_cast* and *typeid* with pointers they work equally well with references.

When To Use RTTI

As far as possible you should use virtual functions in your code. You should resort to RTTI only when you must. While using virtual functions you must have an access to the base class source code. If the base class is part of a library and doesn't contain the virtual function that you need, you are stuck up. At such times you should use RTTI. You can derive a new class from the base class and add your extra member function to it. Then you can detect your particular type (using RTTI) and call the member function.

Sometimes even when we have access to the source code of the base class and want to add a new feature to it we may not do so by adding a virtual function to it. This is because for the benefit of one particular class other classes derived from that base class require some meaningless stub of a virtual function. Instead, if we use RTTI we can place the function that we want to add in a particular class where it is appropriate.

Typecasting In C++

Explicit type conversion is known as typecasting. Typecasting is often overused and a major source of errors. Whenever we use typecasting we are trying to tell the compiler that even though we know the object is of one type we are going to pretend that it is of a different type.

The C style casts looked like this

```
( type ) expression
```

Unfortunately, when this style of casting is used each cast looks different since each may use a different *type*. So if a program isn't working correctly and you wish to examine all the casts there is no guarantee that you have located all the casts. To eliminate this difficulty C++ provides a new casting syntax using four reserved words: *dynamic_cast*, *static_cast*, *const_cast* and *reinterpret_cast*. By using these casts you can easily search for all the casts in any program. This will improve the chances of locating and removing bugs in a program. We have already discussed *dynamic_cast* in the previous section on RTTI. Let us now understand the other three.

static_cast

A *static_cast* is used for conversions that are well-defined. These include:

(a) castless conversions
(b) narrowing conversions
(c) conversions from *void* *
(d) implicit type conversions

These are shown in the following program. Read the comments in the program carefully.

```
#include <iostream>
using namespace std ;

class base
{
} ;

class derived : public base
{
    public :

        operator int( )
        {
            return 1 ;
        }
} ;

class sample
{
} ;

int main( )
{
    int i = 10 ;
    long l ;
    float f ;

    // castless conversion – safe
    l = i ;
    f = ( float ) i ;

    cout << endl << l << f << endl ;

    // explicit conversion - safe
    l = static_cast <long> ( i ) ;
    f = static_cast <float> ( i ) ;
```

```
cout << endl << l << f << endl ;

// narrowing conversions
i = l ;
cout << endl << i << endl ;
i = ( int ) f ;
cout << endl << i << endl ;

// better way of doing narrowing conversions
i = static_cast <int> ( l ) ;
i = static_cast <int> ( f ) ;

void *vptr ;
float *fptr ;

// dangerous conversion through a void pointer
vptr = &i ;
fptr = ( float * ) vptr ;
fptr = static_cast <float *> ( vptr ) ;

derived d ;
base *baseptr ;

// upcasting - safe
baseptr = &d ;
// explicit upcasting - safe
baseptr = static_cast <base *> ( &d ) ;

int x ;

// conversion through a conversion function
x = d ;
// more explicit conversion through a conversion function
x = static_cast <int> ( d ) ;

// sample *sptr = static_cast <sample *> ( baseptr ) ; // error
sample *sptr = ( sample * ) baseptr ;
```

```
    return 0 ;
}
```

Most of the program is self-explanatory. We would concentrate only on the last two statements of the program. When we try to cast a pointer to *base* into a pointer to *sample* using *static_cast* an error is flashed. This means that *static_cast* won't allow us to cast out of the hierarchy. However, the traditional cast would permit this. This means *static_cast* is safer than traditional casting.

const_cast

const_cast permits you to convert a *const* to a non-*const* as shown in the following program.

```
#include <iostream>
using namespace std ;

int main( )
{
    const int a = 0 ;

    int *ptr = ( int * ) &a ;  // one way
    ptr = const_cast <int *> ( &a ) ;  // better way

    // long *lptr = const_cast <long *> ( &a ) ;  // error
    return 0 ;
}

class sample
{
    private :

        int data ;
```

```
    public :

        void fun( ) const
        {
            ( const_cast <sample *> ( this ) ) -> data = 99 ;
        }
};
```

If we are to assign address of a *const* object (*a* in the above program) to a pointer to a non-*const* (*ptr* in the above program) we should use the *const_cast*.

Another place where we can use a *const_cast* is when we wish to change a class member inside a *const* member function. However, this is a workable way. A better way is to define *data* as *mutable*. This way in the class definition itself it would be clear the data member might change in a *const* member function.

interpret_cast

This casting mechanism is the least safe and more often than not a source of bugs. If for some unusual reason you need to assign one kind of pointer type to another, you can use *reinterpret_cast*.

The *reinterpret_cast* can also be used to convert pointers to integers or vice versa as shown in the following program.

```
#include <iostream>
using namespace std ;

int main( )
{
    int a = 65000 ;

    int *iptr = reinterpret_cast <int *> ( a ) ;
```

```
    cout << endl << iptr ;

    iptr++ ; // increases by four
    cout << endl << iptr ;

    a = reinterpret_cast <int> ( iptr ) ;
    cout << endl << a ;

    a++ ; // increases by 1
    cout << endl << a << endl ;
    return 0 ;
}
```

The use of *reinterpret_cast* is not recommended, but sometimes it's the only way out.

Whenever you feel the need to use the explicit type conversion you should take time to reconsider it. You would find that in many situations it could be completely avoided. In others it can be localised to a few routines within the program. Always remember that whenever you are using a cast you are breaking the type system. And that is fraught with dangers.

Exercise

[A] State True or False:

(a) The phenomenon of writing a class within a class is known as composition.

(b) Composition and containership is one and the same thing.

(c) Composition and Inheritance both promote reuse of code.

(d) A function that is a *friend* of a class can access *private* data member of a class but cannot manipulate them.

(e) If an entire class is made a *friend* of another then all the member functions of this class can access the *private* data member of the original class.

(f) Unless you have the source code of a class you cannot declare a function to the friend of that class.

(g) Using a smart pointer we can iterate through a container.

(h) Using a smart pointer we can make an object appear like a pointer.

(i) The overloaded operator -> is called a smart pointer operator.

(j) The pointer to member operator can be used to access particular data members within a class.

(k) Pointers to members are not tied with any specific object.

(l) A namespace definition can be continued over multiple header files.

[B] Answer the following:

(a) Is it necessary that while using pointer to member with data, the data must be made *public*?

(b) When should the *explicit* keyword be used in the constructor? Can it be used with any other function?

(c) How would you change a data member of the *const* object?

(d) If two header files contain same names how would you avoid a clash of names if both the files are to be included?

(e) How would you give an alternate name to a namespace?

[C] Attempt the following:

(a) Write a program which has a class called *base*. Derive two classes *derived1* and *derived2* from it. Store address of derived class objects into base class pointers. Using *typeid( )* and *dynamic_cast* identify the type of the object at run-time.

(b) Write a program that will convert an integer pointer into an integer and vice-versa.

CHAPTER

THIRTEEN

Templates

Templates are a mechanism that make it possible to use one function or class to handle many different data types. By using templates, we can design a single class/function that operates on data of many types, instead of having to create a separate class/function for each type. When used with functions they are known as *function templates*, whereas when used with classes they are called *class templates*. We would first look at function templates and then go on to class templates.

Function Templates

Suppose you want to write a function that returns the minimum of two numbers. Ordinarily this function would be written for a particular data type. For example,

```
int mymin ( int a, int b )
{
    return ( a < b ) ? a : b ;
}
```

Here the function is defined to take arguments of type *int* and return a value of the same type. What if we want to find the minimum of two *long ints*—we would be required to write a completely new function. Similarly, to find minimum of two *floats* or two *doubles* or two *chars* we would be required to write separate versions of the same function. You would agree this is a suitable case for overloaded functions. These are given below:

```
// min for ints
int mymin ( int a, int b )
{
    return ( a < b ) ? a : b ;
}
```

```
// min for longs
long mymin ( float a, float b )
{
    return ( a < b ) ? a : b ;
}

// min for chars
char mymin ( char a, char b )
{
    return ( a < b ) ? a : b ;
}
// etc...
```

Have we gained anything by writing these overloaded functions? Not much, because we still have to write a separate definition for each type. This results into three disadvantages:

(a) Rewriting the same function body over and over for different types is time consuming.
(b) The program consumes more disk space.
(c) If we locate any error in one such function, we need to remember to correct it in each function body.

Won't it be nice if we could write such a function just once, and make it work for many different data types. This is exactly what function templates do for us.

The following program shows how to write the *mymin( )* function as a template, so that it will work with any standard type. We have invoked this function from *main( )* for different data types.

```
#include <iostream>
using namespace std ;
```

```
template <class T>
T mymin ( T a, T b )
{
    return ( a < b ) ? a : b ;
}

int main( )
{
    int i = 10, j = 20 ;
    cout << endl << mymin ( i, j ) ;

    float a = 3.14f, b = -6.28f ;
    cout << endl << mymin ( a, b ) ;

    char ch = 'A', dh = 'Z' ;
    cout << endl << mymin ( ch, dh ) ;

    double d = 1.1, e = 1.11 ;
    cout << endl << mymin ( d, e ) << endl ;
    return 0 ;
}
```

Here's the output of the program:

```
10
-6.28
A
1.1
```

As you can see, the *mymin( )* function now works with different data types that we use as arguments. It will even work on user-defined data types, provided the less-than operator (<) is appropriately overloaded in the class for the user-defined type.

Isn't this code reuse? Yes, but of a different type. Inheritance and composition provide a way to reuse *object* code. Templates provide a way to reuse the *source* code. Templates can significantly reduce source code size and increase code flexibility without reducing type safety.

Let us now understand what grants the templated function the flexibility to work with different data types. Here is the definition of the *mymin( )* function:

```
template <class T>
T mymin ( T a, T b )
{
    return ( a < b ) ? a : b ;
}
```

This entire syntax is called a function template. In a function template a data type can be represented by a name (*T* in our case) that can stand for any type. There's nothing special about the name *T*. We can use any other name like *type*, *mytype*, etc. *T* is known as a template argument. Throughout the definition of the function, wherever a specific data type like *int* would ordinarily be written, we substitute the template argument, *T*.

What Happens At Compile Time

Just seeing the function template doesn't swing the compiler into any real action, except for memorizing it for future use. The compiler cannot generate any code as yet because it doesn't know as yet what data type the function will be working with. The code generation takes place when the function is actually called from within the program through statements like:

```
cout << endl << mymin ( i, j ) ;
```

When the compiler sees such a function call, it knows that the type to use is *int*, because that's the type of the arguments *i* and *j*. Now it generates a specific version of the *mymin( )* for type *int*, replacing every *T* with an *int*. This process is often known as *instantiating* the function template. The compiler also generates a call to the newly instantiated function, and inserts it into the code where *mymin (i, j)* is.

Similarly, the expression *mymin (a, b)* causes the compiler to generate a version of *mymin( )* that operates on type *float* and a call to this function; while the *mymin (d, e)* call generates a function that works on type *double*. Note that the compiler generates only one version of *mymin( )* for each data type irrespective of the number of calls that have been made for that type.

Do templates help us save memory? Not really—because, even when we use templates the four functions (for *int*, *float char* and *double*) do get generated. The advantage is we are not required to type them out. The compiler creates them from the generic version that we pass on to it. This makes the listing shorter and easier to understand. Another advantage is, if we are to modify the function we need to make the changes at only one place in the listing instead of four places.

Here is another function template to help you fix your ideas. This one swaps the contents of two variables.

```
#include <iostream>
using namespace std ;

template <class T>
void myswap ( T &a, T &b )
{
```

```
    T c ;

    c = a ;
    a = b ;
    b = c ;
}

int main( )
{
    int i = 10, j = 20 ;
    myswap ( i, j ) ;
    cout << endl << i << "\t" << j ;

    char ch = 'A', dh = 'Z' ;
    myswap ( ch, dh ) ;
    cout << endl << ch << "\t" << dh << endl ;
    return 0 ;
}
```

This code defines a function template called *myswap( )*. From this template the compiler generates functions that will swap *int*s and *char*s.

Note that standard type conversions are not applied to function templates. When a call is encountered the compiler first looks into the existing instantiations for an "exact match" for the parameters supplied. If this fails, it tries to create a new instantiation to create an 'exact match'. If this fails, the compiler generates an error.

Function Template Override

What if we want the function to behave in one way for all data types except one? In such a case we can override the function template for that specific type. For this we simply need to provide a non-templated function for that type. For example:

```
void myswap ( double a, double b )
{
    // some code here
}
```

This definition enables you to define a different function for *double* variables. Like other non-templated functions, standard type conversions (such as promoting a variable of type *float* to *double*) are now applicable.

Multiple Argument Types

We can as well write a function template that takes different types of arguments during one call. The following code shows such a function template.

```
#include <iostream>
using namespace std ;

template <class T, class S, class Z> void fun ( T a, S b, Z c )
{
    cout << a << endl << b << endl << c << endl ;
}

int main( )
{
    int i = 10 ;
    float j = 3.14f ;
    char ch = 'A' ;

    fun ( i, j, ch ) ;
    return 0 ;
}
```

You must have noticed a small syntax variation in the function template of this program. We have put the template keyword and the function declarator on the same line:

```
template <class T, class S, class Z> void fun ( T a, S b, Z c )
```

This has got nothing to do with the multiple types of arguments that are being passed to the function template. We could as well have adopted the multi-line approach of earlier programs:

```
template <class T, class S, class Z>
void fun ( T a, S b, Z c )
```

Templates Versus Macros

In many ways, templates work like preprocessor macros, replacing the template argument with the given type. However, there are many differences between a macro like this:

```
# define min( i, j ) ( ( i ) < ( j ) ? ( i ) : ( j ) )
```

and a parallel template:

```
template <class T>
T min ( T i, T j )
{
    return ( i < j ) ? i : j ) ;
}
```

The macro given above also performs a simple text substitution and can thus work with any type. However it suffers from several limitations:

(a) The macro is expanded without any type checking.

(b) The type of the value returned isn't specified, so the compiler can't tell if we are assigning it to an incompatible variable.

(c) In the macro the parameters *i* and *j* are evaluated twice. If either parameter has a post-incremented variable, the increment would take place twice.

(d) When the macros are expanded by the preprocessor, the compiler error messages would refer to the expanded macro, rather than the macro definition itself. This makes bug hunting difficult.

To put it one line: macros are no match for templates.

A Template Based QuickSort

The quick sort function is available in most of the libraries. While using this function we are required to provide a comparison function. Since this comparison function gets called many times during any sort, one call to the quick sort function may get translated into hundreds or thousands of calls to your comparison function.

One approach that programmers typically take to avoid the external comparison function is to write their own quick sort function and hard code the appropriate comparisons in it. This makes the program difficult to maintain. If you need to sort five different types of data, or use five different sorting rules, you will need to maintain five different quick sort functions.

Fortunately, C++ lets you resolve most of these problems. By implementing a quick sort function using templates, you can add the type safety you need. The following program shows how to implement the template. Note that the function template (*quick( )*) is a stand-alone function, just like the quick sort library function.

The only difference is that it has been parameterized to accept an object type that can be checked at compile time.

This function template will sort an array of implicit types like *int*, *float*, *char*, etc. It can also sort user-defined objects like strings and dates. To achieve this we have defined classes called *mystring* and *date*. Each of these classes contain overloaded operator functions that define the working of <, <= and > operators. They replace the comparison function that library's quick sort function requires. Two *friend* functions have been implemented which would output the *mystring* and *date* objects respectively. Here is the program...

```
#include <iostream>
#include <string>
using namespace std ;

class mystring
{
    private :

        enum { sz = 100 } ;
        char str[sz] ;

    public :

        mystring ( char *s = "" )
        {
            strcpy ( str, s ) ;
        }

        int operator < ( mystring ss )
        {
            if ( strcmp ( str, ss.str ) <= 0 )
                return 1 ;
            else
```

```
                return 0 ;
        }

        int operator <= ( mystring ss )
        {
            if ( strcmp ( str, ss.str ) <= 0 )
                return 1 ;
            else
                return 0 ;
        }

        int operator > ( mystring ss )
        {
            if ( strcmp ( str, ss.str ) > 0 )
                return 1 ;
            else
                return 0 ;
        }

        friend ostream& operator << ( ostream &o, mystring &dd ) ;
} ;

ostream& operator << ( ostream &o, mystring &ss )
{
    o << ss.str ;
    return o ;
}

class date
{
    private :

        int day, mth, yr ;

    public :

        date ( int d = 0, int m = 0, int y = 0 )
```

```
{
    day = d ;
    mth = m ;
    yr = y ;
}

int operator < ( date dt )
{
    if ( yr < dt.yr )
        return 1 ;

    if ( yr == dt.yr && mth < dt.mth )
        return 1 ;

    if ( yr == dt.yr && mth == dt.mth && day < dt.day )
        return 1 ;

    return 0 ;
}

int operator <= ( date dt )
{
    if ( yr <= dt.yr )
        return 1 ;

    if ( yr == dt.yr && mth <= dt.mth )
        return 1 ;

    if ( yr == dt.yr && mth == dt.mth && day <= dt.day )
        return 1 ;

    return 0 ;
}

int operator > ( date dt )
{
    if ( yr > dt.yr )
```

```
                return 1 ;

            if ( yr == dt.yr && mth > dt.mth )
                return 1 ;

            if ( yr == dt.yr && mth == dt.mth && day > dt.day )
                return 1 ;

            return 0 ;
        }

        friend ostream& operator << ( ostream &o, date &dd ) ;
} ;

ostream& operator << ( ostream &o, date &dd )
{
    o << dd.day << "\t" << dd.mth << "\t" << dd.yr ;
    return o ;
}

template <class T>
void quick ( T *n, int low, int high )
{
    int pos ;

    if ( low < high )
    {
        pos = split ( n, low, high ) ;
        quick ( n, low, pos - 1 ) ;
        quick ( n, pos + 1, high ) ;
    }
}

template <class T>
int split ( T *n, int low, int high )
{
    int pos, left, right ;
```

```
    T item, t ;

    item = n[low] ;
    left = low ;
    right = high ;

    while ( left < right )
    {
        while ( n[right] > item )
            right = right - 1 ;

        while ( ( left < right ) && ( n[left] <= item ) )
            left = left + 1 ;

        if ( left < right )
        {
            t = n[left] ;
            n[left] = n[right] ;
            n[right] = t ;
        }
    }

    pos = right ;
    t = n[low] ;
    n[low] = n[pos] ;
    n[pos] = t ;

    return pos ;
}
int main( )
{
    float num[ ] = { 5.4f, 3.23f, 2.15f, 1.09f, 34.66f, 23.3452f } ;
    int arr[ ] = { -12, 23, 14, 0, 245, 78 , 66, -9 } ;
    date dtarr[ ] = { date ( 17, 11, 62 ), date ( 23, 12, 65 ), date ( 12, 12, 78 ),
                    date ( 23, 1, 69 ) } ;
    mystring strarr[ ] = { mystring ( "Kamal" ), mystring ( "Anuj" ),
```

```
                        mystring ( "Sachin" ), mystring ( "Anil" ) } ;
    int i ;

    cout << endl << endl ;
    quick ( num, 0, 5 ) ;
    for ( i = 0 ; i <= 5 ; i++ )
        cout << num[i] << endl ;

    cout << endl << endl ;
    quick ( arr, 0, 7 ) ;
    for ( i = 0 ; i <= 7 ; i++ )
        cout << arr[i] << endl ;

    cout << endl << endl ;
    quick ( dtarr, 0, 3 ) ;
    for ( i = 0 ; i <= 3 ; i++ )
        cout << dtarr[i] << endl ;

    cout << endl << endl ;
    quick ( strarr, 0, 3 ) ;
    for ( i = 0 ; i <= 3 ; i++ )
        cout << strarr[i] << endl ;
    return 0 ;
}
```

I do not intend to discuss here the actual working of the quick sort algorithm. This topic has been dealt with quite thoroughly in all the standard books on Data Structures. What you need to concentrate here is how to write function template that can work for standard as well as user-defined data types.

Class Templates

The concept of templates can be extended even to classes. Class templates are usually used for data storage (container) classes.

Stacks and linked lists, which we encountered in previous chapters, are examples of container classes. However, the examples of these classes that we presented could store data of only a single basic type, say an integer. If we were to store data of type *float* in a stack we would be required to define a completely new class. It follows that for every new data type that we wish to store, a new stack class would have to be created. Won't it be nice if we are able to write a single class specification that would work for variables of all types, instead of a single basic type. Enter *class templates*. Here is a program with class template in action.

```
#include <iostream>
using namespace std ;

const int MAX = 10 ;
template <class T>
class stack
{
    private :

        T stk[MAX] ;
        int top ;

    public :

        stack( )
        {
            top = -1 ;
        }

        void push ( T data )
        {
            if ( top == MAX - 1 )
                cout << endl << "stack is full" << endl ;
```

```
            else
            {
                top++ ;
                stk[top] = data ;
            }
        }

        T pop( )
        {
            if ( top == -1 )
            {
                cout << endl << "stack is empty" << endl ;
                return NULL ;
            }
            else
            {
                T data = stk[top] ;
                top-- ;
                return data ;
            }
        }
} ;

class complex
{
    private :

        float real, imag ;

    public :

        complex ( float r = 0.0, float i = 0.0 )
        {
            real = r ;
            imag = i ;
        }
```

```
        friend ostream& operator << ( ostream &o, complex &c ) ;
} ;

ostream& operator << ( ostream &o, complex &c )
{
    o << c.real << "\t" << c.imag ;
    return o ;
}

int main( )
{
    stack < int > s1 ;
    s1.push ( 10 ) ;
    s1.push ( 20 ) ;
    s1.push ( 30 ) ;

    cout << endl << s1.pop( ) ;
    cout << endl << s1.pop( ) ;
    cout << endl << s1.pop( ) ;

    stack <float> s2 ;
    s2.push ( 3.14f ) ;
    s2.push ( 6.28f ) ;
    s2.push ( 8.98f ) ;

    cout << endl << s2.pop( ) ;
    cout << endl << s2.pop( ) ;
    cout << endl << s2.pop( ) ;

    complex c1 ( 1.5f, 2.5f ), c2 ( 3.5f, 4.5f ), c3 ( -1.5f, -0.6f ) ;
    stack <complex> s3 ;

    s3.push ( c1 ) ;
    s3.push ( c2 ) ;
    s3.push ( c3 ) ;

    cout << endl << s3.pop( ) ;
```

```
        cout << endl << s3.pop( ) ;
        cout << endl << s3.pop( ) << endl ;
        return 0 ;
}
```

We have created three stacks here: *s1*, *s2* and *s3* and pushed three values on each one. Then we have popped the values from the three stacks and displayed them on the screen. Here's the output of the program…

```
30
20
10
8.98
6.28
3.14
-1.5 -0.6
3.5  4.5
1.5  2.5
```

You can observe that the order in which the elements are popped from the stack is exactly reverse of the order in which they were pushed on the stack.

The way to build a class template is similar to the one used for building a function template. The *template* keyword and *<class T>* signal that the entire class will be a template.

```
template <class T>
class stack
{
    // data and member functions using template argument T
};
```

The template argument *T* is then used at every place in the class specification where there is a reference to the type of the array *stk*. There are three such places: the definition of *stk*, the argument type of the *push( )* function, and the return type of the *pop( )* function.

We have also declared a class called *complex* and then pushed/popped *complex* objects to/from stack. This proves that we can create stacks of user-defined objects too from the class template. To be able to display the *complex* objects through *cout* we have overloaded the << operator. The working of such an overloaded operator has already been discussed in Chapter 11.

We saw that in function templates the instantiation takes place when a function call is encountered. As against this, classes are instantiated by defining an object using the template arguments. For example,

```
stack <int> s1 ;
```

creates an object, *s1*, a stack that can store numbers of type *int*. The compiler reserves space in memory for this object's data, using type *int* wherever the template argument *T* appears in the class specification. It also reserves space for the member functions (if these have not already been placed in memory by another object of type *stack <int>*). These member functions also operate exclusively on type *int*.

When we create a *stack* object that stores objects of a different type, say *float*, space is now created for data, as well as a new set of member functions that operate on type *float*.

As with normal classes can we not define the member functions of a class template outside the class? We can, but it needs a different syntax as shown below:

```
template <class T>
void stack<T>:: push ( T data )
{
	if ( top == MAX - 1 )
		cout << endl << "stack is full" ;
	else
	{
		top++ ;
		stk[top] = data ;
	}
}
```

Note that the expression *template <class T>* must precede not only the class definition, but each externally defined member function as well. The name *stack<T>* is used to identify the class of which *push( )* is a member.

A Linked List Class Template

Let us now implement a general-purpose linked list class using templates. Using this class template we can easily maintain a linked list of integers or a linked list of floats or a linked list of character pointers, or even a linked list of user-defined data types. Let us assume that the user-defined data type stores information about name, age and salary of an employee. For managing this information we can have a separate class called *emp*. This class needs only two member functions: a constructor and an overloaded << operator. The overloaded operator can ensure that *cout* can be used to output *emp* class's data members.

The program that implements the class template to maintain two linked lists—one for integers and another for employee data—is given below.

```
#include <string>
```

```
#include <iostream>
using namespace std ;

class emp
{
    private :

        char name[20] ;
        int age ;
        float sal ;

    public :

        emp ( char *n = "", int a = 0, float s = 0.0 )
        {
            strcpy ( name, n ) ;
            age = a ;
            sal = s ;
        }

        friend ostream& operator << ( ostream& s, emp& e ) ;
} ;

ostream& operator << ( ostream& s, emp& e )
{
    cout << e.name << '\t' << e.age << '\t' << e.sal ;
    return s ;
}

template <class T>
class linklist
{
    private :

        struct node
        {
            T data ;
```

```
            node *link ;
        } *p ;

    public :

        linklist( ) ;
        ~linklist( ) ;
        void append ( T ) ;
        void addatbeg ( T ) ;
        void addafter ( int, T ) ;
        void del ( int ) ;
        void display( ) ;
        int count( ) ;
} ;

template <class T>
linklist<T>::linklist( )
{
    p = NULL ;
}

template <class T>
linklist<T> :: ~linklist( )
{
    node *t ;
    while ( p != NULL )
    {
        t = p ;
        p = p->link ;
        delete t ;
    }
}

// adds a node at the end of the linked list
template <class T>
void linklist<T>:: append ( T num )
{
```

```
    node *q, *t ;
    if ( p == NULL )  // if the list is empty
    {
        p = new node ;
        p->data = num ;
        p->link = NULL ;
    }
    else
    {
        q = p ;
        while ( q->link != NULL )
            q = q->link ;

        t = new node ;
        t->data = num ;
        t->link = NULL ;
        q->link = t ;
    }
}

// adds a node at the beginning of the linked list
template <class T>
void linklist<T>:: addatbeg ( T num )
{
    node *q ;
    q = new node ;
    q->data = num ;
    q->link = p ;
    p = q ;
}

// adds a new node after the specified number of nodes
template <class T>
void linklist<T>::addafter ( int c, T num )
{
    node *q, *t; int i ;
    for ( i = 1, q = p ; i <= c ; i++ )
```

```
    {
        q = q->link ;
        if ( q == NULL ) // if end of list is encountered
        {
                            cout << endl << "There are less than " << c << "
            elements." << endl ;
            return ;
        }
    }

    // insert new node
    t = new node ;
    t->data = num ;
    t->link = q->link ;
    q->link = t ;
}

// deletes a node from the linked list
template <class T>
void linklist<T>::del ( int n )
{
    node *q, *r ;
    int i = 1 ;

    q = p ;
    if ( n == 1 ) // if node to delete is first node
    {
        p = q->link ;
        delete q ;
        return ;
    }

    r = q ;
    while ( q != NULL )
    {
        if ( i == n )
        {
```

```
                r->link = q->link ;
                delete q ;
                return ;
            }
            r = q ;
            q = q->link ;
            i++ ;
        }

        cout << endl << "Element " << n << " not found" << endl ;
}

// displays contents of the linked list
template <class T>
void linklist<T>::display( )
{
        node *q ;
        cout << endl ;
        for ( q = p ; q != NULL ; q = q->link )
            cout << q->data << endl ;
}

// counts number of nodes in the linked list
template <class T>
int linklist<T>::count( )
{
        node *q ; int c = 0 ;
        for ( q = p ; q != NULL ; q = q->link )
            c++ ;

        return ( c ) ;
}

int main( )
{
        linklist<int> l1 ;
```

```
cout << endl << "No. of elements in Linked List = " << l1.count( ) << endl
;
l1.append ( 11 ) ;
l1.append ( 22 ) ;
l1.append ( 33 ) ;
l1.append ( 44 ) ;
l1.append ( 55 ) ;
l1.append ( 66 ) ;
l1.addatbeg ( 100 ) ;
l1.addatbeg ( 200 ) ;
l1.addafter ( 3, 333 ) ;
l1.addafter ( 6, 444 ) ;
l1.display( ) ;
cout << endl << "No. of elements in linked list = " << l1.count( ) << endl ;
l1.del ( 200 ) ;
l1.del ( 66 ) ;
l1.del ( 0 ) ;
l1.del ( 333 ) ;
l1.display( ) ;
cout << endl << "No. of elements in linked list = " << l1.count( ) << endl ;

linklist <emp> l2 ;

cout << endl << "No. of elements in Linked List = " << l2.count( ) << endl
;
emp e1 ( "Sanjay", 23, 1100.00 ) ;
emp e2 ( "Rahul", 33, 3500.00 ) ;
emp e3 ( "Rakesh", 24, 2400.00 ) ;
emp e4 ( "Sanket", 25, 2500.00 ) ;
emp e5 ( "Sandeep", 26, 2600.00 ) ;
l2.append ( e1 ) ;
l2.append ( e2 ) ;
l2.append ( e3 ) ;
l2.append ( e4 ) ;
l2.append ( e5 ) ;
l2.display( ) ;
l2.del ( 3 ) ;
```

```
    l2.display( ) ;
    cout << endl << "No. of elements in linked list = " << l2.count( ) << endl ;
    l2.addatbeg ( e5 ) ;
    l2.display( ) ;
    l2.addafter ( 3, e1 ) ;
    l2.display( ) ;
    cout << endl << "No. of elements in linked list = " << l2.count( ) << endl ;
    return 0 ;
}
```

Tips About Templates

Before we close this chapter a few tips that you would find useful:

(a) The name of the template class (say *stack*) is expressed differently in different contexts. Within the class specification, it's simply the name, as in

```
class stack {     } ;
```

For externally defined member functions, it's the class name plus the template argument name as in

```
void stack<T>::push ( T data ) {     }
```

Lastly, when you define actual objects for storing a specific data type, it's the class name plus this specific type as in

```
stack <float> s1 ; // object of type stack <float>
```

You must exercise considerable care to use the correct name in the correct context. It's easy to forget to add the *<T>* or *<float>* to the *stack*. The compiler hates it when you get it wrong.

(b) Be careful about the syntax when a member function returns a value of its own class. Suppose we define a class template called *sample*. If a member function *fun( )* of this class returns a type *sample*, and we have to define this function outside the template class we need to use *sample<T>* for the return type as well as preceding the scope resolution operator. This is shown below:

```
sample<T> sample<T>::fun ( sample s )
{
}
```

The class name used as a type of a function argument, on the other hand, doesn't need to include the *<T>* designation.

(c) Template arguments can take default values. The values of these arguments then become compile-time constants for that particular instantiation of the template. For example:

```
template <class T, int max = 50 >
class sample
{
   private :
        T arr[max] ;
} ;
```

(d) We can inherit a new template from an existing one. For example:

```
template <class T>
class newsample : public sample <T>
{
} ;
```

(e) Every time we instantiate a template the code in the template is generated anew. If some of the functionality of a template does not depend on type, it can be put in a common base class to prevent unnecessary reproduction of that code.

(f) Templates should be used while creating a type-safe collection class that can operate on data of any type.

Exercise

[A] State True or False:

(a) We can inherit a new class from the class template.

(b) If there is a function template called *max( )* then a specific version of it would be created when *max( )* is called with a new type.

(c) The compiler generates only one version of function template for each data type irrespective of the number of calls that are made for that type.

(d) Using templates saves memory.

(e) We can override a function template for a particular type.

(f) A function template can have multiple argument types.

(g) Templates are type safe whereas macros are not.

(h) Class templates are usually used for container class.

(i) A class template member function can be defined outside the class template.

(j) Template arguments can take default values.

[B] Answer the following:

(a) Write a program that will implement a binary tree as a class template.

(b) Write a program to implement a doubly linked list as a class template.

CHAPTER

FOURTEEN

Exception Handling

Exceptions are errors that occur at run time. The reasons why exceptions occur are numerous. Some of the more common ones are:

(a) Falling short of memory
(b) Inability to open a file
(c) Exceeding the bounds of an array
(d) Attempting to initialize an object to an impossible value

When such exceptions occur, the programmer has to decide a strategy according to which he would handle the exceptions. The strategies could be, displaying the error messages on the screen, or displaying a dialog box in case of a GUI environment, or requesting the user to supply better data or simply terminating the program execution.

Usually C programmers deal with exceptions in two ways:

(a) Following the function calls with error checks on return values to find whether the function did its job properly or not.

(b) Using the *setjmp* and *longjmp* mechanism. This approach is intended to intercept and handle conditions that do not require immediate program termination. For example, if a recursive descent parser detects an error, it should report it and continue with further processing.

Let us look at these methods more closely.

Checking Function Return Value

In C programs a function usually returns an error value if an error occurs during execution of that function. For example, file-opening functions return a NULL indicating their inability to open a file successfully. Hence, each time we call these functions we can check for the return value. This is shown for some fictitious functions *fun1( )*, *fun2( )* and *fun3( )* in the following code:

```
if ( func1( ) == ERROR_VALUE )
    // handle the error
else
    // do normal things

if ( func2( ) == NULL )
    // handle the error
else
    // do normal things

if ( func3( ) == -1 )
    // handle the error
else
    // do normal things
```

There are three problems with this approach:

(a) Every time we call a function we must check its return value through a pair of *if* and *else*. Easier said than done! Surrounding every function call with a pair of *if* and *else* results in increase in code size. Also, too many *if-else*s make the listing lose its readability.

(b) This approach cannot be used to report errors in the constructor of a class as the constructor cannot return a value.

(c) It becomes difficult to monitor the return values in case of deeply nested function calls. Especially so if the functions belong to a third-party library.

setjmp( ) And *longjmp( )*

C does not provide an easy way to transfer control out of a function except by returning to the expression that called the function. For the vast majority of function calls, this is a desirable limitation. You want the discipline of nested function calls and returns to help you understand the flow of control through a program. Nevertheless, on some occasions that discipline is too restrictive. The program is sometimes easier to write, and to understand, if you can jump out of one or more function invocations at a single stroke. You want to bypass the normal function returns and transfer control to somewhere in an earlier function invocation.

For example, you may want to return to execute some code for error recovery no matter where an error is detected in your application. The *setjmp( )* and the *longjmp( )* functions provide the tools to accomplish this. The *setjmp( )* function saves the *state* or the *context* of the process and the *longjmp( )* uses the saved context to revert to a previous point in the program. What is the context of the process? In general, the context of a process refers to information that enables you to reconstruct exactly the way the process was at a particular point in its flow of execution. In a C program the relevant information includes quantities such as values of SP, SS, FLAGS, CS, IP, BP, DI, ES, SI and DS registers. This information is saved in a structure called *jmp_buf* defined in the header file 'setjmp.h'. The *jmp_buf* structure is a system-dependent data type because different systems might require different amounts of information to capture the context of a process.

To understand the mechanics of *setjmp( )* and *longjmp( )*, look at the following code fragment.

```
#include <iostream>
#include <setjmp>
using namespace std ;

class sample
{
    public :

        sample( )
        {
            cout << endl << "Reached constructor" << endl ;
        }

        ~sample( )
        {
            cout << endl << "Reached destructor" << endl ;
        }
} ;

jmp_buf buf ;

int main( )
{
    void process( ) ;
    void handle_error( ) ;

    if ( setjmp ( buf ) == 0 )
        process( ) ;
    else
        handle_error( ) ;  // executed when longjmp is called
    return 0 ;
}

void process( )
{
    int flag = 0 ;
    sample s ;
```

```
    // some processing is done here

    // if an error occurs during processing flag is set up
    flag = 1 ;
    if ( flag )
        longjmp ( buf, 1 ) ;
}

void handle_error( )
{
    cout << endl << "Error has occurred" << endl ;
}
```

When *setjmp( )* is called from *main( )* it stores all the relevant information about the current processor state in *jmp_buf* and returns zero. In this case, the *if* statement is satisfied and the *process( )* function is called.

If something goes wrong in *process( )* (indicated by the *flag* variable), we call *longjmp( )* with two arguments: the first is the buffer that contains the context to which we will return. When the stack reverts back to this saved state, and the *return* statement in *longjmp( )* is executed, it will be as if we were returning from the call to *setjmp( )*, which originally saved the buffer *buf*. The second argument to *longjmp( )* specifies the return value to be used during this return. It should be other than zero so that in the *if* statement we can tell whether the return is induced by a *longjmp( )*.

The *setjmp( )/longjmp( )* combination enables us to jump unconditionally from one C function to another without using the conventional *return* statements. Essentially, *setjmp( )* marks the destination of the jump and *longjmp( )* is a *non-local goto* that executes the jump.

However, this approach is not appropriate for an object-oriented environment because it does not properly handle the destruction of objects. In our program when *longjmp( )* returned the destructor of the *sample* class did not get called. Hence the object could not get properly cleaned up. This is the critical reason why a better alternative should be thought of for handling exceptions in C++.

Exception Handling In C++

C++ provides a systematic, object-oriented approach to handling run-time errors generated by C++ classes. The exception mechanism of C++ uses three new keywords: *throw*, *catch*, and *try*. Also, we need to create a new kind of entity called an *exception class*.

Suppose we have an application that works with objects of a certain class. If during the course of execution of a member function of this class an error occurs, then this member function informs the application that an error has occurred. This process of informing is called *throwing* an exception. In the application we have to create a separate section of code to tackle the error. This section of code is called an *exception handler* or a *catch block.* Any code in the application that uses objects of the class is enclosed in a *try block*. Errors generated in the *try* block are caught in the *catch* block. Code that doesn't interact with the class need not be in a *try* block. The following code shows the organisation of these blocks. It is not a working program, but it clearly shows how and where the various elements of the exception mechanism are placed.

```
class sample
{
    public :
```

```
    // exception class
    class errorclass
    {
    } ;

    void fun( )
    {
        if ( some error occurs )
            throw errorclass( ) ; // throws exception
    }
} ;

// application
int main( )
{
    // try block
    try
    {
        sample s ;
        s.fun( ) ;
    }
    catch ( sampel :: errorclass )    // exception handler or catch block
    {
        // do something about the error
    }
    return 0 ;
}
```

Here *sample* is any class in which errors might occur. An exception class called *errorclass*, is specified in the *public* part of *sample*. In *main( )* we have enclosed part of the program that uses *sample* in a *try* block. If an error occurs in *sample::fun( )* we throw an exception, using the keyword *throw* followed by the constructor for the *errorclass*:

```
throw errorclass( ) ;
```

When an exception is thrown control goes to the *catch* block that immediately follows the *try* block.

A More Practical Example

Let's now try to use exception handling in a more practical situation. We would try to implement a queue data structure in a manner similar to what we saw in Chapter 8. We would use exception handling to report errors in two situations:

(a) When the program attempts to store more objects in the queue than what it can accommodate.

(b) When the program tries to remove an object from the empty queue.

Here is the program that uses exceptions to handle these two errors.

```
#include <iostream>
using namespace std ;

#define MAX 4

class queue
{
    private :

        int arr[MAX] ;
        int front, rear ;

    public :

        // exception class for queue full. Note the empty class body
```

```
class qfull
{
} ;

// exception class for queue empty. Note the empty class body
class qempty
{
} ;

queue( )
{
    front = -1 ;
    rear = -1 ;
}

void addq ( int item )
{
    // if queue is full, throw exception
    if ( rear == MAX - 1 )
        throw qfull( ) ;

    rear++ ;
    arr[rear] = item ;

    if ( front == -1 )
        front = 0 ;
}

int delq( )
{
    int data ;

    // if queue is empty, throw exception
    if ( front == -1 )
        throw qempty( ) ;

    data = arr[front] ;
```

```
            if ( front == rear )
                front = rear = -1 ;
            else
                front++ ;

            return  data ;
        }
} ;

int main( )
{
    queue a ;

    try
    {
        a.addq ( 11 ) ;
        a.addq ( 12 ) ;
        a.addq ( 13 ) ;
        a.addq ( 14 ) ;
        a.addq ( 15 ) ;  // oops, queue is full
    }
    catch ( queue::qfull )
    {
        cout << endl << "Queue is full" << endl ;
    }

    int i ;
    try
    {
        i = a.delq( ) ;
        cout << endl << "Item deleted = " << i ;

        i = a.delq( ) ;
        cout << endl << "Item deleted = " << i ;
```

```
        i = a.delq( ) ;
        cout << endl << "Item deleted = " << i ;

        i = a.delq( ) ;
        cout << endl << "Item deleted = " << i ;

        i = a.delq( ) ;  // oops, queue is empty right now
        cout << endl << "Item deleted = " << i ;
    }
    catch ( queue::qempty )
    {
        cout << endl << "Queue is empty" << endl ;
    }
    return 0 ;
}
```

We have purposefully kept the capacity of the queue small so that it's easier to trigger an exception by adding too many items to the queue.

There are four parts involved in the exception handling mechanism. These are as under:

(a) Specifying The Exception Class

There are two exception classes in our program. They have been specified in the *public* part of the *queue* class:

```
class queue
{
    // private data

    public :

        // exception class for queue full. Note the empty class body
```

```
        class qfull
        {
        };

        // exception class for queue empty. Note the empty class body
        class qempty
        {
        };

        // rest of the class specification
};
```

Here the body of the two classes *qfull* and *qempty* is empty. Hence objects of these classes would have no data and no member functions. The names of these classes are used to connect a *throw* statement with an appropriate *catch* block.

(b) Throwing An Exception

In our application an exception can occur in two situations: when the queue becomes full and we try to store another integer in it, or when we try to remove an integer from an empty queue. Using *if* statements we check whether any of these situations has arisen. If so then we throw an exception as shown below:

```
if ( rear == MAX - 1 )
    throw qfull( ) ;

if ( front == -1 )
    throw qempty( ) ;
```

When the queue becomes full and we throw an exception the constructor (implicit, zero-argument) for the *qfull* class gets called (which creates an object of this class) and control is transferred to the exception handler.

Similarly, when the queue falls empty the constructor of *qempty* class creates an object and the control is transferred to the exception handler.

(c) The *try* Block

The statements in *main( )* that might cause the two exceptions have been enclosed in a pair of braces and preceded by the *try* keyword:

```
try
{
    a.addq ( 11 ) ;
    a.addq ( 12 ) ;
    a.addq ( 13 ) ;
    a.addq ( 14 ) ;
    a.addq ( 15 ) ; // oops, queue is full
}


try
{
    i = a.delq( ) ;
    cout << endl << "Item deleted = " << i ;

    i = a.delq( ) ;
    cout << endl << "Item deleted = " << i ;

    i = a.delq( ) ;
    cout << endl << "Item deleted = " << i ;

    i = a.delq( ) ;
    cout << endl << "Item deleted = " << i ;
```

```
    i = a.delq( ) ;  // oops, queue is empty right now
    cout << endl << "Item deleted = " << i ;
}
```

This code is the application's normal code. We would have written it even if we weren't using exceptions. All the code in the program need not be in a *try* block; just the code that interacts with the *queue* class.

(d) The Exception Handler (*catch* Block)

The code that handles an exception is enclosed in braces, preceded by the *catch* keyword, with the exception class name in parentheses.

```
catch ( queue::qfull )
{
    cout << endl << "Queue is full" ;
}
catch ( queue::qempty )
{
    cout << endl << "Queue is empty" ;
}
```

In our application there might be another class, say *dqueue*, which may also throw an exception called *qfull*. When such an exception is thrown the compiler would not be able to decide which *catch* block the control should be transferred to. This would be an ambiguous situation. Hence to avoid confusion, in the *catch* block the exception class name must include the class in which it is located. In our case it is *queue::qfull* and *queue::qempty*. Had there been a *dqueue* class it could have been *dqueue::qempty*.

The *catch* block is often called an *exception handler*. It must immediately follow the *try* block. In our program the exception handler simply prints an error message.

Once the *catch* block has been executed the control jumps to the first statement after the *catch* block so you can continue processing at that point. If you don't want this you may terminate the execution in the *catch* block (using *exit( )*), or transfer the control elsewhere.

How The Whole Thing Works

Let's summarize the events that take place when an exception occurs:

(a) Code is executing normally outside a *try* block.
(b) Control enters the *try* block.
(c) A statement in the *try* block causes an error in a member function.
(d) The member function throws an exception.
(e) Control transfers to the exception handler (*catch* block) following the *try* block.

You can appreciate how clean is this code. Just about any statement in the *try* block can cause an exception, but we don't need to worry about checking a return value for each one. The *try-throw-catch* arrangement handles it all for us, automatically.

In our program we have purposefully created two statements that cause exceptions. The first,

```
a.addq ( 15 ) ; // oops, queue is full
```

causes the *qfull* exception to be thrown resulting in the message 'Queue is full' being displayed.

Similarly the statement,

```
i = a.delq( ) ;  // oops, queue is empty right now
```

causes the exception *qempty* to be thrown, resulting in the message 'Queue is empty' being displayed.

Exceptions With Arguments

In the previous program our exception classes were empty. Hence while throwing the exceptions we didn't pass anything to the constructor of the exception class. If the situation demands we can have data members within the exception class. We can set these members through the constructor when we build the exception class object. The following program shows how this can be achieved. This program too maintains a queue but instead of two, it uses only one exception class. Through the same class it manages to report the errors of queue being full or empty.

```
#include <iostream>
#include <string>
using namespace std ;

#define MAX 4

class queue
{
    private :

        int arr[MAX] ;
        int front, rear ;

    public :

        class fullorempty
        {
```

```
        public :

            char str[100] ;

            fullorempty ( char *s )
            {
                strcpy ( str, s ) ;
            }
    } ;

    class qempty
    {
    } ;

    queue( )
    {
        front = -1 ;
        rear = -1 ;
    }

    void addq ( int item )
    {
        if ( rear == MAX - 1 )
            throw fullorempty ( "Queue is full" ) ;

        rear++ ;
        arr[rear] = item ;

        if ( front == -1 )
            front = 0 ;
    }

    int delq( )
    {
        int data ;

        if ( front == -1 )
```

```
                throw fullorempty ( "Queue is empty" ) ;

            data = arr[front] ;
            if ( front == rear )
                front = rear = -1 ;
            else
                front++ ;

            return data ;
        }
} ;

int main( )
{
    queue a ;

    try
    {
        a.addq ( 11 ) ;
        a.addq ( 12 ) ;
        a.addq ( 13 ) ;
        a.addq ( 14 ) ;
        a.addq ( 15 ) ;  // oops, queue is full
    }
    catch ( queue::fullorempty fe )
    {
        cout << endl << fe.str << endl ;
    }

    int i ;
    try
    {
        i = a.delq( ) ;
        cout << endl << "Item deleted = " << i ;
        i = a.delq( ) ;
        cout << endl << "Item deleted = " << i ;
        i = a.delq( ) ;
```

```
        cout << endl << "Item deleted = " << i ;
        i = a.delq( ) ;
        cout << endl << "Item deleted = " << i ;
        i = a.delq( ) ;  // oops, queue is empty
        cout << endl << "Item deleted = " << i ;
    }
    catch ( queue::fullorempty fe )
    {
        cout << endl << fe.str << endl ;
    }
    return 0 ;
}
```

When the exceptions are thrown an exception class object gets created through the constructor of the exception class (in this case the *fullorempty* class). When the constructor is called we pass it a message (*char* *). It copies this message into a *public* member (*str*) of the exception class. The *catch* blocks access this *public* member and print the relevant message.

A Few Tips

Now that we have written a few programs that use exception handling a few tips are in order.

(a) It is not necessary that the statement that causes an exception be located directly in the *try* block. It may as well be present in a function that is being called from the *try* block.

(b) Instead of defining the exception class within our class we can use the following alternate syntax:

```
class fullorempty
{
};
```

```
class queue
{
    public :

        void addq ( int item ) throw ( fullorempty )
        {
            // some code
        }

        int delq( ) throw ( fullorempty )
        {
            // some code
        }
} ;

int main( )
{
    queue a ;

    try
    {
        // some code
    }
    catch ( fullorempty fe )
    {
        // some code
    }
    return 0 ;
}
```

Here

`void addq ( int item ) throw ( fullorempty )`

is know as exception specification.

On similar lines the exception specification,

```
void fun ( ) throw ( maxlimit, minlimit, divbyzero )
```

means that *fun( )* can throw the three exceptions: *maxlimit*, *minlimit* and *divbyzero*. Also,

```
void fun( ) ;
```

means that *fun( )* can throw any exception, and

```
void fun( ) throw
```

means it cannot throw any exception.

(c) There can be more than one exception handler for one *try* block, as shown below:

```
try
{
    // code that may generate exceptions
}
catch ( type1 id1 )
{
    // handle exceptions of type1
}
catch ( type id2 )
{
    // handle exceptions of type2
}
```

(d) If an exception other than the ones specified in the exception specification is thrown then a special function called *unexpected( )* gets called.

(e) You can write your own version of *unexpected( )* function by setting it up using the *set_unexpected( )* function as shown below:

```
set_unexpected ( my_unexpected ) ;
```

(f) *try* blocks can be nested.

(g) If none of the exception handlers following a particular *try* block matches an exception, that exception moves to the next higher context, that is, the function or *try* block surrounding the *try* block that failed to catch the exception.

(h) If an exception is thrown before constructor's execution is completed the associated destructor will not be called for that object.

(i) When an exception is thrown, the exception-handling system looks through the 'nearest' handlers (*catch* blocks) in the order in which they are written. When it finds a match, the exception is considered handled, and no further searching takes place.

(j) The exception handling mechanism tackles the errors that occur in class libraries. While writing a class library, we should anticipate what could cause problems to the program using it. At all such places we should throw exceptions. If we are writing a program that uses a class library, we should provide *try* and *catch* blocks for any exceptions that the library may throw.

(k) Exceptions impose an overhead in terms of program size and (when an exception occurs) in time. So we should not try to overuse it.

(l) When an exception is thrown, a destructor is called automatically for any object that was created by the code up to that point in the *try* block.

(m) Standard C++ contains several built-in exception classes. The most commonly used is probably *bad_alloc*, which is thrown if an error occurs when attempting to allocate memory with *new*.

Exercise

[A] State True or False:

(a) *setjmp( )* and *longjmp( )* can properly handle destruction of objects.

(b) A *setjmp( )/longjmp( )* combination can perform a non-local jump.

(c) The exception handling mechanism is supposed to handle compile time errors.

(d) It is necessary to declare the exception class within the class in which an exception is going to be thrown.

(e) Every thrown exception must be caught.

(f) For one *try* block there can be multiple *catch* blocks.

(g) The *catch* block and the exception handler are one and the same thing.

(h) When an exception is thrown an exception class's constructor gets called.

(i) *try* blocks cannot be nested.

(j) Proper destruction of an object is guaranteed by exception handling mechanism.

[B] Answer the following:

(a) Implement an exception handling mechanism which reports stack full and stack empty mechanism for a class called *stack*.

(b) Create a class with its own *operator new*. This operator should allocate 5 objects, and on 5th 'run out of memory' and throw an exception. Also add a *static* member function that reclaims this memory. Now create a *main( )* with a *try* block and a *catch* clause that calls the memory-restoration routine. Put these inside a *while* loop to demonstrate recovering from an exception and continuing execution.

Index

C

R

S